French by Heart

BROADWAY BOOKS

New York

French by Heart

An

American Family's

Adventures

in

La Belle France

REBECCA S. RAMSEY

BROADWAY

PUBLISHED BY BROADWAY BOOKS

Copyright © 2007 by Rebecca S. Ramsey

All Rights Reserved

Published in the United States by Broadway Books, an imprint of
The Doubleday Broadway Publishing Group, a division of Random
House, Inc., New York.
www.broadwaybooks.com

BROADWAY BOOKS and its logo, a letter B bisected on the diagonal,
are trademarks of Random House, Inc.

Library of Congress Cataloging-in-Publication Data

Ramsey, Rebecca S.
    French by heart : an American family's adventures in La Belle
France / Rebecca S. Ramsey.
        p.   cm.
    1. France—Description and travel. 2. Americans—France.
    3. France—Social life and customs. I. Title.

DC29.3.R367 2007
914.404'839092273—dc22
                                2006022430
ISBN: 978-0-7679-2522-8

PRINTED IN THE UNITED STATES OF AMERICA

10 9 8 7 6 5 4 3 2 1

FIRST EDITION

for

Madame Mallet

affectueusement

ACKNOWLEDGMENTS

Warm and sincere thanks to my talented editors and friends at Broadway Books. To Alison Presley, for believing in the book, having a vision of what it could be, and spending countless hours helping me shape it. To Jenna Thompson, for picking up my book downstream, polishing it to a shine, and guiding me through to the end. And to Charlie Conrad, for all of his ideas, support, and direction.

Thanks also to the circle of girlfriends who became my sisters in France; particularly to Leah Radulescu, for giving me the courage to tell the whole truth, even when it made me look ridiculous, to Susan Wallace, for her enthusiasm and creative inspiration, and to Linda Panning, for reading umpteen rewrites of chapter after chapter and still laughing when I hoped she would.

And the biggest thank-you ever to my sweet family. Thanks to my mother, Judy Skaggs, for being my very own personal cheerleader, and to my daddy, Wayne Skaggs, for showing me the world, one drainage research plot at a time. Thanks to Sarah, Ben, and Sam for allowing me to share all their stories, even the embarrassing ones. And thanks especially to Todd, for always loving me through everything, no matter where in the world we live.

I am home now. The azaleas are in full bloom, and I'm back to the world of school carpools and soccer practice, of church suppers and orthodontist appointments, of pork barbecue and pecan pie. But on a painted shelf below my sunny South Carolina window, a bevy of old French alarm clocks with their art deco numbers and little ball feet reminds me of a life when time barely ticked by. A life in which my family walked through each weeklong day arm in arm, shocked by the purple clouds, the black Auvergne soil, the smell of soup cooking for someone's breakfast, and the sounds of our neighbor Alain practicing his trumpet during his two-hour lunch break from work.

In July of 1999, my husband and I boarded an airplane for the heart of France with our baby Sam, seven-year-old Ben, nine-year-old Sarah, and Katie, our dear old cat. We had no idea what would happen to us, but we hoped to fall in love. Four years passed and we weren't disappointed. We drove to the airport again, feeling once more the tug that comes with leaving home.

This is the story of our life in France, of the American family in the stucco house at number 20, allée des Cerisiers, where the neighbors had never met a foreigner and only savages went barefoot.

La Rentrée

"Parents, children," said the stern directrice, standing in the school courtyard in front of the teachers. "It is my *something* to *something* you, *something* to a *something something something.* I am very happy to *something something,* these teachers *something something.*"

What was she saying? I watched the other mothers and copied them.

The teachers looked stiff, trying to smile at the crowd and yet appear dignified. Most had very short hair, some dyed in unnatural colors. I had seen hair like that all over France and had told my husband, Todd, how great it was that the French felt absolutely free in their sense of style. But now, seeing it on a teacher, purplish red hair disturbed me.

We weren't in South Carolina anymore. I smiled at my children as if this were just an ordinary first day of school at Cottonwood Elementary, where all the teachers were sweet and had southern accents, except for one foreigner who was maybe from Ohio.

I looked around the crowd of parents and children. Two French boys in knickers and kneesocks wrestled on the asphalt as their skinny mothers, stylish in their skirts and pointy-toed shoes, pulled them up by their ears, fussing at them and pointing at the teachers. The boys instantly tucked in their shirts and stood straight. Little girls and boys from all over the courtyard flitted to their mothers. Even the little French babies, bundled up as if it were winter, stopped whining and began gumming their passies obediently.

Then teachers began stepping forward and calling out names. I watched as they lined up their children, spoke to them firmly, and disappeared with them through the huge doors. A few of the little ones had to be pulled off their mothers. We could still hear them screaming inside. I willed myself not to cry.

It would be Ben's turn soon. My little first-grader, going off to French school. How would he know what to do? I tried to distract myself by pretending to look around casually. There was the enormous school gate. Why was it so tall and reinforced with huge sheets of metal? Were they bolted on for strength, lest the children unite and try a battering ram in their attempt to escape? Or maybe it was to keep the mommies out. I wasn't sure.

Ben tugged at my hand. A teacher was calling again for *Benjamin Ramsey*. With the accent, I hardly recognized the name.

"Oh," I said, flustered. "Have a great day." I squeezed his hand and gave him the most positive, encouraging smile I could muster. He walked to the back of the line and waved at me, looking so small. I watched his teacher give the children instructions, and then they marched away from me and through the school doors. I waved again, but he didn't see me.

Sarah's class was next. Fourth grade foreign students at École Saint-Pierre were put in a class of their own before being thrown in with the French kids. Nevertheless, her teacher insisted on speaking French to the bewildered children, who looked at one another and shrugged their shoulders. Sarah waved goodbye to me nervously, I blew her a kiss, and she followed the group inside.

I stayed there on the asphalt for a few more seconds, holding on to Sam's stroller, still projecting calm and confidence in case Sarah looked back before the door closed. But she didn't.

· · ·

WERE WE REALLY doing this? I had been thinking about this day for months, wondering how the children would react. From the very first time Todd asked me what I thought about the move, I had been picturing the first day of French school. When it came time to tell the kids about our big impending adventure, Todd and I had been nervous. Their lives of school and friends and soccer and church in sunny Greer were so happy and predictable. What would they think?

We decided to take them out to dinner to tell them. We figured that if moving to France made them happy, we could celebrate, and if it didn't, they probably wouldn't throw a fit in front of people.

"We've got some special news!" we announced to Ben and Sarah after we settled into our booth at the Dogwood Café.

We ordered, the waitress brought us our tea, and Todd cleared his throat. "You know how Daddy has to go to France sometimes on business trips, and you know how sometimes I bring you things back, and how we always said that maybe one day, we'd all get to go?"

"You mean we're going?" Sarah said, clapping her hands. "We're going for spring break?"

Ben didn't look up, but just kept rolling his Matchbox car back and forth across the table. Sam slumped in his high chair, sucking loudly on his sippy cup.

"Better than spring break, Sarah. Kids, what would you think of moving there? To France? We'll take all our stuff— all your toys, all our furniture—and they'll put it in a big container and send it over the ocean, and Katie can come too."

"I don't think a cat could breathe in there," Ben said, still rolling the car.

"Honey, Katie will ride on the airplane with us," I said.

Sarah cheered and bubbled on about wanting to live near the Eiffel Tower. Todd explained that we were moving to central France, not Paris, but it would surely be just as fun. She didn't care. She just wanted to know if she could get a red cape like Madeline's and if the houses were all covered with vines like the books said.

Ben didn't say much. We asked him what he thought.

"At least it's not the special news you told us last year. You know," he said, pointing at Sam drooling in his baby seat. "The last time you said you had special news, we got Sam. One of those is enough."

By the next day, however, the idea of our move had started to sink in. Sarah told Ben that they speak French words in France, which is different than English, and though she already knew plenty of words like *bonjour* and *au revoir* (the only ones she actually knew), he'd have a lot to learn. Ben made up a song that went, "I hate France and France hates me." So we found a tutor, which helped considerably. Béatrice was a lady from Switzerland who played color games and taught them how to count to ten. Todd's French colleague disapproved.

"Learning French from a Swiss? Oh, they'll have such an accent!"

We weren't too worried. We were more concerned the children would pick up our southernized French and end up sounding like Foghorn Leghorn in a beret.

As soon as we arrived in France, we continued the preparation for school. I let them watch as much television as they wanted—shows like *La petite maison dans le prairie* (*Little House on the Prairie*) and *Les mystères de l'Ouest* (*Wild Wild West*)—thinking that since they were all in French, some of it might sink in.

Maybe it had worked. Somehow, by the first day of school the children seemed unreasonably calm, and I was the one with the case of nerves. Todd had insisted on making everybody a hot breakfast from scratch, preaching his standard eastern North Carolina sermon about how sausage biscuits gave people confidence and fuel for the hard work ahead. I couldn't eat a thing. The French sausage had strange little bits in it that I couldn't identify, but that wasn't really the problem. The whole idea of leaving my sweet American babies at École Saint-Pierre, with its stern French teachers and its barren asphalt playground, made me a little nauseous.

On our drive to school that morning, I had hoped that Ben and Sarah wouldn't notice that Mommy was trying not to hyperventilate. I was pretty sure that Ben hadn't. My soon-to-be first-grader sat in the backseat, humming and pulling off Sam's socks just for fun. Ben felt pretty good about school, with his natural seven-year-old confidence. After all, he knew the basics. Todd and I had even tried to work with him, teaching him important words and phrases such as *"Oui, madame,"* and *"Non, madame,"* and *"J'ai besoin de faire pi-pi, s'il vous plait,"* ("I need to go pee-pee, please"). He was even fine with a slight change of name. Béatrice had told me the teachers would probably choose to call him *Benjamin* rather than Ben, as *benne* means "dump truck" in French. I was fine with that. After all, I didn't want people yelling after him, "Hey you, Dump Truck, come here!" We practiced how to say his name, *"Je m'appelle Ba-ja-ma."*

Before we reached the frenzy of the schoolyard, the walk from our parking space near the train station to school had been dreamily peaceful—so cool and pleasant, except for the occasional piles of dog poop on the sidewalks. Ben renamed rue de Bellevue "Poopedy Street," and served as my lookout for more piles to dodge. I was glad to have help. I couldn't keep my eyes on the sidewalk with so much to look at—flowers dripping down from the balconies, little niches for statues of Mary on the sides of apartment buildings, and ancient walls of stacked black volcanic stone, patched with stucco. I loved how the ivy made the houses look like shaggy faces, some with eyes closed, their shutters fastened, and others wide awake with eyelashes of decorative brick. All of them had rippling tile roof hats and their mouths were heavy old doors, which opened and closed as the people who lived there returned from the *boulangerie* with their fresh breakfast baguettes or from their morning walks with their dogs.

What was it about this place that was so enchanting? Even with my queasiness, I couldn't help feeling charmed by it, from the old brass door knockers shaped like a lady's hand to the women, young and old, with their sultry eyes and obvious confidence. As we walked by the cafés I tried not to stare at the people sitting there, their beautiful French words twirling out of their mouths, mingling with the swirls of coffee perfuming the crisp morning air. I wanted to understand it all, the Frenchness of this place. I wanted to be part of it and for it to be a part of me—a part of us, our family. We hoped to have four years or so in France. Could that happen in four years? We were nervous, yes, but our American hearts were open. Could we be French too, just for a little while? French, not by citizenship, but by heart?

Finally we made it to the huge orange gate of École Saint-Pierre, walked in, and found a place on the courtyard to wait. I got my camera out for our annual first-day-of-school pictures and let the children pick where to stand. Sarah found Christy Appleton, an American girl her age who was also starting French school that day. They put their arms around each other as if they were old pals and posed beside the door to the teachers' lounge. I hoped the light was right and you could see their smiles, not to mention the curlicues of cigarette smoke coming out from under the door.

Ben had no one to stand by. I knew there was supposed to be a little British boy his age, but he hadn't arrived yet, so Ben chose to stand outside the gate for his picture. Ben was wearing shorts and a T-shirt that he had sponge painted in Vacation Bible School back home in South Carolina, the one with what is supposed to be three birds stamped on it that actually look more like ink blobs. I had wanted him to wear one of his nice Penney's shirts with a collar, but he said he liked the bird shirt, so I didn't say anything. While I snapped the picture, one sleeve was drooping down nearly off his shoulder and he was biting his lip, trying to not to topple over with his backpack full of school supplies.

I hoped his supplies were the right ones. I'd heard horror stories from former expatriates about how once the stores in France run out, they don't restock. One lady named Ruth told me her little Hannah got yelled at her first day of first grade because she had the wrong type of fountain pen, and that the poor little thing had to eat Tums for breakfast all the way until Christmas.

My French friend Virginie lent me her husband, Yves, to take me school supply shopping for the kids. Auchan, the *hypermarché,* was decorated with big banners celebrating *la rentrée,* the first day back to school. Stressed-out mothers and fathers were everywhere, armed with their lists, ready to fight over the last *cahier de brouillon.* What was that, anyway? Yves didn't know. According to the pocket dictionary in my purse it was a "notebook of disorganization." Was that right? And was an *ardoise* really a "slate"? Using slates seemed primitive to me, but this was France, not the USA.

The farther we made it down the children's lists, the clearer it was to me that Yves had no idea what he was doing. By the time we finally got to the notebook aisle, jampacked with hundreds of different kinds of *cahiers,* grouped according to paper weight, page number, dimensions in centimeters, and line type, Yves sheepishly asked me if I'd mind if he went to look at the CDs. He wanted to find that Shania Twain one where she sang, "Man, I feel like a woman."

After dropping the children off at school I went home and

tried to stay busy until I couldn't stand the suspense any longer and drove to the gate at three-thirty, a whole hour early. Eventually people started double-parking again and honking at one another, and crowds gathered and finally the directrice opened the gates. The mothers poured in and Sam and I found a place to the side and waited with my new friend Linda and a Finnish lady whose name I couldn't pronounce. Sarah came out skipping and started bubbling over about her French teacher and how her British English teacher says "trousers" instead of "pants" and how "pants" is British for "underwear" and how they say "dog dirt" instead of "dog poop" and how she hated the playground toilet, how you have to squat into a hole, and how she liked the spicy meat they had for their second course at lunch until somebody told her it was pig intestine. I was relieved to see her so happy, but I wasn't too surprised. Sarah always had seemed grown up to me and capable, but what about my little Ben? My heart beat wildly in my chest as I searched the crowd for his face.

I almost cried when I saw him. Ben came out smiling in the middle of his little French classmates, and I wanted to run to him, but I made myself stand still and wait, as if this were just an ordinary day. When he walked through the crowd, smiling at me and swinging his book bag, I kissed him on the cheek and hugged him.

"Did Madame Chaput give you any homework?" I asked.

"How do I know, Mom?" he said, shrugging his shoulders and then giving me a grin. "All that lady talks is French!"

I. *La Tornade*

A month before we left for France, a truck pulling a steel shipping container pulled into Kensington Farm, our neighborhood, and parked in front of our house. It was moving day and Mother had come down from Raleigh to help me with the children. We pulled lawn chairs into my front yard, along with the kiddie pool and a cooler of juice boxes, and tried to keep the kids out of the way. Sitting there sweating, we watched the movers swarm into our house like termites, dismantling furniture and loading our life into the steel box. It was a little rusty. I hoped it was waterproof.

"It will be an adventure," Mother said, trying to sound confident as Sam fingered her necklace. I sighed at the bittersweetness and agreed that yes, it would. Then a loud noise came from inside and we jerked around to see a mover slip on the carpet at the top of my stairs, sending towels and boxes flying and ripping the oak banister clean off the wall. I watched it sail like a javelin right out the open door and land in my India hawthorns.

That's when I began to feel like Dorothy, pulled right out of a scene from *The Wizard of Oz,* the one where the twister is whirling and I am in the middle, watching everything pop up in front of me, riding the waves of the wind. There were the towels, and then the banister, and the people—Mother, Todd's boss, Ben's soccer coach and Sarah's choir teacher, my sister-in-law, and the man at the bank. They were all waving and talking to me, though I could barely make out what they were saying.

For six months the tornado had been brewing, starting on a December night right after we had put up the tree and let the kids hang up a few ornaments. Todd had finished the last of the bedtime stories and I had put Sam, our two-month-old, down to sleep. We collapsed on the couch, savoring the stillness of the house in the glow of the Christmas lights, listening to the calm tick-tocking of the mantel clock.

The minute hand twitched forward and Todd broke the silence. "There is a job in France," he said, and raised his eyebrow into a question mark. My heart fluttered. France? Now? We had talked about going for years. As if on cue, the heat came on, blasting through a ceiling vent and rattling the paper chain the kids had draped on the tree. The little yellow house ornament that I had made for our first Christmas there began to spin on its gold thread, then unwind and spin again, caught in its own little cyclone. I pointed it out to Todd and we laughed at the coincidence.

A move to France? I had been in love with France since I was fifteen, daydreaming myself into the travel posters plastered all over the walls of my high school French class. Mademoiselle Wright was young and blond, and she taught us how to order dinner at a brasserie and how to sing "Sur le pont d'Avignon." But the best part was when she would pass around pictures she had taken when she was in college and went to Paris with her boyfriend. It was the first time a teacher had ever mentioned a boyfriend, but this class was about romantic France, after all. When Todd first started with Michelin, we had dreamed of getting to go and touring the countryside. He started French lessons and we hoped for a job transfer. But now, settled, with three kids?

The question mark followed me around like a cartoon bubble over my head everywhere I went—into bed or the shower, to church on Christmas Eve and to my parents' living room in Raleigh as we opened presents. A couple days later we made the drive back to Greer, and as we pulled into the neighborhood, I looked at the houses on our street. We had a nice life in South Carolina. Kensington Farm was a good subdivision, full of perfectly fine vinyl-sided two-story houses, with a swim team, close to the soccer fields and good schools. People decorated their houses for every holiday and there were always pink and blue balloons popping up on mailboxes, announcing more happy children being born into suburbia. The children liked their teachers and I volunteered at school, and on weekends we had soccer games and went to church and spread our mulch like everyone else. And yet that day everything looked gray. Maybe it was the rain. In spite of the hills, the place felt as flat as Dorothy's prairie.

I tumbled the pictures in my mind of the possibilities before us. French school. The gothic black cathedral I'd seen on Todd's postcards from business trips. The flowers. The travel. The French countryside.

The job opening was in Clermont-Ferrand, a city four hours south of Paris. According to the tour books, Clermont-Ferrand was an uninteresting industrial town located in the region called the Auvergne, the lush agricultural heartland of France dotted with crumbling castles and sunflower fields. Some described the city as filled with smoke-spitting factories and car dealerships. One of Todd's French colleagues rolled his eyes whenever Clermont was mentioned. "It's a dirty place," he said. But it sounded fascinating to me, such a mix of modern and medieval, with a thirteenth-century cathedral, a thermal spring, and the Michelin headquarters, all within a mile of each other. And on the horizon was the Puy de Dôme, an extinct volcano. Who needed Paris?

Would we live in the city? Most American expatriates lived together in one of the sleepy little villages on the outskirts of town. But I wasn't interested in that. I wouldn't want to move all the way to France to live right in the middle of a bunch of Americans. Still, the village sounded so quaint, with its bakery, butcher shop, vineyards, and town square. Couldn't we find a village that was still unexplored? Todd said that it would all depend where there was a rental house available. But there I was, picking out a village when we hadn't even decided on whether to move yet. I didn't want to rush my answer even though this was my long-lost dream.

Then Todd tempted me with food. He spoke of fresh cheeses, crusty baguettes, and big loaves of *pain de compagne,* country bread. Potatoes layered with cream and cheese, and coq au vin. Apricots, fresh from the tree, and *clafoutis,* a cherry flan, eaten warm. My mouth watered.

We said yes.

Within two weeks of our acceptance we were summoned

to a meeting with personnel. In the parking lot, a sudden gust of wind blew my hair and fluttered the paper I carried for notes. A guard handed me a badge on a chain and I followed Todd through hallways and past mazes of cubicles. Finally we got to an office where a serious-looking woman sat across from a frightened couple. We joined them at the table, and she shut the door and handed me a three-inch-thick binder on expatriation. And then she talked at us for I don't know how long about French taxes, insurance, school for the children, bank accounts, how our lamps would work but our televisions would not, percentages of pay in dollars and in francs, housing costs, French lessons for spouses, the company's responsibility in case of accidental death, and how France has no closets. Two hours later, it was over. I looked down at my paper. It was blank.

Todd and I wandered out into the parking lot with our eyes spinning and struggled to find our car. We drove home and called our parents. I just knew Mother and Daddy would be thrilled for us, as much as they loved to travel. "Oh," Mother said, with a quiver in her voice. "Well," she said, "I'll call my friends at church. You'll have to be our new foreign missions project."

Daddy sounded serious. "I'm sure it will be good for Todd's career," he said, and then got off the phone and started planning a last-minute family trip to Florida, as if they might never see us again.

Next we called Todd's parents, and Todd's mom didn't hide her feelings. After considerable silence she said, "I guess I might as well curl up and die." I couldn't blame her. She had just gotten Todd's brother and his family back to the Carolinas after the air force had taken them off to Japan and then

New Mexico. Now we were running off to another country with her youngest grandbaby, before Sam had even started reaching for her. Todd's dad, who had been in France with the army in the early sixties, said, "You've got to do what you've got to do," and started recalling how he used to see French men bicycling to work with wine in their baskets and baguettes under their arms.

Within three months that breeze in the parking lot had grown into a full-blown twister. Paperwork of every kind blew around us like confetti, though we tried to rein it in. I walked around the house for a week with a clipboard, writing down the required inventory of our every possession, from boys' briefs to salad forks, complete with a translation in French and estimated replacement value in dollars and in francs, just in case the boat sank. We sold our house, closed bank accounts, were photographed and medically examined, went to French class, got a visa for the cat, and said goodbye to everyone we knew at least a couple times.

• • •

FINALLY, WE LUGGED our suitcases to the airport.

Ahead of us was the very last obstacle, a three-flight marathon; first to Atlanta, then to Paris, then south to Clermont-Ferrand.

Flying to France with three children, an old cat, nine suitcases, four backpacks, a diaper bag, a car seat, and a stroller turned out not to be nearly the nightmare I expected. Sarah busied herself by making up sad songs about lost nine-year-old ponies who would never see Greer, South Carolina, and their little yellow house again. Ben spent his time by drawing

pictures of the cargo ship carrying all of our worldly posses-
sions tragically sunken at the bottom of the Atlantic Ocean.
Thankfully, baby Sam slept most of the way and Katie the cat
was strung out on kitty Valium in the cargo hold. Todd and I
took turns at being comatose and giddy, celebrating that our
move to France was finally happening. If we had forgotten
any essential detail, it was too late now.

As Todd snored at the other end of the aisle, I asked the
cute Air France steward for a drink.

"So you are taking your children to visit France?" he asked
in his charming accent, searching his cart for a Coca Light.

"Oh, no," I gushed. "We're moving there. Today!"

"Ah. How nice for you," he said. "Americans do love
Paris."

"Oh, we're not moving to Paris," I said, smiling. "We're
moving to Clermont-Ferrand."

"Pardon?"

"Clermont-Ferrand," I repeated with some throat scraping, trying to sound more French. "We have a connecting
flight in Paris to Clermont-Ferrand."

"Oh, Clermont-Ferrand," he said, and grimaced. "For
Michelin, no?" he asked, pointing at my husband drooling on
his little pillow.

"Yes. How did you know?"

"Ah, madame, why else would anyone go to Clermont?"
He handed me my glass. "It's not Paris," he said, frowning.
"But maybe you will like it."

2. *Le Début*

We landed in Oz.

There were volcanoes on the horizon—volcanoes, for heaven's sake, not jagged and rocky but smooth and green, weathered into mounds and mountains, one sunken at the top like an egg cup for the moon. There were farm fields in the distance, dotted with little stone buildings roofed in orange tile, and tall, blackish cedars spiking into the purple blue sky. And there were thousands of sunflowers, tight green balls, flanking the roads as if standing offstage, waiting for their cue to raise their heads and burst into bloom.

Inside the air-locked plane we had braced ourselves to be hit by the steamy July heat we knew by heart, but this air was oddly cool and dry, as if puffed into the scene like a special effect. What was this place? Even the people in baggage claim had seemed strange—the woman so boyishly thin yet so outlandishly sensual, with her dark eyes and her silk chemise unbuttoned down to there. She moved in such a sultry way, whispering ordinary things to the businessmen as they stood by the conveyer belt and smoked.

The French people had greeted each other with smiles and kisses on both cheeks, taking each other's bags and talking quietly. I stood and watched from the middle of our pile of stuff while Todd hoisted our heavy bags off the belt and the children flitted around him, getting in the way. We were making a scene, but no one seemed to notice. One by one the French left us. Huddled there alone within the glass partitions of baggage claim, we looked like an exhibit at the zoo.

Someone was supposed to meet us there. The lady in personnel had said that someone, maybe even a family with children of similar ages to ours, would be assigned to meet us at the airport, to welcome us and escort us to the furnished apartment where we'd stay until our things arrived. Americans are always assigned to Americans, she had said, as they would know better than the French what their fellow countrymen would need when they were jet lagged and hungry. But no one came.

I didn't mind—I liked the idea of the five of us seeing Clermont-Ferrand for the first time alone, arm in arm on our yellow brick road, without anyone else to color our opinions or explain how our life here would be. I had talked with a few American expatriates back in South Carolina, and most were malcontents. Not me. This was going to be the big adventure of my life—of my family's life.

"Somebody will show up," Todd said, leaning on the luggage cart. "They have to—they've got our keys."

Finally the conveyer belt turned off and we found a bench of plastic seats to sit in while Todd went to report two missing bags. Sam, tired of sitting in his stroller, fussed and fidgeted. Ben was setting up the suitcases like dominoes and Sarah was whining to take Katie out for a second when Todd called out "Catch!" from behind.

He swung a heavy ring of keys up in a fake throw. There had to be twenty keys on the ring—paper-thin keys less than an inch long and heavy old keys with a single tooth that looked like they belonged in a chateau.

"You won't believe it, but this envelope was just setting up there on the counter with my name on it. It's a good thing we had two bags missing or I wouldn't have even seen it."

Sarah, intrigued by keys and envelopes that magically appear, whispered, "How do you think it got there?"

"Mrs. Thompson brought it, Sarah," Todd said plainly. "You know Beck, Dan's wife, Nora—I worked with Dan back in Research and Development. She must have dropped it off earlier," he said. "She left a note that something came up but she'd call later. There's a map—see, here's the airport and here's where we're going to be, and there's this," he said, pulling out a blue elastic-bound folder labeled "PAPERS VERY IMPORTANTE," and a small paperback titled *La code de la route*, with French traffic signs all over the cover.

"You want to look this over? Before we, uh . . ." I hesitantly asked my husband as he stuffed Sam into the car seat between Ben and Sarah in the back of our small rental car. Todd shook his head.

"Don't need to. There are only a few signs I'm not sure about. I'll just follow him," he said, nodding at the taxi driver, who had loaded eight of our suitcases into his car and was gunning his engine. "No problem."

3. *Rue des Bosquets*

We almost died. At least I thought we were going to.

It was Mr. Toad's Wild Ride into the city of Clermont-Ferrand and all the way to number 18, rue des Bosquets, Michelin's furnished duplex, where we would live until we found a rental house of our own. Todd followed close to the taxi driver, who jerked from lane to lane as motorbikes wove in front of us and behind, and bus only lanes and stoplights and roundabouts popped out of nowhere. Merging into the circle of spinning cars was like throwing ourselves into a life-and-death round of jump rope. I sat in the front with Katie's carrier on my lap, my heart slinging from side to side and dropping down into my shoes, trying to keep our place on the map in case the taxi sped on ahead. On long straight roads I stole glances at the view whizzing past the windows. There were ugly Laundromats next to charming stacked-stone houses with turrets and window boxes. There were cafés with tables outside crowded with people in sunglasses having tiny cups of coffee.

Every building was roofed in ripples of orange tile, and most had quirky features like carved faces or molding or art deco borders of stone. There were restaurants, patisseries, and an Easy Rider L'École de la Moto. Even though the city looked like it was in need of a good power washing, it was stunning. Even the streetlights had baskets of flowers hanging from them, heavy with pink and red blooms.

People were everywhere—thin, tan people with summer clothes on. They were walking, some with dogs, some with children and funny strollers with attached umbrellas propped askew and with running boards where bigger children could stand and have their mother push them too. There were women in aprons sweeping their front steps or opening their shutters upstairs. And there were women with red hair, purple-red hair, and pink hair. People waited for buses and sat on benches, reading the paper or staring into space. There were revolving billboards and half-demolished buildings, one with the kitchen wall exposed to the world, still with the tile backsplash stuck on.

We strained our necks to see the Michelin headquarters. It was right in downtown Clermont-Ferrand. We hung a right and there on the hill was the huge black cathedral with its gothic spires. The city center was crowded with people walking and shopping at stores like Betty Boots, with its racks of shoes brought out onto the sidewalk. There were bakeries on every corner, and people carrying baguettes—unwrapped—in their bare hands. We turned onto rue Lavoisier and a diesel cloud blew into our car through our open windows as we headed up the hill. Rue des Bosquets was the left turn before the Total, a gas station with a rotisserie chicken oven next to the rack of butane tanks by the front door. Beside it was a *boulangerie*, Au Croissant d'Or, which must have been a chain—the kids had noticed the same plastic croissant on a sign on the way into town. The rest of rue des Bosquets was residential.

Back home we had looked up *bosquet* in the dictionary, but this was no street of groves. Rue des Bosquets was a quilt of asphalt strips, marked with potholes and lined with dingy tile-roofed duplexes built in the sixties. But it wasn't so bad. In a month or two we'd be moving, and this would give us a chance to try living in the city. The homes (except for the one in the middle) looked well cared for, all with garden gates, manicured lawns, and window boxes full of red or pink flowers.

The taxi parked half on, half off the curb in front of number 18, the one in the middle with the trash piled up on the sidewalk. The front yard was barely big enough to lie down in and was overgrown with weeds. It had large windows with scrolled down metal shutters—the kind that I'd seen on television police dramas. At the top of the stairs, added for decoration next to the front door, were two blue ceramic bugs of some kind—either bees or locusts. We stared at the house in silence. Katie meowed from her carrier.

"This isn't it, is it?" Ben asked from the backseat.

We got out and the kids examined the trash and got excited, which I took as a good sign. There was "Tony le Tigre," roaring "Grrr," from a Frosties box, and on a large box was stamped the word *trotinette,* along with a large picture of a scooter. Ben asked if the house came with toys.

We opened the gate, with its mod sixties-style ironwork of squares and rectangles, and walked through the overgrown jungle of trees and bushes and roses. The kids were buzzing around like bees. "Watch yourself around these," Todd warned them, lifting a thorny rose branch caught on his shoulder. I had to groan at how gorgeous it was—even with the dingy stucco and mod architecture. I'd always loved roses but never had luck with them in South Carolina. But these were going crazy, let go on their own.

As Todd began to try each of the keys, I started to look around. Across the street there was a storybook scene to rival anything I'd ever seen in a magazine. There were topiary roses, a little wishing well, and a balcony lined with window boxes bursting with red flowers. There was an old man in blue coveralls watering a hanging kettle of pink impatiens, standing so still that he looked planted beside them. He glanced up at us with a kind look, and I think our eyes met—it was hard to tell behind his thick glasses. Of course, he might have just been watching the five of us all crowding the front steps. We must have been quite a sight—Sarah and Ben jockeying for position, Sam fussing on my hip, the cat howling in her kitty Valium–induced stupor, and Todd pushed up against the door, trying the keys one by one. It turns out there were seventeen.

Finally the last key clicked and Todd opened the tall heavy door into a hall with black and gray checkerboard linoleum, textured wallpaper of mottled peach, high ceilings, and the scent of disinfectant. It was dark with all the shutters closed, so the kids scattered and started turning on lights and running in rooms.

We were inspecting the low beds and the armoires in the two back bedrooms when we heard a short, strange repeating melody coming from somewhere, maybe inside the house. We all looked at each other. What was it? It sounded again.

"An ice cream truck!" Ben said.

"No," Todd said, listening to it repeat again. "I bet it's the phone." He headed to the living room.

"This place sure is a crazy," Sarah said from her bed, sinking her head into the long sausage-shaped pillow at the headboard.

It was Nora calling. I had talked with Nora twice on the

phone before the move and had concluded that at least in her mind, she wrote the book on American expatriate survival in France, which, if it were an actual book, would certainly be titled *How to Get Along in This Miserable Country*. At least five times during our first conversation she had informed me that this was her fourth year in France, and she hoped that after this they'd never have to live in France again.

By Todd's "uh-huhs" and "yeahs" and "thank yous," I could tell that Nora was in monologue mode. Finally, he handed the phone to me.

"Welcome to France!" she said. "You knew you wouldn't have screens, right?"

Screens? What was she talking about?

"The shutters you've got in front are the modern kind. You roll them up," she said. "There's a long rod hanging beside the sheers—do you see it?" I said that I did. "Well, go ahead and crank them up. I was in there this morning before I ran over to the airport. You need to air that place out, but watch the kids around those windows. French people don't sue, so they don't care a hill of beans about liability. Kids fall out of them all the time." I opened them up and looked out at the hundreds of tile-roofed houses between us and the cathedral in the distance. Katie jumped up to the ledge and sniffed the breeze. Nora was still talking. "It can get hot as blazes, but if you keep the windows open you can get a good draft running through." She was right. As soon as the second window was open, a cool breeze blew the stale air out of the house.

"There'll be no closets like I warned you but the bedrooms do have armoires—there's a gorgeous one in the back bedroom—I saw one exactly like it at Troc de l'Ile. That's the place to go for cheap antiques—we'll go sometime. Anyway, there's a tub down the hall and a separate little room for the WC—you know, the potty. It's the only one you've got, unless you count the one down in the garage. You've got to take the kids down to see it. It's two footprints and a hole!"

After Nora gave me a short course on how to use the tiny washing machine and the dryer in the kitchen, she said she had to run. "Eventually things get easier. Just be sure to let us help you. Oh, that reminds me—Joan Fillmore and I made you dinner—I stuck it in the fridge. They always stock the apartments with food, but what American kids do you know that will eat duck in a can?"

I couldn't see Nora becoming my best friend, but it was nice that she had brought us a meal. I hadn't even thought about dinner. Or, apparently, a litter box. Katie christened the stairs, and then hopped up on a window ledge for fresh air. Todd and I looked at each other, and then he groaned and got up off the couch. I went to look up *litter box* in the pocket dictionary I had stuffed in a suitcase, while he stared at the map and tried to remember where the big grocery store was that somebody had taken him to once on a business trip. "The only thing I can find is *litter bin,* which is *boîte à ordures,* but I don't know if that has anything to do with cats," I said.

"That's okay. There'll probably be pictures on the bag," Todd sighed and put the map in his jacket. I made him promise me that he would come right back and not die in a car accident on the way. While he was gone, I sent the big kids out to explore the backyard, and stood in front of the oven, trying to convert Fahrenheit to Celsius. When the oven wouldn't start up, I dumped the noodle bake in a saucepan and, after several tries, managed to light the gas stove.

Leaning over the cold pan of spaghetti, my brain started replaying the goodbye scene at the airport. Sarah and her buddy Meg had started crying, which started my friend Kathy crying. Even though I was thrilled to go, I had cried too. And now the bathroom smelled so bad, and there was a huge pile of trash outside, and I was thinking that this house probably had mice. I felt sick to my stomach. What had we done?

The door slammed and Ben rushed in. "You should see it out there!" he said, opening his hands like a book to show me his red stained palms and dozens of ripe raspberries. "There's tons of them!"

"And pears!" Sarah said, pulling me to the front door. "You've got to see this!"

So I turned the gas off, pulled Sam up on my hip, locked the front door (not being sure of the safety of the neighborhood), and we walked around the side of the house, through the weeds past the quince bush and the huge lilac trees. There in the back was a big weedy yard, enclosed by tall walls of stacked stones, unkempt but wildly beautiful with the scattered daisies and cosmos. There were raspberry bushes on one side, and in the shade of the house there was a moss carpet and clusters of wild violets. In the back there were two rusty poles with a clothesline dangling and on the other side a weeping willow tree. Stepping into that overgrown garden, I felt surrounded by a living fence, as if even the stone walls were breathing and wiggling their footings in the soil. Dozens of little pear trees, all pruned flat against the tall stone walls, encircled the yard. They stood like frozen cancan dancers, their branches reaching out like arms holding on to one another. And dangling from those arms were the most perfect little green pears, hundreds, maybe thousands of them.

"I know we have to get our own house," said Sarah, "but can we at least stay till they're ripe?"

4. *First Conversations*

Where was my husband? I crowded Sarah and Ben around the table by the window in the tiny kitchen, squished Sam into the small wooden high chair, and served up spaghetti casserole and milk, which came in a small paper box.

"This tastes funny," Ben said, pushing away his glass.

There were bottles of water in the fridge. Was the tap water not safe to drink? No one had said anything about that, but I gave him the bottled water, just in case, and exchanged Sarah's too and sat down. No sign of Todd, and he had been gone an hour and a half. How long could it take to buy a bag of cat litter and a box?

The doorbell rang. We were on display, sitting there by the open window. There was a teenage boy standing at the gate looking up at us. What did he want? His black hair hung over one of his eyes, as he waved something sharp and silver at me and called, *"Madame, madame."*

What in the world?

He tried again. *"Madame, puis-je couper les arbres?"*

I stood up. I had no idea what that meant.

"Uh, *pardon?*" I shouted nervously out the window.

"Elle est anglaise" (She's English), a beer-bellied man in a T-shirt shouted down from his window next door.

Américaine, I wanted to yell back.

The boy nodded up at the man and smiled.

"Madame, ma-da-ame," he called. *"Puis-je couper les arbres?"* He was making no effort whatsoever to slow down. What had he said? Something about *couper*—to cut. He could have cut us if he had wanted to—he could have jumped the fence, raced up the stairs, and used that sharp thing on us right through the open window.

"Puis—je—couper—les—arbres?" he said again, this time enunciating for effect and waving the silver thing—they were loppers, to trim bushes or trees. Okay, so he wanted to trim the trees. Nora had told Todd that Michelin would probably send someone over to fix up the yard, but this guy didn't look old enough. One of the expatriates had told me that there were gypsies who did that kind of work and that I ought to be careful, though they only stole things and rarely hurt anyone.

"Madame! Puis-je couper les arbres?"

The man next door was still leaning out his window, drinking his beer and watching us. I could hear his television going, but apparently we were better entertainment. There were two women next door on the other side—they were watching too from underneath their patio umbrella. I could see their shadows. Where was the little old man across the street? Couldn't somebody help me?

"Mommy, shut the window," Sarah whispered. Ben got up and hid behind me.

"*Où êtes-vous?*" I yelled back, my voice shaking, meaning to ask "Who are you?" but actually saying "Where are you?"—which of course made no sense. He looked at me funny and then went back to the yelling.

"*Madame, puis-je couper les arbres?*"

"*Non!*" I shouted, embarrassed, and put my back to the window. "Just ignore him," I told the kids. "He'll leave us alone. Sit back down—your food is getting cold." Ben stared at me. "Now," I said sternly.

"*Madame, ma-da-ame!*" he called, holding out his hands. He wanted money?

The beer-bellied man in the T-shirt laughed down from his window. "She's a foreigner and she doesn't understand a word you're saying!"

The nerve! I understood him perfectly. He just couldn't understand me.

My hands shook as I locked the window shut. Where was Todd?

The boy gave up, swung off my gate, and bumped the pile of trash as he walked by, toppling it into the street. The old women came out to the road, talking with their backs to us.

Twenty minutes later Todd was still nowhere to be found, and as I tried to scrub out the noodles that Sam had tangled up in the wooden beads attached to his tray, I started to worry. What was I going to do? I didn't even know my own phone number. Todd had the packet of important papers and phone numbers with him in the car, including Nora's phone number. I searched a phone book, but it was organized according to villages and I couldn't remember which village was Nora's. *You're just tired,* I said to myself. *Don't be paranoid.*

The old man was out again, puttering in his front yard.

And there was the trash, now in the street. I need to do something about that. I wasn't going to let a rude teenager intimidate me into hiding inside my own apartment, even if I did just make a fool of myself. "I'm going out to straighten up the trash," I told the kids, who didn't even notice. They were sitting in front of the television, mesmerized by a game show involving an alien and a balding man in tight orange pants.

I stood behind the front door, trying to work out what to say. What was the word for garbage men? I knew the word for trash can was *poubelle*—such a beautiful word, *poubelle,* for something as nasty as a trash can. I'll use *poubelle*, I decided and tried some deep breathing to slow my racing heart. *How silly to be nervous,* I thought. And then I put Sam on my hip, glad to have a baby to help the conversation, and finally exited my house.

I crossed the street and got my question out to the old man, but with lots of pointing to the *poubelle* and to my watch. It was awful. After three years of high school French and the last two months with a tutor, I sounded like a caveman. "Man for garbage, go, when?" At least he understood and said we'd have to wait until Thursday. He grinned and twirled his shaky finger at Sam, who thankfully smiled back and acted cute. "Your wife?" I asked, nodding at a woman who had left the house and was making her way up the hill.

"Non, madame," he said, and as he smiled at the thought of that, I looked at his blue-gray eyes, all glittery behind his thick glasses. I hadn't really noticed what he looked like before that moment, being so preoccupied with myself, my words, my accent. "I eat my soup alone," he said, and gave a slight smile.

I was charmed.

Five minutes later, Todd finally pulled up to the gate, and as we unpacked the strange mix of groceries with their funny words and pictures on the packages, we all talked at once, telling the stories of the rude lopper boy and the pears out back and the *soupe* man. By the time we got in bed that night, the kids had put tiny coffee cups of roses and daisies and grass in every room of the house. The place smelled like a zoo, and I was pretty sure that the litter Todd bought was for guinea pigs. The French they spoke here scarcely resembled what I learned back home, and my first run of the little washer dyed all the new dishcloths red. We had no idea where we'd find a house, we had one week to find a car and insurance, and two Limoges cups had fallen onto the tile and were now tiny slivers in the little trash can. But in spite of it all, I still had a crush on France. We had made it through the first day of our new life, and there was a coffee cup on my kitchen windowsill filled with wilted grass and a big pink rose, just opening up.

5. Door Number Three

Madame Chabosson was the real estate agent assigned to Michelin's British and American expatriates, even though she spoke no English and foreigners made her nervous. "Uh . . . I am afraid that I will not be able to meet with you for at least ten days," she had said to Todd on the phone the day after we had arrived in a heap from South Carolina. "But I'm sure you understand, Monsieur Ramsey, as it is August, when our entire office except for me, unfortuantely, is on vacation. And I am sure that you will agree," she went on, quivering, "that the time to explore the quartiers of Clermont-Ferrand and its surrounding villages could be good for you. Rest," she said. "Have some good meals. I've yet to meet with an American who's relaxed."

Eleven days later, Madame Chabosson met us at her office parking lot and the five of us squeezed ourselves into her little clown car. Todd sat in the front, holding her papers and keys, and I sat pinned in the middle between Sam's car seat and Sarah. Ben was happy to be tucked into a strange little seat in the very back, which I was pretty sure was part of the trunk. I tried not to think about rear-end collisions as motor-bikes and buses closed in around us, weaving in and out of traffic.

Madame Chabosson spoke French in a high-pitched ner-vous voice and smacked gum as she talked. She was trying to quit smoking, she said.

"Ah," Todd and I said in unison and smiled at each other, glad to have finally understood an entire sentence. Now that we were no longer separated from Madame Chabosson by miles of phone line, her nerves had thrown her French into high gear.

"I'll present to you the three rental houses currently avail-able," she explained, her right eye twitching, and then she said that we were to attend to a matter that was très importante, which unfortunately we missed on account of the gum smacking. I had my dictionary on my lap, but it only kept confusing the issue. I wanted to live on a cul-de-sac, but I wasn't sure about using the word *cul-de-sac,* even though it's a French phrase. It sounded fine, but when I looked it up I found three stars beside the word *cul,* which meant that it was a cuss word. Literally translated *cul-de-sac* meant "ass of bag." Did they say that? I certainly didn't want to cuss at her. I al-ready looked foolish enough, yelling my questions over the traffic and engine noise, on account of the windows being rolled down. My increased volume seemed to emphasize my southern accent and lack of confidence. By the time we stopped at the third house, Madame Chabosson had given up and pulled out her cigarettes.

Luckily, the third was the charm. It was not precariously

built on a cliff, as was house number one, and neither was the
entire first floor taken up with the owner's large boat, as was
the case for house number two. To our delight, house three
was perfect. It was in a small village with narrow roads, stucco
houses with flower-laden balconies, and stacked-stone fences.
No other Americans lived there, and it was even on a cul-de-
sac, named allée des Cerisiers, "alley of the cherry trees." As
quickly as we could get out of the car, Ben and Sarah raced
for the huge cherry tree in the side yard and started fighting
about who got there first. The tree had thick low branches
and was perfect for climbing. The house was a two-story with
an orange tile roof, like all the houses, and had beautiful
wooden shutters instead of the rusty metal ones in our temporary apartment. The balcony stretched across the entire
second floor with a curvy wrought-iron railing, and I could
just imagine flower boxes dripping with geraniums all along
it, like on the other houses on the street.

As I lifted baby Sam out of the realtor's car and put him
on my hip, I felt like someone was watching us. I looked
around and there she was, staring down at us from the balcony just across the narrow street. She was old and had very
short white hair and was wearing an apron and holding a
wooden spoon. Her mouth was screwed up in a funny way.
Had she never heard children speaking English before? As
Todd quizzed Madame Chabosson about rent and utility
bills, the woman in the balcony stopped staring for a moment
to wipe her hands on her apron and unfold the little bistro
chair propped against the wall. Then she settled in to watch
us from her box seat, as if we were a basketball game.

Not wanting to be rude, I nodded up to her and smiled—
just a slight smile, nothing too perky or warm. I had learned

since we left Greer that I couldn't just go around giving out smiles carelessly or people would think I was weird or flirting with them, which had led to problems. The white-haired lady looked shocked at my nod, but then returned it and may have smiled—I couldn't really tell. I figured that after our exchange she would go back inside to her cooking, but as Madame Chabosson fiddled with the keys at the front door, the lady on the balcony dropped her spoon beside her and leaned forward in her chair to examine us with greater scrutiny. Wasn't it nice that she was so interested in us? With the apron and wooden spoon, she cut quite a grandmotherly figure. What a comfort it would be for our family if we picked this house, a sweet little French grandma right across the street.

6.   20, allée des Cerisiers

One step inside the house and Madame Chabosson's eye
stopped twitching. She could tell. We were sold. We couldn't
help ourselves from oohing and aahing at how wonderfully
French everything was—the gravel-floored wine *cave* under
the house, the bidet next to the shower, and the curly
wrought-iron rail on the balcony. And there were five bedrooms! Five! It was a veritable mansion compared to the cliff
house and the one with the ship. The kitchen was tiny, but
unlike in the other houses it came with cabinets, an oven and
stove, and even a refrigerator, though it was dorm-size.

In all our excitement we hardly noticed that the bedrooms
were no bigger than walk-in closets. Neither did we see the
shiny peach disco wallpaper, the tan zigzags on the floor tiles,
and the brown grout that oozed up unevenly between them.
We were having too much fun opening and closing the heavy
doors on every room and hallway with their old-fashioned
fairy-tale keys. The landlord had left all the French doors and

windows open, and as I stood there holding Sam's sweaty sleeping body on the zigzag tile in the middle of the empty great room that seemed so big, I felt the breeze blow a path to the side window. The window framed the Puy de Dôme, the great extinct volcano overlooking the city, like a postcard picture. It was meant to be.

We walked out into the sunshine to finalize the deal, and Madame Chabosson introduced us to a man in blue coveralls, who had just arrived with a toolbox. He was Monsieur Giraud, the propriétaire, the owner. We shook hands.

"They just moved to France from America," she said.

"Ah," he said, smiling. "*Something* you *something* very well *mumble mumble something.*"

"Would you repeat that, please?" Todd asked politely.

Monsieur Giraud did, exactly as before.

Madame Chabosson smiled, so we did too. It must not have been a question.

It was then that I noticed that she was still there, the white-haired lady. But now there were two of them on the balcony, she and a small, frail-looking man. They stood there so still, like a pair of white rabbits watching us.

Monsieur Giraud glanced up and upon seeing them turned his back to them and said in a low voice, "Have you *something* Madame Mallet yet?"

"No, not yet," Todd said.

"She lives across the street," he said, nodding back at her with his head. "But there are many friendly people that live in this *something.* There is another family that you should meet, who would be excellent *something.* And of course there is Madame Fauriaux, who lives next door at number eighteen. She adores children."

Before we left, I felt that I should try to say something to the nice old couple on the balcony.

"*Bonjour, madame, monsieur,*" I said, nodding again.

"*Bonjour, madame,*" they responded together, and smiled politely. The lady pointed to Sam's chubby bare foot, which he was kicking into the sunshine. "Madame, your son has lost a shoe."

"No, he is not wearing shoes," I said, and smiled. This conversation was going great!

"No?" she said, wrinkling her forehead.

"No," I said meekly. "But thank you."

"It's my pleasure," she said, and muttered something to the old man.

• • •

TWO WEEKS LATER we met Madame Giraud at the house, to get our keys and to ready the house for the movers. After a bit of pleasant small talk, she paused and lowered her voice. "There is an old woman that lives across the street," she said slowly, enunciating her French so that I could understand. "She asked that I tell you not to park beside your gate, because it makes it difficult for her husband to exit their driveway." She waited to see our reaction and then raised her eyebrows. "Madame Mallet's old," she said, with a nervous laugh. "And they never go anywhere. You'll see."

7. Madame Mallet Meets the Americans

On moving day, Madame Mallet stayed behind her lace curtain, watching the men unload our furniture. We could easily see her there, a gray shadow taking careful inventory of the strange things that we foreigners had brought all the way from America. She did take a couple of five-minute breaks during the morning, and when the movers left for their two-hour lunch, she ventured out, pulling her husband along behind her, to formally introduce themselves. After exchanging names and polite handshakes, she nodded at Monsieur Mallet, urging him to try out his English on us. The only words he said he knew were from his days as a pilot, and since there's not much place for "air highway" and "ten knots" in small talk, it was a short conversation. They stood uncomfortably close to us. They had eaten something with onions at lunch and maybe ham.

"You have chosen a wonderful street to live on," she assured us. "One on which *calme* and *tranquillité* are valued by

all the neighbors," she continued, eyeing the balcony. We
could hear Ben and Sarah inside, delightedly opening up
moving boxes.

"It's their toys." I explained, smiling, "the first time in two
months." Surely she would understand the children's happy
chattering, even in English, being a grandma type and all. Her
face was blank. I must have said it wrong.

"Yes, this is a very nice street," Todd said.

"We are happy to be here," I said.

They smiled politely and nodded. There was an awkward
moment of silence.

"You have a nice bed, very big," Madame Mallet said. It
was a queen, not a king, so I thought that was strange, but I
said *merci,* and she asked me if I liked to garden. When I said
that yes, I did, her eyes brightened and she took my arm in
hers and led me across the narrow street for a garden tour. It
was a strange feeling, walking arm in arm with this old
woman that I hardly knew. I tried to relax my arm and resist
the urge to pull it back to my side. I had never done this before. The two of us reminded me a little of old photos of my
mother's I had seen of her with her girlfriends posing arm in
arm in front of my grandparents' car. I had only seen women
in America do this when they were helping along an elderly
aunt or grandmother so that she wouldn't fall and break a
hip. This French woman certainly wasn't frail—she did the
leading like the man in a dance. Her arms were bony, but she
crouched down to point out the flowers and herbs as easily
as a young woman. She stopped at each plant and taught me
its French name and its Latin name if she knew it.

"Oh. A *marguerite* is 'daisy' in English," I said in my best
French accent.

"Well, that makes no difference to me," she said, shrugging her shoulders. "I had to learn German when I was in school—not English." Her English was indeed nonexistent, but she was very patient with my French and was excellent at charades. "*Prenez votre temps* [Take your time], Madame Ramsey," she said as I struggled to get the words out. "I'm retired, so I'm not going anywhere."

We walked and talked and carried on our pantomime throughout her yard. She was the general of her estate, conducting as we walked a military inspection. She straightened the dahlias slumping from their wooden stakes and picked up stray twigs from under the birch trees. She stopped in front of a six-foot-tall horseshoe-shaped hedge in her side yard. "It is my summer place to hide," she said, taking me around to the opening in the horseshoe. Inside her leafy bunker there was a lawn chair with an open book on it. "I planted the hedge so that it opens away from the vegetable garden, so that I don't have to take notice of any failures during my moments of pleasure." The rectangular grave of a vegetable garden at this moment contained mostly black dirt and the last of the tomato plants. "The dryness of the summer kept the tomatoes terribly small," she said, shaking her head.

Then we walked around back and she showed me the grave of her beloved cats Minou and Choufleur. She wiped away a silver streak that an *escargot* had made across the gravestone on its way to the violets encircling the grave. "They loved the garden," she said pensively. "Now I just feed the neighbor's cat, the one that belongs to the Laporte family. They are terrible cat owners and feed the poor fellow only when they remember to. I noticed that you have a cat. It is French?"

"No, American."

"Ooh la la," she said, impressed. "The cat made the voyage, all the way from the United States?" she asked. I nodded, and she looked down at the gravestone. "There are no words for one's love for one's animal."

We walked around to the front yard and ran out of things to say.

"You have many different areas of your garden," I said.

"Oh, I have made a map of it," she said. "I consulted with Madame Fauriaux, my chef across the street," she added, pointing to the house across the narrow street with the garden that looked like a fairyland. The wild artistry of our neighbor's yard made Madame Mallet's attempt look like an awkward imitation. Roses were everywhere, from the pink ones next to her *boîte de lettres* to the great tidal wave of yellow ones cascading down from her balcony to the courtyard and driveway below. Bordering the courtyard were layers and levels of greens of every tone and texture, yellowish green, forest green, fluttery leaves, velvety petals, and sharp spears. There were flowers shaped like hearts and butterfly wings, big red and orange zinnias and fine white phlox, like a soft carpet of white moss.

So Madame Mallet consulted with this Madame Fauriaux—the neighbor whom Monsieur Giraud said adores children. She cooked for the Mallets?

"She is your chef?"

"Oh, yes," she said. "She gives me lessons, and I try to be a good student. I have many books to consult, but I ask her, as she is quite alone, having divorced her husband many years ago after a considerable time of unhappiness."

"Oh," I said.

Apparently my tour of her garden was over, as I found my-self being walked to the gate.

"I wish you a pleasant afternoon, Madame Ramsey," she said as she opened it to let me out.

"*Merci,* Madame Mallet," I said as she closed it. "But please call me Becky, not Madame Ramsey," I said, oblivious to the rules of French etiquette.

She looked at me nervously. "*Bettie?*" she said, sounding it out.

"Uh, Becky—like Rebecca," I tried to explain.

"Ah—Rébecca," she said, recognizing the name. "All right." She smiled. "Rébecca."

I smiled, waiting for her to tell me her first name.

She didn't.

"Are you *juive*?" she asked.

Juive?

"You know," she said, folding her hands in prayer and gaz-ing at the sky. I still didn't get it. "You know—'Rébecca, Ben-jamin, Sarah, Samuel' . . . Well, 'Todd,' I don't know about that one . . . *juif.*"

Jewish—she thought we were Jewish.

"No, Madame Mallet. We're Christian."

"Oh. With the names, I wondered."

We looked nervously at each other.

"*Catholique?*"

"*Non, baptiste,*" I said, hoping she wouldn't think I was a snake handler. But then again, did she even know what Baptists were? And was *baptiste* really the French word for Baptist?

"Hmm," she said. "Well, I suppose I'm Catholic, but I don't go to Mass anymore. I prefer to think for myself."

Over the gate she handed me the small tomatoes she had picked and signaled that our discussion was over. *"Au revoir, madame,"* she said.

"Au revoir. C'est Rébecca," I reminded her.

"Au revoir, Rébecca," she said, and smiled.

"Au revoir, Madame Mallet."

Madame Mallet nodded to me and closed the door behind her.

8. *Chèques, Please*

The day after we moved into our house, Todd left on a business trip to Italy.

"I'll be back in a week," he said. "Don't worry, Beck. You'll be fine."

I wasn't so sure. I had gotten brave enough to drive in France only the day before, and that had been just a mile down the road to the *Ecomarché* to buy the beer the movers had requested. I hadn't wanted to get behind the wheel even then, but it was either me or Todd, and I didn't want to be left alone with those guys, stuttering out directions of where to put things.

As Todd loaded his suitcase into the trunk for his trip, the children lined up at the driveway to say goodbye with sullen faces, as if he were Captain Von Trapp and they were being left with the inept governess who had never looked after children before.

I tried to not be offended. Of course we'd survive. We had

once before. While we were still in our temporary apartment Todd had left me for a week's business trip to Paris. We did just fine left behind in Clermont-Ferrand, walking to the market, walking to the park, walking to the patisserie for treats, walking to the gas station for a rotisserie chicken. I still had the paper I had kept by the phone:

Emergency Phone Numbers:
Fire: 18
Police: 17
Medical: 15

Important Words to Remember
robber—*voleur*
choke—*étouffer*
fire—*feu*
poison—*poison*
burn—*brûler*
break—*se casser*
breathe—*respirer*
emergency—*urgence*
Come quick!—*Venez vite!*

While he packed his bag for Paris, I sat down with my dictionary and made out the list, hoping I had thought of all the important words. If I yelled help, would anyone understand me? I had practiced screaming out "Au secours!" inside my head, but would I remember it in a moment of panic? Every night while he was gone I had locked the house up tight, including the metal shutters. We roasted, but we made it.

Todd blew us another round of kisses and backed out of

the driveway. As he switched gears he called to me, "Oh, I almost forgot. We're almost out of those temporary checks that the bank gave us. They called the other day about the new ones. Do you mind picking them up? The branch of Crédit Lyonnais is just down the street."

"Okay," I said, trying to appear confident. Taking care of the family finances was no big deal in the States, but in France everything was more complicated. Luckily Todd didn't mind doing most of it. He didn't seem bothered by the stares, the constant requests to repeat himself. I wondered if the checks could wait, but then I found a bill by the computer. I would have to handle it. How hard could it be?

The next morning I found out.

An American stranger named Cindy called and offered to take Ben and Sarah swimming at the public pool with her daughter Maggie. I had heard of Cindy and she sounded normal on the phone, so I said okay, and then hung up and scolded myself. What was I doing, sending my children off with a lady I didn't even know, someone who would change their clothes and send them into the pool, maybe into the deep end? But it turned out that Cindy looked like a perfectly fine mother, very nice in fact, and didn't have alcohol on her breath, so I said thank you and sent them off. They would go first to Décathlon, she said, to buy Ben a Speedo since the French do not consider swimming trunks to be hygienic, so they wouldn't be back for several hours.

"What's a Speedo?" Ben asked.

"Go on and get in Miss Cindy's car," I said, patting him on the back. "Have fun!"

This would be a perfect time to get my errands done. I got Sam dressed, put him in the stroller, and walked to the bank.

When we got there the door wouldn't open. I checked my watch. It was ten o'clock. Was it some kind of holiday I didn't know about? I shook the door handle to be sure.

"Do you have a problem, madame?" grumbled an old lady in an apron who was clearing cups and saucers off the outdoor café tables next door. A young man with a mustache looked up from his table to watch our exchange.

"Uh, it's closed today?" I stuttered.

"Oh, you're a foreigner. No," she said. "The bank is not closed today. *Le bouton.*" She pointed at the door.

Bouchon? Didn't that mean "cork"? Or "traffic jam"?

"*Le bouton,*" she repeated, putting down her tray and reaching for my hand. "Push it." She grabbed the pointer finger of my right hand, guided it to the bank door, and pressed the top of two buttons to the right of it. I had thought they were doorbells for the upstairs apartments.

As she walked away, laughing with the man at the table, I felt my face flush. The door buzzed and a green button lit up. I left the stroller on the sidewalk, as I had seen others do, opened the door, and pulled Sam in with me. The door closed behind us, leaving us in front of another door and another pair of *boutons.* Standing there, I felt as if I were in some kind of decontamination chamber. Through the door I could see a line of four people in front of a redheaded clerk behind the counter. I pushed the top *bouton.* Everyone looked at me blankly and then frowned at Sam. The clerk nodded at me and must have pushed a *bouton* of her own because there was a buzzing noise and the red light turned green. I opened the door, took my place at the end of the line, and put Sam down next to me. He was just learning to walk well, and held himself steady by clenching my pants leg with one hand. With the other, he fingered the potted plants. When I told him no he chose to try out the stomp-on-your-foot game that his brother taught him on the man behind me.

"*Desolée.*" I said to the man. I was a pro at saying *desolée,* the French word for "sorry." It sounds like *desolated, destroyed,* made wretched, gloomy. In our few weeks in France, I had made things wretched or gloomy for French people so often that I had the word *desolée* down pat. The short man nodded grimly and returned his stare to the wall. At the front of the line, an old man was unloading a bag full of rolled centimes— the little coins worth less than a penny. As the clerk counted them out, I worked up a sweat trying to humor Sam with my keys and then a pen and paper and then a pack of Kleenex. Sam shrieked with delight as he sat on the floor, pulling tissue after tissue out like a magic trick, sending the little parachutes drifting across the room. I took them from him and cleaned up the mess. People kept clearing their throats. Sam whined and I gave him the Kleenex back. He began to eat them. I let him do it.

Finally it was my turn. Holding Sam tight between my knees, I did my best job to say clearly and slowly, "*Bonjour, madame. J'ai besoin de mes nouveaux chèques.*" (Hello, madame, I am in need of my new checks.) A pained expression came over the clerk's face and it tightened as I spoke. She disappeared into a back room. People behind me began sighing. Sam broke free and began to circle me as if I were a Maypole.

The clerk returned with a short man in a suit. She stood behind him, as if she feared I might reach across the counter and strangle her.

"*Bonjour, madame.* May I help you?" he said slowly, enunciating his French.

"*Bonjour, monsieur. J'ai besoin de mes nouveaux chèques, s'il vous plaît.*"

"You would like to order new checks?" he continued in French.

"No, I *have* ordered new checks. Already."

"Your name, please."

"Rebecca Ramsey."

The man and the woman looked concerned.

"Would you repeat that, please?"

"Rébecca Ramsey," I said, trying to add the throat scraping.

They looked at each other.

"Could we see your driver's license, please?"

I handed my French license to them and watched them both inspect it. They looked through the box on the back table. They murmured to each other and shook their heads.

"I'm afraid that you are in error. There are no checks for Rébecca Ramsey," the man said with the throat gargling.

"But my husband ordered them. He said you called."

The two looked puzzled. "Maybe Rébecca is a man's name in England," the woman whispered to the man.

"And your husband is Rébecca Ramsey?"

"No, *I* am Rébecca Ramsey," I said, adding the throat gargling.

People in line began to clear their throats and cough.

"Ah, well, you didn't say that. Do you have his driver's license?"

"No, he has it." Why would I be carrying my husband's

driver's license? "The address is the same. I think my name is on the checks."

"This is highly irregular. In the future you should know that the checks will be listed under the name of the person who orders them. We must do things correctly, you know."

I nodded and signed the paper they gave me. I couldn't wait to make my escape. At the clerk's nod, I said a quick *merci,* scooped Sam onto my hip, and pushed the button to exit into the no-man's-land between the doors. Almost out! I pushed the *bouton* for the second door. Nothing happened. I pushed it again. Still nothing. Out on the sidewalk waited an old lady carrying a big purse and a tiny dog. Her pink hair was teased up into a cotton candy pile on her head, and she frowned at me through the glass. The white dust-mop dog she held in her arms yapped, "Move, stupid," in dog French as the lady pointed at the buzzer. I tried again. Nothing. My heart raced and Sam squirmed as I looked back to the clerk for help.

Several people in line called directions out to me. It might as well have been Swahili. Finally a young twenty-something in a black turtleneck rolled his eyes and left his place in line. Just as I thought he was about to help me, he reached down to pull the doormat on which the inside door was caught. The door shut with a bang, trapping me inside.

What is he doing? I thought, panicking. I desperately tried again.

Voilà! The door buzzed and unlocked.

Oh. So the first door had to be completely closed before the second door would open. With my face as red as steak tartare, I raced back to the safety of my house, Sam bumping along in the stroller.

Once we got home I locked the door behind me. "Sam, how about some comfort food?" I said to him. "You want a *pain au chocolat,* buddy?"

Sam nodded wildly and started drooling. Chocolate croissants were his favorite.

I put Sam in his high chair and handed him a whole one. He dug in with both hands, smearing chocolate everywhere. *He's fine,* I thought, picking up my emergency word list off the floor where it had fallen. In fact, we all were doing fine. So what if we were constantly embarrassing ourselves? Ben and Sarah were fairly happy and Todd was surviving work. I looked out at my quaint little street, at the flowers on the balconies and the cherry trees. Madame Mallet had her shutters open and was airing out her comforter. My neighbors never closed their shutters at night when it was hot. Why did I?

After I finished the last tasty morsel of my *pain au chocolat* and washed the chocolate off Sam, I tucked the list of emergency words neatly inside the phone book. I was pretty sure that life was going to be okay. If some emergency did happen, the words would probably come. But there was no way I was ever going back to that bank.

9. *Plenty of Time*

Our first month on allée des Cerisiers, it was hard to get used to the open windows and open doors and the sounds flowing back and forth between our houses. We could hear the plates and the silverware clanking from the Mallets' at mealtime, and I'm sure they could hear all the goings-on at our house as we adjusted. We were all stressed out—from trying to understand our electric bill and our children's homework, to trying to figure out the traffic rules and relearn how to parallel park, and from trying to find food at the supermarket that the children would eat, to trying to figure out what cuts of meat I had bought and what animal they had come from. We were so tightly wound that at least once or twice a day we'd be yelling at each other about something. I would run around, closing the windows and doors, but I would see Madame Mallet's gray shadow peering out at us behind her curtain.

We had been in the house less than a week when she told me at my gate that I shouldn't carry Sam around so much while

I do my housework. "Put him in a playpen, Becky," she said, wagging her finger at me. "It isn't good for your back." I nodded and said that she was probably right, but in my head I was thinking it was time to put curtains on the windows.

Then she pointed at my skirt and gave me a thumbs-up sign. "You're wearing a skirt! How beautiful you look, Rébecca!"

"Merci beaucoup," I said.

"I didn't know you had one."

"Pardon?"

"A skirt. I thought all you Americans wore were *'les jeans.'* You look very chic."

"Merci, Madame Mallet."

"And your hair. It's different, isn't it?"

"Oui," I said. "But I don't like it." I didn't. My first trip to the hairdresser's was a failure. I had tried to tell the lady I wanted layers, sure that *les tissus* was the term for that, but later found out that I had requested that my hair to be cut in fabrics. Ben had giggled and said I looked like that big Egyptian lion except my nose was still on. And I did sort of look like the Sphinx.

Madame Mallet asked me where I went to have it cut and I explained that it was at Happy Hair, next to the *hypermarché.* I had hoped that if their name was in English, maybe they spoke some. No one had.

"No wonder it turned out like that," she said. "Only the Algerians go to the *hypermarché* to get their hair done."

"Well"—I coughed—"it's time to go to get the children."

"Maybe while you're out, you can find yourself a *garderie* for little Samuel. You need some time to yourself, free of all three of your little *marmots.*"

"Uh," I said, "maybe in a week or so. He has a cold right now."

"That's because you never dress him properly. You're not in South Carolina anymore, my dear."

Our honeymoon was over.

The kids complained that Madame Mallet wagged her finger at them every time they went barefoot in the yard. The finger wagging was a French thing. They stuck out their right index finger and wagged it back and forth like a windshield wiper. I couldn't get my finger to do it well, but Madame Mallet was an expert. One day I walked out barefoot to get the mail. The gravel was a little sharp on my feet, but I was too lazy to get my shoes. Within seconds there was Madame Mallet, leaning over her balcony, wagging her finger at me. "I see where the children get their bad habit," she said.

I laughed and said, "Maybe so. But in South Carolina it's hot, and kids don't always wear shoes to play in the yard."

"That may be," Madame Mallet called down to me. "But you're in France now. In France only the savages wear no shoes."

No wonder the children disliked her.

Every day she asked them for a *bisou*—a kiss on both cheeks, a sign of respect that comes naturally to French children but not to mine. Sarah would do it but Ben wouldn't.

"I like your daughter, but your son is *sauvage*," she said one day as Ben ran from her to climb the cherry tree. I tried to explain that it was difficult for him, not understanding the language, being thrown into French first grade, leaving all his friends behind, and being kind of a nervous kid anyway. I thought he was coming along pretty well, considering that his first week in France he started virtually every conversation with "No one ever asked me if I wanted to move here."

"All he needs is some of this," she said, demonstrating a kick to his behind.

We talked nearly every day, and I liked her less and less the more we talked. Every conversation would start out nicely— she would instruct me on how to keep the house cool by closing the shutters in the heat of the day and then leaving the windows and shutters open at night. Or she would tell me the best place to buy fruit or how to cook rabbit or lamb. But by the end of the conversation she'd share some crazy story she had heard on television about Texans cloning their cats or on why Americans were so fat.

I would grit my teeth and try to smile, telling myself that for the next three or four years I had to live with this woman. *At least my French is improving,* I would say to myself, and shut the door and groan. Then later that evening I would find on my doorstep a bag of *noisettes* (hazelnuts) freshly picked from her tree, or some hollyhocks tied with raffia, or a jewelry box for Sarah that a catalog company had sent Madame Mallet for being such a good customer.

And then came the conversation that made me reconsider house number one on the cliff. It started when I asked her if we were the first Americans she had ever met. Madame Mallet looked at me, paused, and then said, "Oh, no. I wish that were the case." Then she explained that at the end of World War II she had moved down south to Beaucaire to work in her aunt's café. "I met plenty of American soldiers there." Then she scowled. "They were all terribly rude," she said, shaking her head. "Complete savages. They were wild and drunk and behaved worse than animals. They were drinking so fast that they threw their money at us. I remember stepping on the dollars that had fallen to the floor. And when they had no more in their pockets, they paid us with petrol from their trucks—you could hardly get it on the black market back then. All they wanted was *pastis,* and when it ran out my uncle said to just give them syrup water—they were too drunk to notice."

"Maybe they were scared and far from home," I said, shocked.

"Scared?" she said, raising one eyebrow. "The war was over then and they were just waiting their time."

"Well, I'm sure they weren't all that way," I said, thinking of the old photographs of my mother's father.

"*Ah, si.* Every American I met was exactly that way," she said, wagging her finger in my face.

"Madame Mallet, my grandfather died in that war," I said, angry and flustered. "He was killed here in France." Madame Mallet stared at me blankly. "He died on my mother's first birthday. He's buried in Normandy." I searched her face for a trace of empathy.

"It is sad, I'm sure, but many families have lost many men," she said. She kept talking, but I stopped listening. I was glad that Mother didn't have to hear this. I thought of the padlocked footlocker of my grandfather's things that Mother kept in the basement and the dozens of times my brother and I begged her to open it. I remembered the flag folded into a tight triangle, the photo albums and scrapbooks, the yellowed postcards and the Limoges teacup that he had sent back from France.

My grandfather had given his life for people he didn't even know. And Mother had paid a huge price for that.

Madame Mallet was still talking. Her father was part of the Maquis—the French Resistance. He died of his wounds after the war ended. "The Americans didn't come over until the end," she said, pointing her finger at me. "They knew what was going on over here, but they didn't get involved until they were bombed at Pearl Harbor." She stared at me and then added, "And they made a lot of money during the war."

I was furious. How could I live by this woman? The ingrat-itude! The prejudice! I stuttered and tried to respond. Sam be-gan to fuss on my hip and I used that as an excuse to leave our conversation.

After that exchange I avoided Madame Mallet. Arguing with her would do no good. My father was a champion of debate, but I never won bouts of verbal sparring. I could put together a decent argument if I had time, particularly if it could be in writing, so that I wouldn't get flustered or leave out important points, but to do it right then and there—and in French? That day it was all I could do to keep myself from crying, and that made me even madder.

I talked to French people about her, and they were nearly as shocked as I was. "She's *spéciale,*" Camille told me, grimacing. "Not 'special,' as you say in English, you know—wonderful or great, but *spéciale,* as in strange—peculiar." That was an under-statement. This woman was going to ruin France for me. And I *loved* France—it was the big adventure of my life.

So instead I decided to make Madame Mallet disappear in my mind—as I had before with other disagreeable people I had encountered in life. I knew it was a passive and unhealthy scheme, but I didn't care. I'd have to hide behind my front door occasionally and stay inside more than I would like, but even-tually she'd lose interest. I was even prepared for it to take a good while, knowing how stubborn she was. But she watched my every move, my very own one-woman paparazzi.

I began closing the shutters more often and insisted the chil-dren play in the backyard, which wasn't much fun since there was only a clothesline back there. I made up excuses to hurry in or out or pretended I didn't see her. But she wouldn't give up. It seemed like all I had to do was open my door, and there she was, opening her door too, or standing at the mailbox. I'd think that the coast was clear, that she was inside watching her favorite talk show, so I'd go out to swing Sam in the yard, and she'd spring over to my gate. She'd have pictures of herself as a little girl and of herself as a young woman, dressed in a uniform that she explained was a British women's uniform—the uniform adopted by AFAT, Auxiliaires Féminines de l'Armée de Terre. I'd pull into the driveway and she'd come over with photos of her father when he worked at Michelin when all they made were bicycle tires. There he was along with other bearded men, standing with their tires in front of Place de Carmes, where Todd worked.

She told me stories of her thirty years of work there and shook her head and called Michelin *"la bande de bandits,"* who stole away her good years for little reward. She told me about her motorbike accident on her way to work when she was in her early twenties and how her leg aches now whenever it is about to rain. And she showed me pictures of her cats Minou and Choufleur and talked about how long they lived with her and how they died. She told me that she had told her sister that when she died, she wanted to leave everything she owned to be sold and given to a home for abandoned animals, since her cats had given her more joy than any human she had ever known.

All that talk made me enjoy her company again, even though I didn't want to. She still loved giving me the finger wagging for various crimes I had committed, like shopping at the local flea market. "Everything there is either stolen or full of termites," she said. I shook my head and laughed and knew that I had a choice: I could either stand there and discuss it with her, or I could just start leaving things in my trunk until after dark. The dark path of least resistance won out.

Our first New Year's Day, we turned a corner. Madame Mallet came over to wish me a *"Bonne Année,"* and asked for a *bisou* to bring good luck for the year. Up until that morning we had always had an awkward moment in greeting each other, she leaning forward, forgetting for a moment that I wasn't French, and me standing there feeling I should be doing something with my hands. But after that kiss, we started greeting each other every day the French way—at least her version of it. My French friend Virginie told me the proper way to do it, but I reminded myself that she was raised in a chateau outside of Paris. She said that you only touch cheeks and make the kissing sound—lips are never to come in contact with skin. Unfortunately Madame Mallet had her own style. She zoomed in at the lower cheek, perilously close to my mouth, and planted her moist lips on each side. After the *bisou* she'd always stand so close to me that I would find myself backing up. No problem, she'd just inch closer, and I would try not to focus on her morning breath.

I even learned to argue with her, and she loved it. She would squint her eyes and listen hard, probably because my French was so bad, but she'd always give me time and would consider what I had said. She'd say I was too optimistic and naive and it came from the lack of history of my young but powerful country. I'd tell her that she was a *cynique* and that she was prejudiced, and she would insist that she wasn't, but that people should stay in their own country, where they're happy. "So I should go home then, back to America where I belong?" I asked.

"Well, not you," she said, and harrumphed.

At the end of our first year in France, I prepared to take the kids back home for a monthlong vacation in the States. The day before we left I made the mistake of telling her that we would be making the trip without Todd, since he had to work for a week before joining us. Madame Mallet's jaw dropped open, and then she started talking. How could my husband force me to go alone? How could I ever make it by myself with three children and a stroller and a car seat and layovers in Paris and Atlanta? I interrupted her to explain that Todd had to take a business trip to Australia, which sent her on a full-fledged anti-Michelin tirade.

"La bande de bandits!" she shrieked. And then she started yelling really fast, and I couldn't keep up. I waited, and finally she took a breath, wiped her nose with her handkerchief, and commanded me to write her to let her know that we had arrived safely.

"But Madame Mallet," I protested, "my written French is even worse than my spoken French." She shook her head, and wagged that index finger at me, and then pulled me closer to her side.

"All that you have to say, *ma chérie,* is *'Je pense à vous'* ['I'm thinking of you']," she said. I said that I would and gave her an extra kiss on both cheeks.

That first week at home I made Mother drive me all over creation to find some postcards to pick from. I was sure Madame Mallet was eyeing my house and checking her mailbox every day, so I sent it off as soon as I could. We had a wonderful five weeks, and when we returned, guess who sprang out into the street the moment the taxi pulled away? Madame Mallet didn't even give me a chance to brush off my rusty French. I struggled to talk and then apologized. "I guess I've forgotten all the French I learned," I said.

"Ne vous inquiétez pas, Rébecca," she said, holding on to my arm. "I'm retired, and I'm not going anywhere. We have plenty of time."

10. *Monsieur Rougé, the Piano Man*

When Mother used to tell people that we were moving to France, they didn't seem to get it. They might act impressed for a moment, but then they'd start going on about their vacation to Paris in '84, and how we should be sure to pay the extra for the elevator ride all the way to the top of the Eiffel Tower.

"No," Mother would try to say patiently, "they're not going for a visit. They're *moving* to France. They're taking everything—even the piano!"

Mother told everyone about the piano. The monstrous upright piano was a perfect symbol of the immensity of what we were about to do. She could just imagine it wrapped up in plastic bubbles inside a shipping container, riding the waves all the way to France. We weren't just sightseeing—we were moving in. We'd have bills to pay and French neighbors, and we'd send her brilliant grandchildren to some lucky French school. Some real French movers would lug that piano into a

real French house, and Sarah would take piano lessons, probably from a French teacher, maybe even at the *conservatoire*.

Reality wasn't so impressive. The piano was moved into a
real French house, but a month later when the piano teacher
heard its voice, she cringed. *"Mon Dieu,"* she said, "it needs
work." She handed me a business card. "Maybe Monsieur
Rougé can fix it. Perhaps he knows *magique."*

So I called him and requested a *rendez-vous.*

"Rougé Pianos" was written in fancy letters on the side of
his van, alongside a keyboard and the words *"Philippe Rougé,
Le Maître du Piano."* When Monsieur Rougé opened the
door and unfolded his long legs onto the street, my first
thought was that he looked like a piano key himself, all in
black and white, slender and polished. His clothes were neatly
pressed, and his long face was blank, until he scowled at the
dust clouds that rose as he stepped onto our gravel driveway.

"Bonjour, monsieur," I said.

"Bonjour, madame," he said in a baritone voice, shaking my
hand and stomping his feet on the welcome mat. I thanked
him for coming and opened the front door into the foyer.
"I'm afraid it's here," I said, embarrassed. The door missed the
edge of the piano by a mere inch. The piano crowded the en-
tryway like an elephant.

"The movers couldn't take it up the stairs," I tried to explain. "We had no choice."

It was true. I wanted it upstairs in the *salon,* the living
room, where pianos should be. And they had said they could
do it. The five skinny guys in sandals who moved us in had
groaned and cussed and wrestled our upright piano right up
the tile steps, making it all the way to the landing, but the pi-

ano was too wide to make the turn without lifting it. It weighs a ton, so they sweated and groaned and cussed all the way down, their sandals squeaking on the tile, their legs struggling and quivering under the weight. Then they stepped out on the porch for a break, lit up cigarettes, and laughed and teased one another. Todd and I tried not to stare at them as we talked out by the boxes on the street, but we could tell that something was about to happen.

"*Vas-y, Louis,*" someone called out, and then Louis, a guy with dark eyes and a movie star chin stepped inside the front door and sat down at the piano. With a sheepish grin and a cigarette bobbing up and down on his bottom lip, he began to play a lilting, tinkling sonatina. As the other guys laughed and applauded, the youngest one with hair stuck up in wrong places stepped out of the group and signaled for the others to stand aside. They laughed and egged him on, and he snapped his eyes shut and began to sway to the music. Like a clumsy ballerina he leapt onto the driveway, sashayed around the roses, and then gave his grand finale, a pirouette under the cherry tree. So our piano had a christening in our new home, and there it remained, just inside the front door.

It was a horrible place to put a piano. Our beautiful instrument was always covered in dust from the driveway and had become a shelf for book bags and the day's mail. Stray notes and pencils crowded the sheet music, and occasionally pens or pencils would slide under the wood apron and get stuck between the keys. Monsieur Rougé grunted at the sight and shook his head in disapproval. He played a note and immediately recoiled as if the piano had pinched him.

"Oh la la la," he said, as if shaking his head. "La, la, la, la," he scolded again, ticking off the la's like a metronome. "How old is it?" he asked, putting his hands on his hips, like a doctor in favor of euthanasia.

I said that I was not sure, but I thought it could be around seventy or eighty years old. He lifted the lid cautiously, as if opening a coffin, and peered inside. "La la la la la," he said in disgust.

What in the world could be so bad? So it was old. Pianos do get old. The old man that sold my mother that piano had had a house full of old pianos, and people snatched them out of his hands before he could even get them fixed. I was in third grade when old Mr. Storm led Mother and me down into the cool musty air of his basement. It was like a piano hospital, jam-packed with them, some whole and some in various states of reworking. There were boxes of hammerheads and screws and a workbench cluttered with tools and piano wire. After some time Mother picked out an old upright and wanted to know what I thought. I thought she was kidding. That piano towered over me like a monster with its yellowed ivory teeth and crackled, gunky skin.

The next thing I knew our basement was full of piano pieces as Mr. Storm hauled it in and helped Mother take the whole thing apart. By the next day, the Ping-Pong table was covered with newspaper, rubber gloves, and cans of poisonous chemicals, and Mother was stripping off the black shellac. When she scraped back the thick crackled lacquer and found flawless mahogany underneath, she was beside herself, like a junkie high on stripper fumes. Just a few days later she was rubbing in tung oil, revealing the silky richness of the wood. Mr. Storm came over with the new keys, helped her put everything back together again, and tuned it up. Talk

about a miracle! I couldn't stop staring at the glistening reddish brown wood, the elegant tapered legs, and the brass pedals. And I loved the curve of the shoulder of wood that
flipped down to cover the keys. It wasn't square and boring
like other pianos'. Our piano was like a sculpture that sang.

Regardless of its sentimental history, Monsieur Rougé was
not impressed. He played a scale. "La la la la," he said, shaking
his head. Taking his tools out of his black leather bag, he began to dismantle the piano, first removing the lid. Meanwhile,
I tried to make excuses.

"I know moving a piano is not good for it," I said. What
could the problem be? Maybe something had happened during the move. To me, my piano looked the same and sounded
the same as always.

"C'est abîmé, complètement abîmé!" Monsieur Rougé said
with a heavy sigh, staring at the inside workings—the wires,
the hammerheads, and the soundboard. I wasn't sure what
abîmé meant, but I knew it wasn't good. I stood there feeling
like a bad parent as he pulled two pencils and one pen out of
the piano's innards. "Perhaps you are missing these," he said,
and handed me a gum wrapper to boot.

"You fixed middle C," I said, smiling, hoping he would
laugh along and allow me some dignity. Monsieur Rougé
harrumphed and then declared, *"C'est impossible. C'est impossible, Madame Ramsey."* He waited for my reaction.

I didn't know what to do. Was he not going to tune it?
Should I ask him to try? Should I pay him? Did he want
more money?

Monsieur Rougé waited a moment and then responded to
my unasked questions with the typical French shoulder
shrug—the one that says, *"Tant pis*—too bad for you."

I tried anyway.

"Can you do the best you can?" I begged.

"Non, madame," he said, "I cannot." And then his French sped up and he began to wave his wooden pointer around, showing me the felts worn bare, the three large cracks in the soundboard, and the drips on the wires and wood of what looked like petrified sap. He played a note and cringed, closing his eyes in disgust.

"I could tune it, but you would not be happy."

I didn't know what to say.

"It would not be correct," he said.

Maybe he thought he had hurt my feelings or had been unduly harsh, because then the stiffness of his face softened. "I understand if there is a sentimental attachment to this piano, if it was given to you by your grandmother or had some such history," he said as he began to reassemble the piano and put his tools away. "I could arrange to rebuild the piano if you like. It would take at least six months and would cost about the same as a new piano." He took a fountain pen and book out of his briefcase and in beautiful handwriting wrote the brand and serial number, "Lindeman & Sons Piano Company, New York, New York #121969." "I will research its age and send it to you along with some information on new and used pianos in my showroom. I have a very nice selection," he continued. "I have sold pianos to many Michelin employees, most notably the Michelin family themselves." I tried to look impressed as he named the individual sons who had been clients.

He didn't know it, but at that point my relationship with him was over. There was no way that I would ever consider trading in my dear *abîmé* piano, and it would be silly to have two pianos in the house. Besides, I always thought our piano sounded much better than others I had heard. New freshly tuned pianos sounded too soft—too shy, too wishy-washy. I loved the way my piano echoed in my ears without even pressing the pedals, like a saloon piano from an old Western.

I paid Monsieur Rougé his two hundred francs. At least he would leave my house and take all his fancy piano talk with him. Not all was lost. Now Sarah could play middle C. It's kind of hard to play much without it.

A week later we received a big white envelope in the mail. Inside were several glossy brochures with pictures of beautiful new grand pianos and baby grands and simpler pianos. None was as beautiful as mine. In a letter he included the age of my piano. I wish I could remember what it said. I threw the letter away, so I guess I won't ever know, not that it's important. All the other pianos were fine, but I'm keeping mine. I need a piano that's at home in my house, wherever we live. And if it has great legs, curvy shoulders, and a voice that means business, what more could we want?

II. *Bijoux for My Birthday*

Of all the things I wanted for my thirty-fifth birthday, a trip up the stairs to Madame Mallet's bedroom was not on the list. Talk about disturbing. I felt like Batgirl being led right into Catwoman's lair, forced into the very hideout where she spies on us day and night. I saw it all. There was the lace curtain, the door to the balcony, a worn place on the beige carpet where she must do her snooping. She'd been standing there watching us only a couple of months, but we hadn't been the only ones. I felt a kinship for the previous renters, whoever they were.

The Mallets' boudoir was creepy, but it looked like I had expected, with dark paneled walls, a faded floral bedspread on a low bed, a couple of bedside tables, and an armoire. The most frightening thing, however, was what I saw through the lace curtain: the jar of Nutella on my kitchen counter. And the bread. No one had put the bread away. There they were, as clear as day, sitting on my kitchen counter in front of the flowery wallpaper. *What a plain view she gets of my naked life,* I thought, straight from her own bedroom. And this was during daylight hours. At night, when the kitchen's all lit up with stage lights, I must really put on a show.

I should buy a robe, I said to myself. *Today.*

"Ne bougez pas!" she barked at me, fussing with the clasp of the necklace she had draped around my neck. *"Clément,"* she called over her shoulder. More shivers ran up my back. *Please don't let her call her husband in here,* I prayed. It was weird enough to be standing in their bedroom at all, their private place where they changed their clothes, et cetera. Apparently God thought it would be funny, because in a split second there we were, the three of us at the end of her bed, Madame Mallet barking out directions as Monsieur Mallet's shaky fingers fiddled with the tiny chain at the nape of my bare neck.

The whole thing would never have happened if I just could have kept my mouth shut. It happened all the time. She asked me a question and I tried to answer, and before I knew it I had committed to cook rabbit for dinner or start making Sam wear a hat. This time Madame Mallet wanted to know why Todd was at home before seven in the middle of the week and was setting up the grill while I was playing soccer with the kids in the yard.

"So now your husband does all the cooking too?" she asked. (Ever since she learned that he does his own ironing, she loved to give me a hard time.)

"Non," I said, explaining that it was my birthday and he was grilling salmon for dinner.

"And what did he give you for your birthday?" she asked.

I considered lying to her, and I had two good reasons to do it. First, she and Todd weren't getting along very well at that moment, and this would make matters worse. She wouldn't understand that between Todd's business trips and the kids' homework, neither of us had time to think about birthday presents. I was fine with forgetting the whole birthday thing, knowing that the next time I found a treasure at the flea market I could call it my birthday present and he'd have to go along. Madame Mallet wouldn't get that. Second, any explanation would require a lot of French, and I was tired. But for some reason I stood there struggling to explain while she shook her head and scolded me with the click of her tongue.

"Well," I said, "I really don't know what to ask for."

"Les bijoux! [Jewelry!]," she said. "You never wear any jewelry, and you really need some. Every woman looks prettier with some jewelry. Rings, bracelets, chains, maybe some gold earrings." Then she started rattling off more jewelry vocabulary, which I didn't understand, so she took my hand and pulled me toward her house. I put Sarah in charge of the soccer game and closed our gate behind me. If I had known we were headed to her bedroom, I would have made up an excuse.

So there I stood at the foot of her bed, shifting my weight from one foot to the other in an attempt to distract myself from the urge to run screaming out of her lookout point back to the comfort of my house. I tried focused breathing techniques, and when that didn't work I tried to stare at a knot on the dark wood paneling. Finally Monsieur Mallet got the clasp fastened and made himself scarce, and Madame Mallet handed me a mirror. Before I could get a good look, she snatched it off.

"No, no. Too short," she said. She plundered her jewelry box and pulled out several necklaces, which she neatly laid on her bedspread. "This one is serpentine, this one is a *sautoir,* and that one is called a *collier,*" she said, pointing to the choker.

They were really pretty. *Maybe she's right,* I started thinking. She must have been in full brainwash mode, because in a couple of minutes I closed her gate behind me, lugging two big catalogs full of baubles and chains and dreaming of how together I'd look as the New Accessorized Me.

"Guess what you're getting me for my birthday," I said to Todd over a plate of grilled salmon.

"I give up," he said. "What?"

"Madame Mallet says I need some jewelry, and I've been thinking she might be right."

"Jewelry?" my husband asked, gawking at me as if I had asked for ironing lessons. "You've got to be kidding. You never wear the jewelry you've got."

"Maybe I just don't have the *right* jewelry," I said. Todd glared at me in disbelief. "Maybe I'd wear it if I just had the right stuff."

That night I pored over the catalogs, skipping right to the silver section. Ever since Mother had had a color analysis at her garden club and discovered we were both winters, I'd been wearing silver. By the looks of the silver section, French women must all be summers or springs. But I did find a few things that I liked and showed them to Todd over breakfast on Saturday.

"Okay, no problem," he said, after I finished my laundry list of suggestions. "Load 'em up, kids. We're going birthday shopping."

As everybody scrambled to find shoes I followed him to the closet.

"Do you want me to write these things down?"

"Nope. Got it."

"Are you sure?"

"Yep."

"Silver, not gold," I called as he herded the kids to the car.

"Uh-huh."

"Antique-y—not a thick chain." Todd nodded and buckled Sam in his car seat. "Delicate. Small—not showy," I said.

"Right."

"Fourteen inches. I like wearing them long."

"Right, fourteen inches."

"Do you know that in centimeters?" I called down from the balcony. "It'll be in centimeters."

Todd gave me a look. "I think I can figure that out," he said, and started up the car. "See you in about an hour or two," he said. "I've got to get batteries while I'm out."

I knew right then it wouldn't happen. It wouldn't be fourteen inches.

. . .

"WOW," I SAID, sixty-five minutes later, looking at the small silver necklace in the little white box. It was short and made of twisted silver wire laced with small silver beads. Was it a bracelet or a necklace? I lifted it from the box. It couldn't have been more than eight inches long.

"What do you think?" Todd asked. He looked at me with his big brown eyes, like a kindergarten kid hoping for approval.

"It's great, honey," I said holding it up to my neck. The circumference of my neck had to be longer than that necklace.

"Do you like it, Mom?" Sarah asked.

"I sure do. Here, put it on me." I handed it back to Todd. He put it around my neck and pulled it right against my windpipe as he fiddled with the clasp. I stuck a finger through to give me some breathing space. It itched my skin.

"They didn't have much silver to choose from," Todd said. "The lady tried it on for me. Is it too snug?"

"Well, it is a little," I said. Hadn't he noticed that my neck was the American version, not a pencil-thin French one?

"You could probably take it back, if you want."

"No, no. I just need some time to get used to having it so close," I said. "I like the beads."

Todd smiled. "You look great in it," he said, pushing Sam in the swing. I tried to sit in the lawn chair and relax and breathe naturally, but the necklace was closing in on me. *I've got to get out of this dog collar,* I thought, figuring I could rip it off with one good jerk. Then I looked at Todd and the kids grinning at me and told myself to behave. Maybe I just needed a dress with the right neckline.

· · ·

A FEW DAYS later, Madame Mallet asked me about my birthday present. "Show it to me," she commanded. As I walked upstairs to get it, I tried to think of what to do. Madame Mallet wouldn't like the necklace, would say that it didn't fit, and would try to get me to take it back. Later she would probably accost Todd about it and lecture him on how to select proper jewelry for a birthday. He'd hate that.

In the quiet of my bedroom I fumbled through my little jewelry box and pulled out the beaded chain. There beside it was my favorite necklace, a silver chain Todd had given me years before. At a time when we couldn't really afford spur-of-the-moment gifts, he had picked it out on a business trip without any help or suggestions and brought it home as a complete surprise. I grabbed them both and took them down to show Madame Mallet.

"This is very pretty," she said, picking up the older present. "But I don't care for the other one. Did he give you both?"

"Yes," I said.

"You're a very lucky woman," she said.

"Yes, I think you're right," I said, and went inside to put on my new necklace. If I wrapped it around my wrist twice, it could make a pretty bracelet. And if I wore it with my favorite necklace, Todd would hardly recognize the New Accessorized Me.

12.   *Emergency Room*

My children used to save their rowdiest behavior for when their grandparents came for a visit, which explains why Ben was running wildly through the house, whooping and hollering, while my mother-in-law was clinging to her coffee, barely over her jet lag. It was five o'clock on a November afternoon in our first year in France, and we had just come in from school when Ben flew through the dining room like Superman, tripped on a chair leg, and went splat, facedown on the tile floor.

I knew the scream.

We had surely heard it enough. In Ben's short seven years of life, we had toured emergency rooms all over the East Coast. The first visit was when he was eighteen months old and fell out of the car on a camping trip to the mountains. We found the nearest hospital and I sat in the waiting room and cried, listening to Ben screaming while Todd wrestled him into a body board so they could stitch him up. Since then he had broken his arm, had a second set of stitches, cut his wrist by falling on a glass of water (while standing on the kitchen counter—don't ask), and had a freak accident with a pool light. After that, he fractured his leg on a trampoline at a family reunion in Kentucky, and two weeks later we carried him through the ER doors again, this time at my in-laws' in Fayetteville, North Carolina. He had swallowed a coin. It turned out to be a dime. We saw it plain as day, a perfect circle of white on his X-ray.

And now it looked like his tour of emergency rooms would go international. I was sure he needed stitches. I had climbed up to the top of his bunk bed, where he was hiding under a blanket, all balled up with a washcloth to his cheek. It was still bleeding, three-fourths of an inch wide. I could see the little white layer of fat under the skin.

It always happened when Todd wasn't home. At least he was in town, at a meeting at work. I left a message, took a deep breath, and searched the emergency list for Docteur Allezard's phone number. How would I say it in French? What was the word for *stitches*? I got out the dictionary. My shaking hands felt huge and cumbersome in the thin pages of my pocket dictionary as Ben cried and screamed.

> Stitches = *les points de suture*
> Cheekbone = *la pommette*
> Tile = *le carreau*

Mary, my mother-in-law, went to talk to Ben while I practiced what I was going to say.

I found Docteur Allezard's phone number and made the

call. As usual, his wife answered. Unlike back home, the only person at the doctor's office was the doctor. His wife served as his receptionist at home and forwarded calls.

With much stuttering and several pauses, I told her what had happened. She said that for stitches we'd need to take him to a *clinique*. She calmly gave me directions and then had me read them back to her, to make sure I had them right.

Ben wouldn't come down from his bed. A French hospital and a French doctor? It was too much to ask. French kids? Okay. French teacher? He'd try. But a French hospital? No way. He drew the line. He stood his ground. I pleaded with him, then ordered him, then yelled at him. It was no use.

Finally I heard the jingle of Todd's keys in the door. Thank goodness. I caught Todd up on the news of the clinic, and he went in and sat on the floor of Ben's room. "Tell me when you're ready," he said, "and then we'll go."

Ben sat there for a while as Todd waited. After a couple minutes of silence, Ben came down the ladder, crying.

I left Sarah and Sam with Mary, and we headed out.

I buckled myself beside Ben in the backseat. "We'll go to Jouetland tomorrow, Ben. You know, that toy store," I said. "We can get a game for your Game Boy." Before the move I had always vetoed Game Boys as toys that weak parents buy their whiny children because they felt guilty. Then I became one of those guilty parents, thinking of all the time on the airplane, how Ben didn't have any choice in this move, and how we were taking him away from all his friends, the school he loved, and the only home he knew.

"We can even hook up your Game Boy with a friend's so that you can play together," Todd said from the front seat.

"But Daddy, I don't have any friends," Ben said, and then burst out crying again, twisting his face into a long, forlorn openmouthed wail.

I put my arms around him and pulled his sweaty head to my shoulder.

We finally found our way. The sign said CLINIQUE, but the place was deserted. Was this right? We parked and walked through the emergency entrance. There were rows of empty chairs in a sterile-looking hallway and not a person in sight. We walked down the hall, peering in rooms, searching for anyone. In a back room there was a lady in white scrubs counting bandages. She led us into a room, took a look at Ben's wound, and went to get a doctor.

Ben sat on the examining table. "Are they going to give me a shot?" he whimpered. "What are they going to do?"

"I don't know, sweetie," I said, smoothing his hair, trying to swallow the lump in my throat. "But you've done this before. They'll probably take a good look at it, and then they might give you a stitch or two." Ben began to cry, but wiped his eyes when the nurse came in.

She was pretty and young and wore her blond hair in a ponytail, and she smiled more than most French people do. She took a look at the cut and kissed Ben on the forehead and told him that he was *a-dor-able*. The doctor came in, a stern, short man with no bedside manner. He examined him, explained that four or five stitches would do it, and then he led us out of the room to wait in the hall.

I didn't want to leave him. Todd and I stood outside the door, watching through the window as they had Ben lie down and draped a white sheet over him, all except for his little pale face. The doctor was speaking to him as he worked.

Ben answered back in French a few times. He could speak French! It was the first time I had ever heard him. He was too embarrassed to speak it in front of me.

When it was all over, the doctor invited us in, showed us his stitches, and left.

"Where do we pay?" I asked the nurse.

"Pay?" The nurse shrugged her shoulders. "Oh, let's not worry about that until you come back to get the stitches out. Or you could just bring it by sometime when you are in the neighborhood."

Todd and I looked at each other. Was this for real?

A week later I picked the kids up from school and headed for the clinic to get Ben's stitches out. The waiting room was crowded this time with a dozen or so French people, who were enjoying being entertained by my loud English-speaking children. Sam was trying to move the furniture around, Ben and Sarah were bickering, and I was constantly looking at my watch. My friends had said they never had to wait long at the clinic. What was the problem?

After thirty minutes or so, a doctor came out and asked me just who I was and what I had come for. I was in agony, trying to explain it in my bad French, in front of all those people, with Sam pulling on my pant leg and trying to open my purse.

"My appointment is for today," I said. "To have my son's sutures cut off." (I didn't know how to say removed.) I found my appointment card. "See," I said. "It is for Tuesday, the eighteenth."

"Madame, this is the eighteenth, but today is Thursday. There is no Tuesday the eighteenth."

"I did not write it," I said.

Someone snickered.

"But it is the eighteenth," I said.

The doctor felt sorry for me and took me and the kids back to a room where a nice brunette nurse removed Ben's stitches.

The nurse gave Ben a *bisou* and shook my hand. "Have a good day," she said, and dismissed me.

"But what about the cost?" I said.

She looked bothered. "Oh, that office has closed for today. Can you come back sometime next week?"

I said sure, and we left.

A whole year later, we could still see the four little stitch marks. The kids at school teased him about looking like a pirate. But I told him it made him look brave. "I wouldn't worry about it," I said. "You know, I read that Harrison Ford still has a scar from his childhood and girls go crazy over him."

"Who's Harrison Ford?" Ben asked.

"You know, *Raiders of the Lost Ark*."

Ben looked puzzled.

"Han Solo," I said.

"Ohhh," Ben said. He bit his lip for a second and then grinned and waved an imaginary light saber.

13. Joyeux Noël

Our first December in Auvergne was a little dreary. The sky was perpetually gray, with cold wind and rain. It was a week before Christmas, and none of my neighbors had put wreaths on their doors or fake snow on their windows or light-up Santas or manger scenes in their yards the way people did back home in Greer. So far all I had seen were the glittery snowflakes that teams of men in blue coveralls had hung from all the streetlight poles.

When I went out to get the mail I asked Madame Mallet about it, whether the French usually did more decorating for the Christmas season. She looked insulted.

"What do you want? It's a religious holiday, not a party. Besides, New Year's is right around the corner, and we French really celebrate that. We send cards, have big dinners and parties, and give presents. I have no idea what Christmas is like in the United States, but here it's just for family. Since Clément and I don't go to mass anymore, we'll probably just stay inside the house, wallowing in our sin. But we usually have company for New Year's. I suppose my niece Matilde will come over with little Spermatazoïde."

"Pardon?"

"Spermatazoïde. Have I not told you about him? He was conceived by artificial insemination, since Matilde's François is not as manly as she always claimed he was. Anyway, that's what I call the child. Of course she calls him something else. Gabriel, I think, her little angel. Or 'Little Prince,' that's what she says most of the time. Imagine. Treating him like royalty. The way Matilde fusses over that child, he's going to grow up wanting to know what she did with his crown.

Madame Mallet pointed up at our balcony. "I noticed that you bought a Christmas tree." There through the glass French doors was Todd putting the lights on. "I've got something for it. I'll be right back." I waited at her gate, watching Todd and the kids upstairs. The tree was only three feet tall, so he was putting it on top of a table to keep Sam away from the ornaments. It was a sad-looking tree, but most of them at the lot that morning had been like that, more like bushes than trees, with stray branches sticking out at odd angles. When we had brought it home, our neighbor Alain had shaken his head and said there were nicer trees downtown, but we didn't care. The kids loved it, though Sarah worried about it being nailed to a wooden platform. "Won't it die without any water?" she had asked the man who had sold it to us.

"Of course it will," he had answered, "It's already dead. It's for Christmas, not Easter."

Madame Mallet came back out to the gate with a box of silver balls. "Here," she said. "A catalog company sent this and I have no use for it."

"Thank you," I said. "The kids will love these."

"Oh, it's not anything that great. It might just as well decorate your tree as clutter my trash can."

.   .   .

AFTER LUNCH I headed across town to help decorate our little church for Christmas. Christ Church of the Auvergne was listed as *Temple, Culte Protestant* on the Clermont map, and I must admit that I did feel a bit like a cult member, being that we members were all English-speaking expatriates who wore similar clothes and shared peculiar habits, like a tendency to laugh loudly. But I loved that church, the tiny gothic stone chapel, with its crazy pump organ that sounded like a bagpipe, the wooden pews that were falling apart, and the stained-glass baby boy behind the pulpit. We were like pilgrims worshipping there, wrapped in our coats and hats and gloves, huddled in that church. I didn't even mind how our feet froze into ice cubes on the stone floor and how puffs of breath came out of our mouths as we sang the hymns.

Unlike First Baptist back home, there were no committees to carry out the church work or a custodial staff to clean it. We members had to cut the grass or plant the flowers, buy the bread and wine, not grape juice, for communion and decorate for Christmas and Easter. If we didn't do it, it didn't get done.

So someone volunteered to direct a Christmas pageant for Christmas Eve night, and all the kids signed up. Sarah wanted to be an angel and Ben a shepherd, and we made Sam a sheep. The only rehearsal would be an hour before the pageant started, and we left the costumes up to the kids.

My friends and I put out candles and greenery at all the stained-glass windows, hung an arrangement on each of the huge wooden doors next to the old wrought-iron scrollwork and hinges, and added ribbons and holly to the ends of the pews. With the advent wreath lit, it looked like a Christmas fairy tale.

After we finished decorating, I returned home to find Todd waiting for me. Ben and Sarah were driving him crazy, begging and pleading to go on the shopping trip he'd promised them. Père Noël, the French Santa, was supposed to arrive at Auchan that day, and Ben wanted to be sure that Père Noël knew that he wanted the cowboy Playmobile set, not the castle one.

I hated Auchan. I had tried to do my shopping other places, but in spite of my animosity for the place, I kept coming back to it. It was a huge and impersonal super store, but it did have an international aisle with a section labeled *Américain,* which included jars of peanut butter and boxed brownie mix and sometimes even a fajita kit, with tortillas and *sauce piquante.*

My French friend Virginie had scolded me for shopping there and took me around to four other groceries—different ones for meat, fruits and vegetables, paper products, and canned goods. "It's so much better than Auchan," she said. "The staff can answer your questions, and the food is of much better quality." But I just wanted to get my food and go home and not frighten grocery clerks with my American accent. Besides, who has time to visit four grocery stores every week? So I stuck it out with Auchan, in spite of the hugeness of the place, the crazy carts with their four wheels rolling in different directions, the irritating way people in line would stand right next to me as I tried to punch in the pin number to my *carte bleu,* and the breakneck speed with which I had to bag my own groceries.

And now my children wanted to go there, just for fun.

I tried to be a good sport.

The place was packed. Auchan was closed on Sundays and after seven p.m. the rest of the week, so everybody in town was there to do their last-minute Christmas shopping. They mobbed the special displays loaded with extra holiday treats, filling up their carts with stuffed goose, duck, oysters, boxes of chocolates, foie gras, pâté, and special sausages available only during the holidays. It was a gastronomic heaven. After touring the food and the toys, we walked back to the front of the store. Père Noël looked like Santa, but a deflated version, with sunken cheekbones and red wine breath. Sarah and Ben hopped on his lap and told him what they wanted until the camera man interrupted and said it was time for the picture. At the last second I lunged forward with Sam, stuck him on Père Noël's lap to get him into the picture. After the light flashed, Sam turned around, saw the grim-looking Santa, and started screaming bloody murder.

We had to come back after Christmas for the photo. It turned out great. Ben and Sarah were smiling and Sam looked confused. Père Noël appeared a little hostile.

The pageant was a success as well. Sarah wore a halo and her *Star Wars* Princess Leia costume, which was white and flowing, and stood among the heavenly multitude between a Barbie princess angel and a bride angel, complete with veil. Ben was a perfect shepherd in his bathrobe and sandals and completed the look with a stick from the backyard. During the rehearsal, our little sheep kept running off with Baby Jesus and falling on top of Mary, but by the time the pageant started, Sam was content to just wander. Ben tried chasing him down with his stick but finally gave up. Sam was a sheep. Ben figured that he should let him graze.

After the pageant, we all stood in the back of the chapel and shared cookies that we had brought from home, and thermoses of hot chocolate and cider. The shared friendship warmed us, and then we all went on our way.

On the way home, we went for a drive like we always did on Christmas Eve. We saw the lights at Place de Jaude in Clermont, with its huge Christmas tree and skating rink. Then we drove around our little village, oohing and aahing at the snowflakes all lit up in the shadow of the ancient buildings.

Finally, we tucked our exhausted children into their beds, and within a few minutes they sailed off to dreamland. A few hours later I snuggled next to my dear husband and thought about our French Christmas. Noël was indeed different in France, more like "Silent Night" than "Joy to the World." The French had no spray snow on their houses, no wreaths on their doors, and no light-up manger scenes in their yards. But as we woke the next morning, gathered around our tabletop tree, and celebrated our first Christmas in France, I whispered a prayer of thanksgiving—for the babe in the manger of course, and for a newfound taste of heavenly peace.

14. French Skin

There is no question as to when I started thinking so much about breasts and their significance. It was January, and we had been in France about six months. I was weaning Sam, and my swollen, milk-engorged grapefruits ached in my nursing bra. I hadn't expected to have such trouble. At fourteen months, Sam nursed only at night and only for comfort. No, it wasn't good for his sleep routine, and after three kids I should have known better. But our new life was stressing us out, and letting Sam nurse himself to sleep was the only bedtime routine I could muster by the end of the day. But when our sweet toddler grew horns and started torturing me with hourly demands for a nightcap, I was desperate enough to make a change.

Surprisingly, it was an easy switch for Sam. He didn't seem to care that Mommy's warm, fleshy milk jugs had been replaced with a flavorless bottle of water. Mommy's body, on the other hand, had a tantrum. My breasts liked their routine and weren't about to go out of business.

I tried everything to relieve the pain. I drank lots of water and then dehydrated myself. I bound myself up like Disney's Mulan, singing, "Be a man . . ." Nothing worked. I even tried sticking red cabbage leaves in my bra. In the warm sun I smelled like coleslaw—all I needed was a little vinegar behind the ears. There was no way to avoid it. I would have to go to the doctor.

There are certain words that they never teach in French class—"engorged," for example. Armed with a French-English dictionary, my best bra, and new courage brought on by sheer agony, I went to see Dr. Allezard.

We had visited Dr. Allezard once before when the children caught a stomach bug, complete with *la diarrhée*. He was a handsome, serious man with dark eyes and sat very straight at his desk, as if sitting taller would help him understand me better. He had leaned forward, listening intensely as I struggled in French to describe the children's symptoms. When I struggled for the word for "dehydrated," he decided that it was time to take over. He cleared his throat and began to speak loudly in English, carefully enunciating each word.

"Do . . . the . . . children . . . throw . . . down?" he asked.

"Yes," I had said, not wanting to correct him with my French being what it was.

During this visit, however, he decided to speak in his own language.

"I am sorry that I have no robe or covering for you," Dr. Allezard said, offering me a chair as my brain raced to translate his words. "French women don't use them. I think they are more *bien dans leur peau* [comfortable in their skin] than American ladies, no?" He paused as I was still translating and then switched to English. "To . . . search . . . for . . . infection . . .

Madame Ramsey," he said, "I . . . must . . . look . . . for . . . your . . . breasts."

Well, *bien sûr!* Even as a modest American, I would have considered ripping off my shirt in the waiting room if he'd do something about my aching bosom. I was desperate enough to be grown up about it. Standing up at his desk, I took off my shirt and bra. He put on gloves and examined me. No nurse. No separate examining room. Just me and him and Sam gazing hungrily at my chest.

As Dr. Allezard gently poked and prodded, I focused my eyes on the doorknob. Was it locked? I tried to make my mind go blank. *"More comfortable in their skin,"* he had said. Next to the French, he did have a point. During our first months as American expatriates, I had developed a lightning fast reach for the TV remote. Naked breasts were popping up everywhere—in commercials for everything from shampoo to gelatin, and even on the news. Before long my big kids and I stopped noticing. (I think Todd still noticed.) Bigger-than-life billboards, however, were a little harder to ignore. Plastered beside a stoplight near our home was a woman in a tight sweater, her breasts as big as two tire swings. It wasn't her pretty face that stopped traffic. As my mother would say, her buttons were showing.

Probably the most bizarre billboard was a yogurt ad captioned, LIVE YOUR FANTASY. Above the words, a large black bird proudly sported huge yellow breasts of lemon halves.

"I don't get it," I thought out loud on our way home from school. "Why would a bird want breasts?"

"I guess because they're pretty," my ten-year-old daughter replied from the back seat. I looked at her in the rearview mirror. Her innocence stunned me. She was looking wistfully out the window, her hair in two rumpled braids, and the slightest ripples on her shirt. Somehow she was free of it, so far anyway—the self-consciousness, the critical eye toward her body.

She was saved by France, at least in part—by the rosy, fleshy women in paintings in the cathedrals and museums, the bosomy beauties on pedestals in the park, and the coffee table nudes in homes of her friends. It was bound to rub off on her, this wonderful love and acceptance that the French have for their own bodies. I envy it. I love how no one ogles over the topless women at the city pool or at the beaches—except for the tourists climbing all over one another to snap pictures. I have to admit, I stole a few glances myself. I guess I'm just fascinated that these grandmas and moms and twenty-somethings alike are so *bien dans leur peau*. No one appeared to be worrying about stretch marks and cellulite as they lay on the sand or chased their children in the surf.

There was a statue in a rose garden downtown that be-came one of our favorites. It was a woman—a real woman—with thick thighs and round breasts. She stood facing a fountain, as if under the shower, holding back her long hair to let the water rinse through it. "I like that girl," Sarah told me on a walk. It made me happy. I was sure that when we moved back home she might lose her fantastic accent, and she'd probably forget a lot of the words that once flowed so easily, but I hoped she'd always stand tall like that stone woman in the park, at peace with the skin God gave her.

But this story had a happy ending for me as well. Thanks to Dr. Allezard, I got gauze to bind my breasts, a prescription to dry up my milk, and a single-use rental breast pump to re-lieve my pain. Plus, I developed an oddly intimate relationship with Monsieur Gronot, my neighborhood pharmacist, who insisted on showing me how to use the electric pump, despite the long line of curious onlookers waiting behind me. They called it a *tire-lait*—"milk-puller" in English. Let me tell you, the translation fit.

I took the pump home to the privacy of my bedroom, plugged it in, and within a couple minutes I became half the woman I used to be. The pump pulled so hard that I was afraid it might vacuum me right into its little metal box, where I'd call out, *"Au secours!"* and no one would hear me. But thankfully it didn't, and soon I felt much better. I even learned to love my dried-up milk duds. Though I wasn't ready to bare it all at the beach, I didn't scowl so much at myself in the mirror anymore. My skin might not be perfect, but it fit me just fine.

15. Project Benjamin

Ever since Ben got Le James Bond 007 Trousse d'Espionnage for our first Christmas in France, I learned to expect lots of slinking around and hiding behind the shower curtian, so it was no surprise to see him standing in the foyer, peeking out the front door.

"What are you doing?" I whispered.

"She's out there," he whispered back. "And I want to get my Nerf ball—but not with her out there."

I looked at Ben's feet. Sure enough, no shoes. It was a warm spring day, but Madame Mallet would object to him running around barefoot.

"She's trimming the hedge," I whispered. "That takes a good while. Just put on some shoes if you don't want her to say something."

"Oh, I'll just go play in my room," Ben sulked.

I was getting sick and tired of Madame Mallet picking on

my son. It seemed like the sweeter she was to me, the meaner she was to Ben. She noticed every nitpicky thing about him. Whenever he climbed the cherry tree, she'd leave her yard to come over and remind him that cherry branches are brittle and Monsieur Giraud, the owner of the house, would not be happy if his tree was destroyed. When a stray ball dropped into her yard, she would come out squawking and then disappear into her garage with the ball. Ben stopped playing ball in the road, but that wasn't enough. Whenever he and Sarah and the neighbor kids would race through our yard playing tag, it was Ben who'd get the finger wagging. When he stood on our balcony and shot his water gun onto the street, she gave him the finger wagging again.

"She doesn't understand boys at all," I told Todd.

"Maybe you should talk to her about it," he said.

Easy for him to say. I knew it wouldn't help, but I consented to try.

"Boys need to run," I said.

"Boys need discipline," she said.

I tried again to explain Ben's sensitive nature, how stressed he had been, and that he needed some room to work it out. Madame Mallet repeated the advice she had given me before. "He just needs what my niece in Lyon gives her girls—a quick stick to their legs. They are very well behaved."

. . .

ONE SUNNY SATURDAY morning, I was talking to Madame Mallet at her gate when our smoke alarm went off. Todd was upstairs cooking bacon, and he always forgot to shut the kitchen door. She stopped in midsentence at the loud beeping, and I explained. She had never heard of a home smoke alarm before.

"That's ridiculous," she said. "Why do you need a smoke alarm in a house built of concrete?" Then she began a discourse on the silliness of Americans building their houses out of wood, since stone and concrete lasts forever.

"Ben worries about the house catching on fire," I said. "I know we don't need it, but getting a smoke alarm was the only way we could get him to sleep upstairs."

"But he's so wild," she said, shaking her head. "It's bizarre that he would worry so."

"Oh, that's not all," I said, and told her that he worried about getting to school late, and if his homework was exactly right, and what if the alarm on his watch went off again during class and he couldn't turn it off.

Madame Mallet looked amazed. *"C'est vraiment bizarre,"* she said.

The next time she saw Ben, she put her hands on his shoulders and told him that he was in France now, where people are sensible and build their houses out of stone and concrete. And if some freak event happened, she assured him, the *pompiers* were highly trained to handle any emergency.

"Huh?" Ben said. "I'm not afraid." He turned to me and said in English, "What's she talking about?" I smiled nervously and muttered that I would explain later.

Project Benjamin had begun.

Before we left for a summer month in the States, I mentioned to Madame Mallet that Ben was a little apprehensive about traveling home without Todd. That wasn't the half of it. I was trying not to be insulted, but Ben was showing absolutely no confidence in my ability to get all three kids and myself through the Paris and Atlanta airports and home to Raleigh. He begged Todd to fly home with us, and when that didn't work, he simply refused to go.

"It's not you, Mom," he would say with his fibbing face on. "I just don't want to leave without Daddy."

That was a lie. He knew the truth—that I never had flown anywhere but to Texas by myself and didn't know what to do in airports. I didn't know where to go or what I had to do at customs or which bus or train to take where. It's not that I liked depending on my husband—it's just that it always took one of us to do the navigating and standing in line, and the other one to shepherd the kids and watch the bags. I'd always been the shepherd.

As we were loading up the trunk to head for the airport, Madame Mallet came over to talk. "*Viens,* Benjamin," she said, pulling him into her yard. He looked to me, and I nodded to him to go ahead.

"So what did she say?" I asked later.

"Oh, she just went on and on about how airplanes were safer than cars and she gave me a four-leaf clover from her yard," he said, opening up his palm to show me. "No big deal," he said, and tucked the clover into the folded paper his daddy had given him. On the paper Todd had written out step-by-step instructions for where to go and what to do in each airport, just in case I forgot.

. . .

SUMMER ENDED AND soon we were back in the routine of school life. Things had been pretty quiet between Ben and

Madame Mallet. Maybe it was because we were starting our second year, but life was almost peaceful. Ben no longer played ball in the street and Madame Mallet lessened her harsh words. It seemed that they had reached a détente.

If only Ben and Sarah would work out a détente of their own. It was a Saturday, and Madame Mallet and I were again talking at her gate while the kids were playing and arguing in the yard. Ben was bouncing the tennis ball against the side of the house and yelling at two-year-old Sam to leave him alone. Sam, who had an identical ball in his fat little hand, was running around Ben, crying and reaching up to take Ben's ball. Sarah had to be right in the middle.

"Just give him the ball and take the one he's got—they're the same thing," she yelled in a motherly voice.

"Well, if there's no difference he can just keep the one he's got," Ben yelled back. "He gets everything he wants! He's just a spoiled baby."

Sam stormed after him, shouting, "I not a 'poiled baby!"

"I think I know Ben's problem," Madame Mallet said, pointing at him. "He is jealous. He is the middle child and he is jealous of his brother."

No kidding, I thought. "Yes, I think you're right," I said.

Then Madame Mallet advised me on how I might treat his need for more attention, suggesting time alone with me or with his father and additional responsibilities for him around the house of which he can be proud. I resisted the urge to say that we were doing those things already. This was a big step for her. For the first time, Madame Mallet was beginning to understand our eight-year-old *sauvage.*

I didn't know it, but this diagnosis of hers was the next step of Project Benjamin. Next was a gift-giving campaign—

first a wallet, then a digital watch that she got from one of her catalog companies. I forced him to go and say thank you, and that is when the kissing started.

"It's gross, Mom," Ben said. "I'm afraid if I move just a little too much, she's gonna get me on the mouth!"

"Well, why do you do it, then?" I asked.

"Oh, I guess she's not that bad of an old lady."

One afternoon we came home from school and Ben was moping around and dragging his book bag in the gravel because someone on the playground had called him a moron. Madame Mallet came over and went right to Ben. She put her arm around him and cooed, "What's the problem, *mon chéri*? You with the beautiful brown eyes. Why are you sad today? Did you have a bad day at school?"

"Non," Ben answered, not wanting to explain. "I'm just tired."

Madame Mallet looked at me accusingly. "Is he not sleeping well?"

"Uh," I stammered. "He seemed fine to me."

The next morning Madame Mallet pulled me aside as we were loading the car for school. "I think I have just what Benjamin needs," she said, leading me over to her house. "Does he like jelly at breakfast?"

"Uh, *oui.*"

"I have some very special jellies," she said, leading me into her dark garage to a cabinet full of canned goods. "They are made by the monks at the Abbaye de Sept-Fons. They're full of fruit—not sugar, like the ones at Auchan—and are good for your health." She began handing me jars. "Does he like apricot? Strawberry? Cherry?" I took an apricot and a strawberry and thanked her.

"If he likes them I can help you make an order," she said as I put the jellies on the floor of the car and buckled Sam into his car seat.

As we headed out of the neighborhood I told Ben about Madame Mallet's plan to make him feel better. "What?" Ben asked, raising his eyebrow and then grinning. "That's a little crazy." He beamed and didn't say a cross word to his brother and sister all the way to school.

A few days later, Madame Mallet asked me, "What is Benjamin doing in the backyard?" I laughed. I had been wondering when she'd get around to asking me. She said that she had seen him digging a hole with a shovel over by the hedges, and she had come over to ask him about it. Madame Mallet continued telling the story. "I said, 'Are you planting a tree?' He said no. I said, 'Are you planting flowers?' He said no. 'Well,' I said, 'what are you doing?' He looked up at me like a little lamb and said 'I'm just making this.' And he pointed to the hole. So Rébecca, what is he doing?"

I said, "He is just digging a hole!" We both laughed. "With his daddy in South America for two weeks, I decided that if digging a hole makes him happy, then it was okay with me." We laughed again, and she shook her head in puzzlement.

"That Benjamin," she said. "He is a complicated boy."

I never did tell Madame Mallet, but I found out later what the hole was for. He was setting a trap, and he was going to fill it with water balloons and then cover them with grass. Sarah's birthday party was coming up, and he figured that a really good spy could surely catch a few fifth grade girls.

16. *Madame Bernard's Elixir of Youth*

I was admiring the artful display of the cough drops in Monsieur Gronot's pharmacy one day when a little old lady wobbled in with her cane and asked for a bottle of youth. "Why it's right here, madame, next to the hemorrhoid creams," Monsieur Gronot said, guiding her to the neat row of little pink bottles with gold caps.

Youth in a bottle? Were they serious? I hid behind the *pastilles* and listened to the old lady ask how well it worked, and what it did, exactly. Monsieur Gronot said that he didn't really know, that he hadn't read the literature as yet.

If I hadn't had such an American accent, I might have spoken up and told the lady about the secret I had discovered a few months prior when I stopped at an antique shop on a whim. Who would have ever guessed that I would stumble into a fountain of youth of sorts, a homemade syrupy concoction that seemed to work magic on the human face as well as on hand-me-down furniture? It was shocking.

Madame Bernard owned the place, Antiquités Bernard, and assured me that her potion was completely natural, a family recipe passed down through hundreds of years, composed of some French words I didn't understand and a touch of honey and cloves. You could even drink it, she said, although she didn't recommend that, and neither did she sell or give out the potion to anyone but family. It remained in old bottles and cans in the ramshackle barn behind her shop, where her son-in-law brought broken-down tables and armoires back to their former glory. That was fine by me—I didn't need a can of my own. An occasional whiff from the oak buffet Madame Bernard sold me was enough. The top drawers, the wood of which must have been especially dry and porous to be so odorous, filled my house with the fragrance. That's what had gotten into me. I may not have looked it, with occasional gray wires sprouting up right in the bareness of my hair part, but there was an energy zinging through my blood that I hadn't seen since my college days, when I used to go jogging—for fun.

It all started with a clipping Mother sent me about how we should never forget to stop and smell the roses—carpe diem, as they say. I was on the way to the grocery store and Sam had fallen asleep in his car seat when I saw a little sign that I had never noticed before on the highway. ANTIQUITÉS, it said in hand-painted letters meant to look medieval. I decided to forget the bread and milk and to seize the moment. So I took a hard left down a cow path through a farmer's field, following more medieval lettering. The signs led me through the stone wall–lined village of Gordes, and when they stopped, I was in someone's driveway in a quaint little courtyard with an old ivy-covered farmhouse on one side, a stone cottage on the other, and a run-down barn off to the side.

No one came out. I put Sam into the stroller and wheeled him over to the tiny arched door of the Hansel and Gretel cottage with a shingle hanging that said ANTIQUITÉS and peeked through the window. My heart skipped a beat at the great stuff inside. Even in the dim light I could see the shimmer of copper pots hanging from the wooden ceiling beams and stacks of linens on a long farm table. Wasn't anyone coming? And then a large woman came out, taking off her apron and drying her hands in it.

"Bonjour, madame," she said, reaching out to shake my hand. "I'm sorry that it took me a minute. I was wringing Clotilde's neck, and she was putting up an awful fuss."

"I'm sorry?" I said.

"Oh, you're a foreigner," she said, smiling big. "British?"

"No, American."

"Ah, American, well, well. That's even better." Madame Bernard was a sturdy-looking woman with a face as round and smooth as a dinner plate. "And look at that beautiful child. Sleeping without a care in the world."

"I saw the sign and didn't know if you were open," I said nervously. Didn't she say she was doing something to somebody's neck? If we went missing, no one would find us for weeks.

"Oh, we're always open, seven days a week. You just come when you like. We have been here for four hundred years," she said, and took a long skeleton key out of her apron pocket. "Not me exactly. I've only been here for seventy-eight. Anyway, I was saying that Clotilde—she's this old hen that my great-grandson named . . . Imagine, naming a hen after a person. She's awful—he doesn't even like her. But he'll like her tonight. Do you like coq au vin?"

I said that I did as she unlocked the door. A powerful smell rushed out of the cottage, like honey and cloves, maybe. How could this woman be seventy-eight? Her hair was dyed an unnatural purplish red, so there weren't any telltale grays. But where were the wrinkles?

"Ooh, the scent is strong today," she said, and took a big whiff. Then she started talking while my eyes tried to take everything in—the huge walnut armoires, the glass cases full of little treasures—figurines, necklaces, tiny statues of Joan of Arc and other saints, the tall dark furniture lining the walls and stacks of linens and old La Mode magazines slipping out of boxes onto the brick floor. "My son-in-law just finished up restoring that armoire over there—the Louis Philippe one. We brought it over just this morning. It's the honey polish that you smell. And look what it does." Madame Bernard stroked the glistening wood grain. It was beautiful—probably eleven feet high, simple lines, with turned-out feet. She turned the gold key and opened the heavy doors. Another cloud of polish floated out. The deep shelves were also refinished. Even in the finest armoires the shelves are often left rough-hewn and unstained. These shone like silk.

"You like beautiful furniture, huh?"

I said that I did, and she took me around her shop and showed me each piece, documenting the style and the age, as well as who sold it to her and brief histories of their families. The grandness of the furniture took my breath away. All the furniture we had brought from South Carolina was either cast-off hand-me-downs or pine stuff we had bought at Naked Furniture and painted or stained ourselves. These armoires and buffets looked like furniture grownups had, the kind you saw in decorating magazines. I had always hoped that someday I might have real furniture like that. Now with an entire selection laid out before me, I was love struck.

My heart ached for subtle wood grain and details—carvings, cornices, pretty hardware. I had to have something. Why, I needed something—a place to put things. After all, I had no closets and only four kitchen cabinets. Todd couldn't expect me to go on living like that. He had always said that we would do like most expats and bring home a few pieces of furniture to remind us of our time here.

But these pieces were huge—not that I minded. It might be too intimidating for Todd though, to start off with something like that. Maybe a smaller piece.

"Do you have anything smaller, a small buffet, maybe, for dishes?"

"I know just the thing," she said. "But it's not ready yet. Victor, my son-in-law, is working on it. Come with me."

Madame Bernard led me out of the cottage, through the stone patio and around all the fountains and urns and stone benches, through the grass, down the worn path to the ramshackle barn on the side.

She opened the barn door and the smell of honey and cloves rushed at me again. There on the dirt floor, standing beside a tangle of broken-down furniture, stood a young man with his back to us. He had wavy black hair and was working on a buffet, leaning over it like in a jeans commercial. In fact, he had on jeans, instead of the usual blue coveralls that French men wore whenever they did any physical labor. He also wore a T-shirt that showed off his muscular arms. I felt my face flush.

"Victor," Madame Bernard called over the classical music coming from his boom box, "I've brought an American lady to see the buffet."

"Bonjour, madame," the man said in an older man's voice, turning around and brushing a shock of black hair from his eyes with the back of a polish-stained hand.

I struggled to say something, standing there like an idiot before this beautiful man with his black wavy hair and blue-gray eyes. Madame Bernard started talking about the buffet. She was saying that it was *noyer,* which I was pretty sure meant "to clean," and I said that yes, it was very *noyer,* that he had done a very fine job on it, very fine indeed. Madame Bernard looked at me funny, and I wondered if *noyer* did in fact mean "to clean," and a half second later I was pretty sure that it didn't. Madame Bernard and her gorgeous son-in-law looked at each other nervously, and then she pointed at the bull's-eye knobs, saying that they indicated the piece was about one hundred years old.

Victor stood there in those jeans, looking like Warren Beatty. His face did have a few lines, if you looked close, but just a few. He was perfect.

The buffet was beautiful too. It was perfect, actually, for my dishes, and it had character. There were two open shelves at the top, braced at the sides with carved swirls of wood that looked like backwards treble clefs. The base had two drawers with the bull's-eye knobs, and two bottom shelves closed by cabinet doors. It was walnut, stained with the honey-colored polish.

"It's beautiful," I said, running my hand over the dry cabinet doors. "What a difference—the before and after. How do you do it?"

"It's the treatment," he said.

"A family secret," said Madame Bernard. "It works on any wood, anything it touches for that matter."

"Anything it touches?" I asked. Was I crazy to wonder? Victor's young face, his young hands? And she and her young smooth face—she breathed it in too.

"Anything," she quickly replied.

"Everything it touches?" I asked again.

Madame Bernard stared at me for a moment. "Everything," she said, looking at me with her hazel eyes. "Anything," she said, and then whispered, "Anyone."

She knew.

"It revives, repairs," she said, instinctively touching her face. "Even the fragrance of it has an effect."

I bought the buffet. I had to talk it over with Todd, but it was fine with him. It was a bargain price, I pointed out, and could house all of our wedding china and table linens. I left off the part about the youth-inducing aroma. He wouldn't have believed me.

On delivery day I was cleaning up the breakfast dishes when their car turned into our cul-de-sac. I looked down from the balcony and saw them—Madame Bernard and War-ren Beatty, and there was my buffet, wrapped in blankets, tied down in the little wagon hitched to their car. But where were the helpers who would move it up the stairs? I had told them that there would be stairs. And Madame Bernard had said that stairs were no problem. The shelves could come off and the two drawers could be taken out, but the wide base weighed a ton. I remembered struggling to pull it away from the wall in the barn so that I could see the back. Not even the three of us together could handle it, let alone Victor by himself.

We made our greetings and handshakes. "May we see where to put it?" Madame Bernard asked. I showed her in, and she wiped her high heels on the mat.

"It goes upstairs," I said apologetically, waiting for the look of surprise and then embarrassment on their faces. "But," I said, "you may leave it here and my husband can ask a friend to help him take it upstairs."

"No, no," Madame Bernard assured me, "it should be no problem. Just show us where to put it."

I took them up the tile steps and into the living room to the space on an empty wall.

"Do you think Victor can lift it by himself?" I asked Madame Bernard.

"Oh, no, Madame Ramsey, I will help him."

"Oh, no, no," I said. I wasn't raised to stand by and let somebody's grandmother move my furniture up the stairs. "I can't let you do that. I'll help your son-in-law," I said.

"Madame Ramsey, I don't wish to offend you, but I've done this many times before, and I'm not sure that you . . . Well, I've done this many times." She didn't think I could handle it. I wasn't sure that I could either, but I couldn't let her do it.

"Victor's used to me," she whispered. "And you are our client, not our assistant. Be assured that this is routine for us. But we could use a rope, if you have one, please."

I reluctantly agreed and went in search of a rope. When I came back, they were carefully navigating the buffet onto the porch. Madame Bernard's high heels were scratching in the gravel.

At the foot of the stairs they began to tie the rope around the big oak base, and then around Madame Bernard, first around her waist and then around her hands. Victor got in back.

"Are you sure I can't help?" I asked.

"No, thank you," they replied in unison.

I stood at the bottom and gritted my teeth as she mounted the steps, feeling guilty, watching this seventy-eight-year-old woman inch along with her heels on the tile, sweat beading on her forehead. I didn't know what to do with my hands, just standing there, waiting for Victor's legs to give way and my big beautiful antique buffet to plow his gorgeous body under it. I could just imagine having to call 18, which was the number for emergency medical help. Or was it 17?

It seemed that it took forever, but thankfully, after much wheezing and groaning and several stops to readjust hands and rope, Madame Bernard reached the top, her fingers white from the strain of the weight. She and her son-in-law set down the buffet with some heavy breathing, and then she effortlessly pushed it right into the place on the wall.

I offered them water, which they politely refused, and then paid them the rest. They counted it, thanked me, and headed for the stairs.

"Wait," I said, searching my purse for tip money. "Please," I said, trying to hand it to them. "For the delivery," I said.

"No, no, Madame Ramsey," Madame Bernard said, looking embarrassed. "Delivery is always free."

At least a smile then. Couldn't we share that? "You will not need to exercise today," I said to them as we neared the door, and then laughed. They looked nervously at each other and then back at me.

"You are strong," I tried to explain, flexing an imaginary muscle for emphasis. Madame Bernard and Victor squinted at me. Didn't *forte* mean "strong"?

"Merci beaucoup!" I called as they hurried back to their car.

For the rest of our time in France, the buffet remained in our living room. The walnut boards must have been exceptionally porous to have soaked up the treatment so well. When I opened up the drawers, I could still smell the honey and cloves. I kept our napkins in the top left side, figuring that close facial contact couldn't hurt. At dinner I dabbed the honey-smelling cloth to my mouth and snuck in an extra breath under the napkin.

I could tell it was affecting me, but not the way I had expected. I still had the gray hairs springing up from my part, but that was okay. I'm not sure that my wrinkles lessened, but I did notice that ever since the buffet moved in, my energy level shot through the roof. I got lots done and I didn't think I could stop if I wanted to. Some nights I'd wake up needing desperately to fix something—*revive and repair,* as Madame Bernard would say.

I told Mother the whole story, and she wanted to go antiquing on her next visit. She'd been looking for a little side table for the living room. She insisted that this fountain of youth business was all foolishness, but I noticed that she was particularly interested in something in pine, certainly the most porous of all woods.

17. Todd's New Pal

The French secretaries at work loved my husband. So did the lady behind the counter at Au Croissant d'Or and the woman at the gas station. Everywhere he's gone in life, little old ladies love him. Once on a business trip to Nova Scotia, Todd found himself in a hotel full of old women partying in the hallway, keeping him awake with their loud Frank Sinatra music. "Come on out, young man, and have a drink with us," they yelled through his keyhole. "We're old and our husbands are all dead!"

It was unanimous, except for Madame Mallet. We couldn't understand it. It was the fall of our second year in France, long after Madame Mallet had started giving me and my savage children *bisoux,* but all Todd got was the finger wagging. When he didn't mow the grass, she complained, and when he did mow the lawn, she rushed out to critique his technique.

"Vous êtes un mauvais jardinier!" (You're a bad gardener!), she said, wagging her finger in his face.

His awkward smile froze in disbelief.

"Pardon?"

"The grass is still wet. You must wait for it to dry."

"But I had to do it when I had time."

"Oh, Monsieur Ramsey, there's always time to do things correctly."

Back in the privacy of our home, Todd wasn't so polite. "I should have told her that I'm not *en retraite,* sitting on my butt waiting for the grass to dry."

"She's just an old woman with nothing much to do," I said. A battle between the two of them could make my life miserable. "Try to get to know her. Maybe when she knows that you're really a nice person she'll stop acting like that."

"I'd rather have a stick in my eye."

A month later, we were on the brink of World War III. Ben and Todd and our American friend Mike who was visiting on a business trip had been tossing the baseball back and forth in the street when a stray ball fell into her yard. Apparently she had seen it all happen behind her lace curtain and was waiting to see what they would do.

Todd rang her doorbell.

No answer.

He rang it again.

Still no answer.

As Todd waited by the gate, Mike, being full of goodwill and American ingenuity, figured that he could save the neighbor some trouble. In a split second he had hoisted Ben over Madame Mallet's fence.

Madame Mallet flung open the balcony door, puffed up and red in the face. *"Qu'est-ce que vous faites?"* she screeched down at Todd. "You know you're not supposed to be in my yard. You rang the bell! I saw you! No one gave any of you permission to enter my yard."

Todd stood on the street, dumbfounded.

"This is my property and you will respect that! If you want to live like that you need to move to the high-rise apartments with the Algerians!"

"But he was just trying to get his ball," Todd said.

"Just who do you think you are, coming onto my property without permission? This is not public land! It is ours— our flowers being crushed, our fence being pulled on, and for that matter, the street is not your property to play on either!"

"But my friend was trying to save you the effort of getting the ball."

"Save me the effort? By coming onto my property uninvited? Over my fence? I think not! They may do that sort of thing in your country, but you are not in the United States anymore, *monsieur,* and you must respect the way we do things here!"

Madame Mallet huffed inside and shut her door behind her.

That evening we closed all the shutters and were teetering on the edge of nuclear destruction. Todd sat in his easy chair, plotting out strategy.

"Oh, yeah," he said in a calm madman kind of way. "Tomorrow morning we're going to have a little talk. We need to set a few things straight."

"You know, honey, Ben did go into her yard without permission," I said. "I've read that French people really do have a thing about that—everybody with their gates and fences and all."

"Let me get this straight," he said tightly, the vein in his forehead beginning to pulse. "Don't tell me that you're going to stand there and defend her! You're taking *her* side?"

"Please," I begged. "Don't make matters worse. You go off to work every day, but I have to practically live with this woman."

Todd groaned and pretended to read the paper.

The next morning I nervously watched their little talk from behind my curtain, trying to analyze every wince, every pointed finger. Things looked calm enough. When they shook hands and parted I was relieved.

"What did you say?"

"Oh, I just told her that we would never go in her yard uninvited again, but that I had some concerns about her as well."

I bit my lip.

"I told her the kids were scared of her and weren't used to having strangers tell them what to do. I said that they're American kids and don't like kissing people other than their family. Don't worry. I think we reached an understanding."

They may have shaken hands, but not much changed. A week later when Todd's car wouldn't start, Madame Mallet was right by his side, ready to turn the knife.

"What were you thinking, buying a Japanese car? The Peugeots and the Citroëns aren't good enough for you?"

"Oh, we've always had Japanese cars in the States, and we've never had any problems."

"When you buy the next one you should pay more attention to where it comes from. These Parisian cars are nothing but trouble."

"No, I bought it in Clermont," Todd said.

"You may have bought it here, but it comes from Paris. You can tell by the code on the license plate. All that stop-and-go traffic—I hope you have a good mechanic," she said, chuckling to herself as she shut her gate.

Madame Mallet had a way of needling Todd over any sign of weakness. She loved to watch him pack the car for an overnight trip, knowing our propensity for forgetting things. Inevitably we'd pull back into the driveway five minutes after our departure to retrieve a backpack or some necessary piece of baby paraphernalia.

"Stroller," I moaned as we merged onto the highway for a long weekend away.

Todd pretended he didn't hear me and began to hum along with the radio.

"Honey, did you remember the stroller?"

"Don't need it," Todd said. "I'll put him on my shoulders."

"For three days?" I asked. Sam had been ten pounds at birth and at two years looked like a little fullback in training. "We have to go back."

"I'm not going back," he said, staring at the road. "They probably have strollers for rent."

"For rent? Come on, they're not going to have strollers for rent."

Todd grumbled under his breath and took the next exit to turn around.

"You could just leave the car here," I said before we turned into our cul-de-sac. "Maybe she won't see you."

Todd parked the car before the turn and crept around the corner to our house. Unfortunately the gravel crunching beneath his feet on the driveway gave him away. In a second she was on her balcony, laughing.

"You would forget your head!" she said. "You might want to start making out a list." Todd gave a fake chuckle and jogged back to the car with the stroller.

The first time in my life that I ever heard Madame Mallet say anything positive about my husband was on the morning after the Bush/Gore Election Day. I thought she wanted to talk politics when she stopped me at my car. No, she wasn't interested in discussing chads and Florida ballots—though of course later she was happy to criticize the pitiful election process of the most powerful country in the world. She was waving around the morning's issue of *La Montagne,* the local newspaper.

"Did you see? Did you see?" she asked, excitedly opening it up on the hood of my car. On the front page was a big color picture of my husband and an accompanying interview with him about the election. (Ever since Madame Chabosson, our real estate agent, gave her friend at the paper Todd's name and number, he's been listed in their rolodex under "A" for American.)

"He's handsome, huh?" she said, happily examining the picture. "And the ring," she said, pointing to the college ring on his finger, in the foreground of the photo. "Is it a family ring?"

"A family ring?"

"You know, is he of nobility?"

I laughed and shook my head. "Not that I know of. We don't have that in the States."

"Maybe he just hasn't told you," she said. "Didn't you say he has Welsh ancestry? It looks like a family ring to me."

I decided to leave well enough alone. Besides, it couldn't

hurt their relationship. Maybe it would even buy him a little respect.

Around cherry-picking time, Madame Mallet kept eyeing our tree, the branches heavy with fruit. "Your cherries are ripe," she said to Todd. "But I suppose you'd rather just buy your cherries at the store than climb a ladder and pick them yourself." Surprisingly, he laughed it off and went looking for buckets. Maybe it was all the talk of his rumored nobility. Whatever the reason, he decided to pick a pailful for Madame Mallet. I was glad to see him trying to improve things, and took a place by the window to watch their exchange.

All was going very well. There was a polite handshake, he handed her the pail, and then . . . what was that? She was wagging her finger at him! It must have been a joke.

It wasn't.

"I just don't believe it," Todd said, trudging up the stairs.

"Didn't she like them?"

"Becky, I tried. That's it—no more. I'm done. We're finished."

At my look of disbelief he shouted, "She fussed at me for taking off the stems! Can you believe it? She said the cherries would spoil faster without them. I picked all those cherries for her, and that's all she could say. The ungrateful old bat!"

A few days later Madame Mallet caught me at the gate. "Do you know what your husband did?" she said with a giggle. "He picked a whole bowl of cherries for me—and took off every single stem."

"Madame Mallet, they don't grow cherries in South Carolina. How was he to know that you don't take the stems off?"

"No cherry trees? Why not?"

"I guess it's too hot and humid," I said. "They grow lots of peaches, but no cherries."

"That's ridiculous. If you can grow peaches, you can grow cherries. Don't you people know anything?"

Okay. She *was* an ungrateful old bat.

A few weeks later, we were waiting for a taxi to take us to the airport for our second summer trip home. Madame Mallet was standing in her garden, watching Todd and me take our window boxes of geraniums off the balcony railing and down to the shade of the cherry tree.

"Rébecca," she called from her garden. *"Qu'est-ce que vous faites?"*

"We're putting them in the shade," I said.

"Bring them over here, *ma chérie,*" she said, moving a couple of potted plants. "I've been wanting to get my hands on those pitiful plants."

We carried all eight of them over and laid them at her feet.

"Todd, what is your wife doing? How are flowers supposed to grow without sufficient soil? Don't you allow her a gardening budget?"

She was teasing him. This was new.

"Honestly! I'd say you were both Scottish—to be as stingy with your dirt as this! It is obvious that neither of you have *les mains verts* [the green hands]. Bring them over here and let me see what I can do with them."

So we brought them over and thanked her, and she pointed to our suitcases on the front porch.

"Now do you have everything?" She smirked at Todd. This time he let out a big laugh, which seemed to delight her.

"Monsieur Ramsey, I don't think the plane will turn around for anything you leave behind."

She waved us goodbye and three weeks later when our taxi emptied us out at our little house, she appeared by our sides once again. She passed kisses around to the kids and me and then called to Todd. *"Regardez,"* she said, pointing over her fence. There were our flower boxes, dripping with red and pink geraniums and thick green growth.

"All it took was a good bit of dirt and a little fertilizer. And I think you all have been watering them too much. You have to go easy on the water, Monsieur Ramsey. You people were drowning the poor plants."

I don't know what came over him, but Todd leaned over and gave her a thank-you kiss on both cheeks. Before he could straighten back up, Madame Mallet wrapped her arms around him and said, "You don't know how long I've been waiting for you to do that!" The kids and I started laughing, and Madame Mallet wouldn't let go of him. She grinned and said to us over his shoulder, "He's my pal."

"That was nice of you," I said to Todd as we pulled the suitcases into the house. "I think you've got a new best friend."

"Better than a stick in the eye, I guess," Todd said, smiling slightly.

18. *Glinda*

If we did indeed move to Oz, as I initially thought, then there was no question as to who on our street was the Wicked Witch of the West, though I had discovered she was not entirely wicked. Still, Madame Mallet liked to jump out from behind her trees occasionally to make the children nervous and to scold me, fussing about such silly things as how my car scattered gravel from my driveway all over the yellow brick road. "Allée des Cerisiers is a private street," she screeched, "and keeping it neat is just as much your responsibility as any other neighbor's." I agreed and started sweeping, but she never approved of my sweeping technique and always insisted on taking over.

Thank heavens there was another woman who lived next door, a force of complete goodness and light who offered a balance between good and evil and cast a spell of peace and happiness over the entire cul-de-sac.

Madame Fauriaux, the *voisine* that the lady who owned our

house had said adored children, was a perfect Glinda the Good Witch, though she measured only four-foot-five inches, had dyed reddish brown hair, and wore a housedress and an apron instead of satin and tulle. Ben said that when Madame Fauriaux smiled, she hunched up her shoulders and squinted her left eye like a pirate—a very nice pirate. Everyone and everything loved her, from each of her neighbors to the garbage men to the birds that flocked to sing to her and to the roses vining and climbing all over the side of her house.

Even the Wicked Witch of the West went to her for counseling. When I first moved to allée des Cerisiers, I thought that Madame Fauriaux cooked for the Mallets, until I learned that *chef* means "boss" in French. Madame Fauriaux was definitely the garden *chef* of the *quartier*. Fortunately for Madame Mallet, Madame Fauriaux was happy to share all her gardening secrets—how she coaxed so many blooms from her dahlias and chose the right fertilizer for her tomatoes. Madame Mallet listened intensely, and then when Madame Fauriaux would go inside, she'd gossip to me about how her *chef*'s unhappy marriage ended in divorce. Madame Fauriaux never mentioned it to me. Whoever her husband had been, he must have been awful to mistreat such a kind and lovely woman. Just to look at her, one might wonder if she would have enough gumption to keep even a Sunday School of children in line, let alone a gang of hoodlums. But I saw her in action one day, so I didn't doubt her powers.

It was evening in early June, about the time for the lightning bugs to come out, when I turned into our little circle and saw them there—three teenagers, sitting on the curb outside my garden wall, looking for trouble. There was a girl in a halter top and low-riding bell-bottoms and a couple teenage boys with slack-jawed expressions and a moped, which they leaned against, smoking cigarettes. The boys would take turns chasing and pawing at the girl, and she would laugh and shriek at them and strut around. Then the boys would buzz the bike down to the other end of the street and back again into our quiet corner. It was hard not to notice them because all the windows were open, but we tried to ignore the buzzing and the shrieking and the music, and figured it was just a onetime thing.

It wasn't.

They came back the next day and the next, and brought their friends and stayed later and later into the night. Both nights I saw Madame Mallet watching them from behind her lace curtain. I didn't mind them too much as long as they behaved themselves, but Madame Mallet was beside herself. In fact, I felt kind of sorry for her. She had finally gotten the barefooted Americans to stop playing ball in the street, and now these hoodlums were coming in and wrecking all her peace and quiet. None of them was from our *quartier*, she said. And then she went on a discourse of the young lady's reputation, using some vocabulary words with which I was unfamiliar.

"Behave yourself, Astrid," Madame Fauriaux scolded, and then said to me, "Close your ears, my dear. You don't need that sort of French lesson."

The next night the noise was especially loud, and when our kids couldn't even hear their bedtime story Todd decided he had had enough. Having had no training on how to deal with teenagers, he walked out on our balcony and told them to keep it down out there, that our kids couldn't sleep with all the racket.

Laughter rose from the pack. As Todd stormed in, they were mocking his American accent, hopping about, throwing their cigarette butts, and staring and grunting up at our balcony.

"Don't you dare go back out there," I said to him, watching him pace, red-faced and muttering. "Madame Mallet just came out. She'll get them." There she stood in her yard, hands on her hips. I waited for the fireworks. Todd joined me at the window, watching her from behind our lace curtain.

Madame Mallet was sizing up the group, surveying them over her hedge, planning her attack.

She walked to her gate.

They were going to get it, and we wanted to see it all. As many times as she had waved her finger and squawked at my husband, a full-grown man built like a football player, these scrawny slack-jaws were in for it.

Madame Mallet grasped the handle of her gate. But what was she doing? It looked like she was checking the lock. It couldn't be! We stood there dumbfounded as she turned tail and scurried inside.

What had happened to our wicked old witch? Where were the yelling and the finger wagging? Where were the screeching and the hopping? Todd sat down, fuming, and I went to get him some Tylenol.

The next day Madame Mallet was back in witch mode, jumping about and pointing at what the teenagers had left us. On our wall, right where they had congregated, was a five-inch line of blue spray paint. *What a poor excuse for vandalism,* I thought, and laughed when I saw it. "Ooh la la," I said. "I think we've been punished. That'll teach you." I elbowed my husband. But Madame Mallet didn't think it was funny.

"I'm going to call the police the next time I see them," she said, eyes blazing. Madame Fauriaux and I studied the unimaginative graffiti while Madame Mallet continued to rant and rave. Madame Mallet pointed her crooked finger at me and said, "You call Monsieur Giraud and tell him about what they've done to his wall." Madame Fauriaux didn't say anything but stood there pursing her lips in thought.

"I have an idea," Madame Fauriaux said. "Just wait." She smiled at me the way she does with one eye squinting—her nice-pirate look. I walked away, wondering what she was up to. What could she possibly do to them, a sweet lady like that? Offer them a freshly baked *clafoutis* if they would agree to leave peaceably?

I should have never doubted her powers.

That afternoon the rebels were early. My kids had just started their homework when we heard them fly into our corner on their bikes. There was laughter, the usual shrieking of the lone female, the beat from the boom box, and then there was quiet. I ran to the window to investigate.

It was Madame Fauriaux. She was walking toward the rebels, holding up a camera as if it were a fairy wand. *"Bonjour, les enfants,"* she said sweetly, and then started snapping pictures from various angles of each of them beside the blue paint. About ten shots were enough, and then she cheerily said *"Au revoir"* and walked back to her yard. Immediately the kids hopped on their bikes and sped away, and we never saw them again.

"What a great idea." I said to her after our bad boys had cleared out. "What are you going to do with the pictures? Save them for the police if they come back?" I asked.

"Oh, Rébecca, I can't do anything with them," she said, smiling and hunching her shoulder. "There wasn't any film in the camera."

19. Ambassadrice to the Second Grade

A year after we moved to France, somehow I ended up as the United States ambassador to the second grade.

Maybe it was the chance to set foot in Ben's classroom that did it. After watching my children disappear every day into École Saint-Pierre, with its huge metal gates and stern French teachers, I wanted to know what they did in there. We parents only got to go inside once a year, for a formal lecture by our children's teachers. We squeezed ourselves into our children's desks and the teachers rattled off as fast as they could the curriculum, grading policy, and standards for national testing. It lasted about an hour. After translating wildly for about twelve minutes, the foreign parents were exhausted and spent the remaining forty-eight making out grocery lists in our heads and feeling guilty. I wanted more. I was spoiled, I suppose.

We moved from Cottonwood Elementary, a megaschool in South Carolina where people were volunteer crazy. I helped out there too—until it got too weird. Every morning, marching in behind the children were platoons of mothers and grandparents, armed with little scissors and construction paper, ready to fill any empty wall space with paper vowel elephants or motivational noun rockets. Everybody was talking about how great it was, but to me it looked like something out of *The Twilight Zone*. It could've been jealousy. During my years teaching high school, I kept expecting those mothers to show up at my door, but they never came. They were probably hiding out at Starbucks, claiming volunteer disability, their hands destroyed by carpal tunnel from all that cutting and pasting in elementary school.

École Saint-Pierre, however, had no open-door policy, preferring to keep their *portes* locked tight. From day one we were firmly told that parents were not permitted to come inside without the expressed invitation of *la directrice*. But we were welcome to stand with our children in the courtyard and gaze up at the building. "Look, Mommy." Sarah pointed. "My room is on the fourth floor—the one with the snowflakes in the windows."

So when Ben's *maîtresse,* Madame Barot, sent home a note inviting the foreign moms to come in and share about their home countries, I signed up immediately.

I was given an hour and a half to tell about my home country and what it was like to go to school there. But what could I tell them that they didn't know? According to Ben's buddy Raphael, everybody knew about the United States already—at least about George W. and dubbed reruns of *Dallas.* Being a teacher, I began to gather up stuff. I borrowed a picture book on America from a French friend, pulled out some American notebook paper and the old classroom wall map of the United States that I bought at the flea market downtown, and made an accompanying cardboard map of France to the same scale.

"Do you think it will hurt their feelings to learn that France is just the size of Texas?" Ben asked. I told him that I didn't think so. He said that to be safe, I probably shouldn't go in looking too American. I promised him no jeans or white tennis shoes.

The day finally came, and I think it went pretty well. The kids asked me about cowboys and hamburgers, and I told them about yellow school buses, playgrounds, art and music programs (hoping they still existed), and how children eat a half-hour lunch rather than the two-hour three-course meal. I explained that second-graders used pencils rather than fountain pens, and kids learned cursive in third grade rather than first. Alphonse wanted to know why we ran the Indians out of their homeland, and Guillaume asked if American boys wore boxers or briefs.

Then a little girl with braids named Colette raised her hand. "I heard that all Americans have guns to keep the robbers away. Do you have a gun?"

"No, no," I said. "Where we live is very safe, as safe as it is here, probably. In some parts of big cities like New York or Chicago it might not be as safe. But that is probably true in big cities in France too, like Paris, for example."

Madame Barot skeptically looked down her nose at me from the back of the classroom.

"You are comparing Paris to New York?" she said. "People do not have guns in Paris. One has to watch for pickpockets, but I always feel safe there. It is not a fair comparison."

"Uh, well, you may be right," I said, a little embarrassed. She was right. I just hated for the kids to have such stereotypical views of the United States. "Where I'm from in the United States, however, few people have guns for protection," I said. "It's a very nice place to live. But they may have guns for hunting."

Jean-Paul spoke up. "If I lived in the United States, I would get a gun. I would be James Bond. I'd work for the CIA," he said, shooting up the air around him with his index fingers. The class laughed. Madame Barot rolled her eyes.

Then Alphonse raised his hand and wanted to talk about global warming, but Madame Barot interrupted and announced that I had brought a snack.

I had found it in the international aisle of the grocery store, between the tortillas and the litchis: *les crackers de table* and *beurre de cacahuètes* (crackers and peanut butter). French people don't eat peanut butter, finding it too rich (as if the big chunks of butter on their ham sandwiches are not), so I spread it on very thin. It was as if I had offered little Americans gooey Brie on baguette. But after the first nibble, everyone wanted seconds. Finally it was Madame Barot's turn.

"No, thank you," Madame Barot said, trying to smile. "I'm not hungry right now."

"Madame Barot," the children teased, "it's good!"

Finally, she consented. "Okay, okay. Not too much, please."

I spread it very thin. The children crowded around and giggled.

"It is not bad, but it's very rich," she said. "But how could a child eat a whole sandwich of this for lunch? It's so heavy."

"Oh, you should try it with grape jelly. With a glass of milk it's great," I said.

Madame Barot was horrified.

At the end of my visit, Madame Barot shook my hand, thanked me for coming, and led the class in applause. On my way out, Colette and Guillaume asked if I'd write down the name of the *beurre de cacahuètes* for their mommies, so I jotted it down on the American notebook paper I had brought. They said merci and handled it as if it were gold.

20. Madame Mallet to the Rescue

Back in 1946, Mademoiselle Astrid Pourchot, later known as Madame Mallet, was trained as a nurse in Paris and was quite good at it, according to her. She would have stuck with it, in fact, if it hadn't been for the whining sick people she had to care for. And the uniforms. Madame Mallet hated the uniforms, which were donated by the British WACs, who obviously had no style sense. Each evening after work she would roll down her combat boots and exchange her uniform jacket for a nice tight sweater for the walk home. She didn't like the clothes, she didn't like the work, and she didn't like Paris. The only thing she liked about it was the pride of serving her country, and she could do that by being a good French patriot back home at the Michelin factory.

So she hung up her blood-pressure cuff, thinking she would never use it again, except perhaps to nurse a husband back to health, if she ever got one. Years went by, and then she married. Her husband was ridiculously healthy, and then we moved in.

Thank goodness the Americans were just so pitiful, not knowing anything really—that gates should be closed at night lest wandering thieves think it an open invitation, or that children should be allowed to run on the balcony half-dressed, breathing in the morning air so satiated with the viruses blowing up from Africa. And the baby! Why, they had never even bought a pair of shoes for the child. They happily pushed him about in the stroller with naked feet and on chilly mornings dressed him in socks. For the children's sake, she felt she must intervene. How much longer could she stay behind her curtain?

Then Benjamin, the middle child, prone to accidents, exited the father's Japanese car one Saturday afternoon with his arm in a cast, after having sprained his ankle only three weeks prior.

That was it.

She had no choice.

She had to cross the line.

"It's his bones!" she shrieked down at us, hanging half out of her bedroom window. "It's his bones that are weak! Is he eating properly?"

"*Bonjour, Madame Mallet,*" I said. "Yes, yes. It's not the food he eats. It's that he falls out of trees!" Madame Mallet gave me the same skeptical look as the last time she had advised me on his diet and I had insisted that the diet wasn't the problem. I could tell what she was thinking. "That Rébecca is quite stubborn, almost rebelliously so, though she means no harm. Apparently no one has taught her anything about raising children." Madame Mallet had none of her own, it was true, but in France, practical advice was public knowledge. I imagined her thoughts. "I must take them on, train them, and educate them in the life skills they desperately will need to survive here. Perhaps it is that America is such a young country, that Americans still act as pioneers, living the rugged life, not used to refinements, like shoes and gates and vitamins."

So Madame Mallet crossed the street and began her tutelage, carrying an offering of three broccoli spears. She handed me the basket at the door, saying, "Broccoli is rich in calcium, for his bones." She said it slowly, making sure that I understood.

I tried to receive my instruction in the medical arts with grace. Madame Mallet was an enthusiastic teacher, but firm and not open to debate. Though it was sometimes quite annoying, and I often retreated into my house after her little talks irritated with the gall of this Gaul, I admit that there was always genuine care behind her words—for me and for my equally ignorant friends as well.

"Rébecca, I have noticed that many of your friends are fat," she would say every once in a while, perhaps thinking that I didn't understand her well the previous time she had broached the subject and therefore couldn't have yet shared her dietary suggestions with my friends. "Are Americans not aware that one must not take in more calories than one expends? Perhaps the American diet should include more fruits and vegetables than foods high in fat and sugar." Each time it blindsided me, leaving me speechless. So we weren't skinny toothpicks. My friends were beautiful, but she didn't see it. She would continue, "And of course there are many ways in which one may burn more calories—daily exercise through calisthenics or walking. Even gardening burns calories," she said, pointing to my barren yard.

At some point, however, her aid transformed from mere

words of instruction to hands-on nursing. The first time it happened I hardly blamed her. It had been a November day our first year in France, and we must have been quite a sight, just home from school, stepping out of the car with the children crying and me still shaking. Assessing the situation, Madame Mallet must have felt that she had to take charge. She walked over to provide assistance.

"Becky, *ma chérie,* what in the world happened?"

"After school, it was a man," I managed to utter through trembling sobs.

"Yes, a man?"

"He was . . . uh . . ." I tried to think of the word for "drunk" and couldn't. Finally I acted it out, weaving around and rolling my eyes. This frightened Sarah.

"Don't do that!" Sarah screamed.

"He has one arm. And he asks me for money." At that point I could only speak in present tense.

"Only one arm?"

"Yes, and the other arm . . . blood is falling from it."

"Blood?"

"Yes. And it makes us all scary."

"And you didn't give him money. Did he hurt you?"

"No, he asks for money and I say I don't speak French. He says he can speak English."

"How generous of him." Madame Mallet chuckled, probably hoping that some humor might help calm things.

"So I say no. I have no money and the children go into the car. I start the car and he falls on my door."

"Oh."

"And he puts his blood on my window. He screams at me and kicks the car."

At this point the children started crying and I wondered why I was standing there explaining this to this woman while my children needed to go inside. So we went inside.

Two minutes later Madame Mallet rang the bell at my gate. I opened the door and saw a blur of her hand coming toward my face, and before I could do anything that old lady had forced some kind of pills into my mouth. They were horrible.

I spit them out into my hand. They were little and white. Madame Mallet laughed, embarrassed, and shrugged her shoulders. What did she think she was doing? What were the pills? Did she actually think I would want to take someone else's medicine?

"What is that for?" I said, coughing the last one out.

"It's only for the stress, Becky," Madame Mallet said. "They're homeopathic. I take them all the time."

Luckily the second medicating event happened without any violent confrontation. Todd had just left town for a two-week business trip to Singapore. It was not a good time to be ill.

Three hours after he had closed all our shutters for the night, thrown his bags in the trunk, kissed us all goodbye, and zoomed off into the sunset, I was in full flu mode—wandering around like a zombie, sitting next to the heater, and then finally lying on the couch, wrapped in two blankets, my head throbbing, my throat painfully sore.

Two days later, the shutters were still closed and the expatriate ladies had worked out a schedule for the delivery of milk and casseroles, as well as school pickup and drop-off for Sarah and Ben. Sam was still little, so he was to stay home with me and teach himself how to climb onto the chair in the kitchen and get out the Play-Doh, which he pinched off in little pieces and dispersed among the scattered papers and dishes on the table. "Look, I made snow, Mommy," he said. I nodded from the couch, semiconscious.

Luckily, none of my friends dared brave the germs to enter our den of despair—not that I would have let them in anyway. There were Kleenexes everywhere, dirty dishes covering the countertops and the kitchen table. Little green army guys and Legos covered the tile from Sam's bedroom to the couch, except where I had kicked them out of my little path from the kitchen to the couch to the bathroom to my bed. Luckily, Sam had more of a self-preservation instinct than Ben ever did, because as I drifted in and out of sleep, my two-year-old was babysitting himself. It was a Wednesday, the day French school was over at noon so the kids could do their extracurricular activities. Ben and Sarah would come home early. Needless to say, we would skip the piano and the fencing lessons.

In my groggy haze, I heard Mary Ann's car pull up and the slam of two car doors.

"Hello, we're home," Ben called.

"Mom, I'm coming up to take care of you," Sarah said.

Thank goodness for Sarah.

"Gross!" Sarah shrieked. "Oh, Mommy, Katie's been sick."

Every time I got sick, that dumb cat got sick too. "Can you take care of it?" I begged her. "Please?"

"Oh, okay."

There was silence.

"Momma, I think I'm going to throw up."

Ben came to my side and stared at me.

Moments later, Sarah appeared beside him.

"I just can't do it. It's in little piles, all up the stairs to the kitchen."

"Okay," I said, and tried to steady myself in an upright position. I pulled my robe around me. I would get it.

I went to get a roll of paper towels and a trash bag but then heard the door downstairs. Had Ben gone out again? He better have worn his coat or Madame Mallet would let him have it.

I was just trudging to the bathroom, trying to get my brain to start up and figure out where I usually put the cleaning spray, when I saw her.

There in my stairway, sidestepping the piles of cat vomit and pulling herself up by the handrail, was Madame Mallet. She hadn't seen me yet, as she was concentrating on holding the rail and not stepping in vomit. I must have gasped, and she looked up at me.

"Oh, Rébecca," she said with great pity. "*Ma chérie,* why didn't you call me?"

What was she doing in my house, climbing up my stairs? How did she get in? I wasn't even dressed—no makeup, bed-headed, with dirty tissues falling out of the pockets of my robe that had the hole under the arm. And the house. She had to dodge cat vomit, for heaven's sake.

"What a state you are in!" Madame Mallet reached the top of the stairs and felt my forehead. "My dear, have you seen a doctor? Why, you're burning up! What is your fever? You must be at least forty-one."

"Uh, I don't know. My thermometer broke."

"And where is your husband?"

I started to answer, but she interrupted. "Michelin has sent him away again, huh? To the United States?"

"*Non,* Singapore," I said. I knew this would get her going, and I didn't care. It would feel nice for someone to feel sorry for me.

"Singapore!" she shrieked. "Leaving you here alone to go to Singapore!"

Madame Mallet started on her usual tirade about *la bande de bandits* and how they stole away the best times of her life. I was listening, but I was more concerned about the bottle she was taking out of her bag and what she was going to do to me with it.

I wanted to tell her that I get tonsillitis every year, that that might be what it was, that I was just waiting to make sure it didn't go away on its own before I called the doctor. Instead I just stood there. What was the word for "tonsillitis"?

And what was the bottle for? It held a clear yellow liquid and had a label on it, but I wasn't wearing my glasses. Madame Mallet took the cap off the bottle and soaked some cotton balls from her bag with whatever it was and reached for my arm. I was still trying to think of the word for "tonsillitis" and so I let her hold my arm. Her hand felt so strong and I was so tired. Then she yanked the sleeves of my robe and nightgown up my arm and started rubbing a wet cotton ball all over my bare skin.

It felt good.

I let her do it.

"How is that?" she asked, switching to the other arm.

"It's good," I said, closing my eyes and feeling myself drift. Madame Mallet took another cotton ball to my face, and it felt so nice that I stayed on the stairs and let her do that too. Madame Mallet was saying something about a pharmacy in Issoire, something about euros or francs. I just stood there at the top of the stairs, with my unshaven legs, wearing Todd's floppy socks, letting her take care of me.

After she treated me, she offered to call the doctor to come to the house, but I had regained full consciousness and didn't want her going into the living room. I could hear Sarah scurrying around cleaning the dishes off the table in case Madame Mallet let herself wander around the corner. Ben and Sam were hiding, most likely afraid that she might start doctoring them.

I promised I would call the doctor, and she let herself out. "Sarah," she called, "you call me if your mother needs anything. And you might want to call the vet about your cat."

"No, she just drank the milk out of the cereal bowls again. It happens every time my mother gets sick."

"You just tell your mother that if I don't see the doctor's car parked on our street by this evening, I'm calling him myself. What is it with you Americans? Are you so used to your primitive health-care system that when you come over here you'll wait till you're dying before you call somebody?"

I did call, and Dr. Allezard came right over. I made the kids go to their rooms and sat on the couch and took off my shirt, and he sat beside me and examined me.

"You have *une angine,* Madame Ramsey," he said, and gave me three prescriptions. I put on my sweats, wondering what an *angine* was, and headed for the pharmacy down the road. Monsieur Gronot, the pharmacist, and I had a special relationship ever since we bonded over the breast pump, so I didn't mind him seeing me like that.

"Madame Ramsey," he scolded. "Why didn't your husband come for your medicine and leave you home in bed where you belong?" He was eyeing my three children out the window. They were wrestling again and yelling at each other in the backseat of my car.

"He's in Singapore," I said.

The pharmacy man looked at me sadly and added another vial to the others on the counter.

"Take these too," he said, showing me the tiny white pills. "Take several at a time—three or four. They're for the stress. They taste awful, but they're very calming." He peered out at the tangle of arms and legs thrashing about my backseat.

It was awfully sweet of him to offer me something to relax. "You know, it's perfectly fine to give them to the children too, just two or three at a time. They're homeopathic so you don't have to worry."

I thanked him, and as I opened the door he asked, "Do you have anyone, a neighbor, perhaps, that can look in on you?"

"*Oui, merci,*" I said.

He had no idea.

21. *Pâté for Cats*

A half hour's drive from our house into the countryside, nestled between the sunflower fields and a high green hill with a crumbling castle tower, was a huge set of buzzing electrical transformers with a web of power lines draped through the sky. In its shadow was Monsieur Blanchard's Pension Canine et Féline, Katie's home when we were away. In spite of the buzzing, it was a peaceful place, almost mysteriously so, as if the canopy of electricity created some kind of magical force field for the dogs and cats.

There were two fine kennels right in my own village, but ever since my friend Mary Ann told me about Monsieur Blanchard, I drove the thirty minutes, and I would have driven more if I had to. People might wonder why, if they hadn't met Monsieur Blanchard. The *pension* was far from luxurious, and it wasn't particularly pretty either. There was only a gravel parking lot and an iron gate enclosing several low cement-block buildings still awaiting the application of stucco. There were large expanses of grass and weeds, with dog trails around the chain-link fence. It didn't look like much, but there was something weirdly wonderful about the place, magnetic even. I could detect it on the telephone, the first time I called. I was a little nervous, since I found speaking French to strangers on the telephone to be nearly impossible.

"Hello . . . Uh . . . I have a cat. You take the cat? Four days?"

I steadied myself for the usual response, the stuttering, the loud talking, or worse—nervous giggling. But to my surprise, the man on the other end of the line responded to me pleasantly, as if I were just another elegant French woman, kindly asking me when I would like to leave Katie and explaining calmly (but not too slowly) how to find the *pension*. I thanked him, hung up the phone, and felt strangely content, completely at ease.

In addition to being a gentleman, Monsieur Blanchard was generous. One Christmas that my parents came to visit, we deposited Katie there and left on a trip to Germany. The next day we all came down with the flu and had to cancel the trip. When Todd went back to the kennel and tried to pay for Katie's one-night stay, Monsieur Blanchard said, "Oh, don't bother, really. Your family is sick *and* your mother-in-law is visiting? You have surely suffered enough!"

If I had known the transforming effect Monsieur Blanchard would have on Katie—and on me—I would have ignored the kennel in my village with its fancy sign and busy parking lot from the start and tried him first time around. It might have saved her a few months of melancholia.

By all accounts Katie came to France as a sickly old cat

with little hope left. Though her depression was never professionally diagnosed, all the classic symptoms were there—the sluggishness, the unkempt look, and the sudden disinterest in her little gray mouse with the bell on its tail. Not even a pile of fresh laundry left warm on the table could get her tail twitching like it used to. Most days she would stay holed up in our guest room, shedding her hair all over the chenille bedspread, waiting for the day to end so that the children would go to bed and she could drag herself up the steps to our side for a momentary dose of affection—if we still cared.

I had hoped that the move to France might shake her out of her listlessness—that a change of scenery might be good medicine. Sadly, this was not the case—until she met Monsieur Blanchard. After Katie's first stay at the *pension,* we noticed a change but wouldn't allow ourselves to think much of it. She returned home from her long weekend curiously refreshed and frisky. She walked around in a flirty little way, and there was a sparkle in those eyes that we hadn't seen in years. *It must be the fresh country air,* I thought.

Then the spring break came and we left her for a week. The changes in Katie's personality and behavior were so bizarre that I began to wonder what kind of voodoo magic was going on in there—not that I was complaining. It was wonderful to see her jumping about like a kitten again, chasing dust bunnies under the buffet and licking Sam's fingertips as he slept. It was a little strange, but wonderful. But when Katie started taking up sleeping quarters in the bathtub, I knew it wasn't just a rediscovery of her youth. This was kind of scary. I was afraid that the next thing I knew, I'd come home to find her sitting with her paws on the table, sipping a tiny cup of café au lait and poring over a *Gala* magazine.

As I drove the car through the fields of wheat and rapeseed on my latest trip to the *pension* after our monthlong summer vacation in the States, I started obsessing about Katie. Had she survived? While we were out gallivanting all over the Carolinas, had she been pining away for us? Was she starving or dead? What would I tell the kids if Monsieur Blanchard had buried her in the sunflower patch out back?

After all, Katie was still a sickly cat, even if the short vacations with Monsieur Blanchard had greatly improved her outlook on life. We tried to do what we could for her. We held her to the Expensive Nonfat Vet's Office Cat Food diet, as well as the two-pill-a-day prescription for her thyroid condition. And I had always classified anyone who would give a fourteen-year-old cat two pills a day as a sad, lonely person. When Dr. Rechou, our French veterinarian, pulled out a blood-pressure cuff the size of a Band-Aid and velcroed it around Katie's little paw, I tried to stifle a laugh. "I've never seen one of those for a cat," I said.

"Oh, yes," Dr. Rechou said seriously, "we must measure her blood pressure. It is essential." When he wrote out the prescription, I raised my eyebrows and tried to make a joke, which probably sounded like, "In the United States, this costs so much that it is terminal disease." Dr. Rechou was not amused and glared at me over his spectacles, saying indignantly, "We will do what's right, of course."

So before we left for our summer trip to the States, I learned how to force Katie to take a pill, which she hated, and had shown Monsieur Blanchard the proper technique. I demonstrated how to pry open her little cat jaws, how to jab the pill to the back of her throat, and how to get her to swallow by holding her mouth closed and blowing into her little cat nostrils. He had the proper instructions but didn't seem to like my method. Had he followed through twice a day, every day, for five weeks?

I pushed the intercom button on the big green gate and waited.

"Allô?" Monsieur Blanchard's voice called from the box, and then I saw him waving his hand out the dog building. He was in his usual uniform, blue coveralls and muddy rubber boots, and as he walked closer I could see the smile below his handlebar mustache. This was not an "I feel sorry for you because your cat is dead" kind of smile, so I breathed a sigh of relief and reached out to shake his hand.

Monsieur Blanchard hesitated. "My hands are dirty—I'm so sorry—here," he said, and pointed for me to shake his forearm. I did and we laughed. As we walked through the yard to the building, Monsieur Blanchard went through the necessary how-do-you-do's and then let me in on the good news. His cheeks reddened as he told me of Katie's new fascination with the outdoor pen he had built onto the kennel. "She spends all of her time out of her cage now. She wanders and does as she pleases. And she's made friends with all the other cats."

My Katie? Friends with other cats? I found that hard to believe. Katie hated all other cats and hissed her mouth dry at the kennels back home. At the Pooch and Purr, the workers would make themselves scarce when it came time for Katie to go home. After a few awkward moments of me alone at the cash register, someone had to volunteer to don leather gloves to pry Katie from her cage, and then nine times out of ten they'd end up asking me to do it. Why, even Dr. Rechou called me once, struggling in English to make sure I understood: "You come for your cat. She is angry." Friendly? This I had to see.

Monsieur Blanchard led me into the cats' room and I searched the dozen large cages for Katie. "Kettie loves to look out at the moon at night," he said, pointing out the window. He saw me searching the cages and nudged me to look out the door. Sure enough, there she was, lounging outside on the deck between a long-haired black cat and a Siamese. She looked over at me and then looked away and flicked her tail.

"Ka-tie. Hi, Katie," I said in my mommy voice. I held out my hand for her to sniff. Katie looked at me suspiciously and then sniffed.

"She's beautiful," I said, not sure of how to say that her coat looked good.

"Yes, I think she has been happy," said Monsieur Blanchard. "She took her medicine every day. There was no problem. She loves pâté."

"I'm sorry?" I said.

"Pâté. She loves pâté."

"Oh," I said. *"Oui?"*

"Oui, particularly the pork," he said, lifting Katie into her cat carrier, "though she likes the duck as well."

Monsieur Blanchard pointed at a greasy spot by her food dish in her cage. "I just put her pill in a little bit of pâté and she adored it." He looked at me thoughtfully, like some kind of counselor, and said, "You might consider giving her pill to her this way as well. I think that it's better for her spirit."

I picked up our expensive nonfat cat food and followed him out to his desk. Bad mommy! All those months of jabbing pills down her throat.

Monsieur Blanchard reached into a little refrigerator and

pulled out a carton to show me. "Here's the pâté that I spoke of. It's delicious."

I gave the carton a closer look. "Pâté for cats?"

"*Non, non.*" Monsieur Blanchard laughed. "This is a treat for you as well. Go to Auchan and buy it and have some with a good baguette. You'll love it."

All the way home Katie meowed to me, like a kid just back from summer camp itching to tell me every detail of her adventures away from home. When we got to the house, she ran around to every room. Her steps looked lighter, friskier, and she had even lost that spread around her middle. Instead of retreating to the guest room downstairs, she plunked herself right in the middle of the Lego fort the kids were building on the coffee table.

"That's a little weird," Ben said. It was just the beginning.

For the rest of our days in France Katie continued sleeping in the bathtub and had pâté twice a day. Every now and then after the kids went to bed, Todd and I would have a little too, with a cracker or a piece of bread. We toasted to Monsieur Blanchard for adding another bit of pleasure to our lives—and to Katie's. We tried to get used to the lap hopping, and we had to start leaving a door to the balcony open during the day so that she could get out in the sunshine. She talked with the cats that ran through our yard, and when night came, just like Monsieur Blanchard had said, she stood looking out the glass, gazing at the moon.

22. Les Pêcheurs

I liked to listen to Catholic radio in France. The broadcasters had kind voices and spoke slowly and clearly. Plus they repeated things a lot. I thought it was good for my French, though I still got confused sometimes. It probably would have helped if I were Catholic. One day a nice lady's voice was saying the Hail Marys and got to the part where it goes: *"Mère de Dieu, priez pour nous pauvres pécheurs . . ."* It didn't make sense, "Mother of God, pray for us poor fishermen." *Fishermen? She called us all fishermen?* I wondered about it for a while. Maybe the word *fishermen* was another word for being Christian, being that we were supposed to be fishers of men, as the Bible says. Or maybe it had to do with the people out fishing when they should be in church. They would need our extra prayers.

I decided to risk it and ask Madame Mallet. She hooted out loud.

"Pécheurs, ma chérie, not *pêcheurs!"* she said, laughing at me, and went into the house to tell Monsieur Mallet.

It sounded the same to me. I went inside and looked it up in the dictionary.

Ah. *Pécheurs* is sinners. *Pêcheurs* is fishermen.

. . .

THE NEXT SUNDAY afternoon Madame Mallet saw us loading the kids in the car and came over to investigate.

"So where are you people off to on this sunny afternoon? Don't you Christians ever obey the commandment to rest on Sunday? Or is that one you Americans choose to ignore?"

I didn't want to tell her where we were going, but I swallowed my pride and braced myself. "We are going fishing."

Surprisingly, she didn't take the bait. "How wonderful," she said. "I used to love to go fishing when I was young. We'd go up to Mont Mouchet and fish in the streams. The trout there, oh, they were incredible. Where are you going?"

"Outside of Riom," Todd said, hurrying us into the car.

"Goodbye, my little . . . sinners," Madame Mallet chuckled.

"What'd she say?" Todd asked as we backed out of the gate.

"Long story," I said. "I noticed you didn't tell her where outside of Riom we were going."

"She doesn't have to know everything."

Todd didn't want to tell her because he knew she'd give us a hard time about going to a stocked pay-per-kilo fish pond rather than out in the wild. It was the very kind of convenience she hated.

I wasn't sure about it myself. We usually went for a hike on Sunday afternoons. The French have books of planned hikes called *balades,* public walks through private land, that usually start at the town hall of some ancient little village and wind through a farmer's orchards or sunflower field, ending up back in town or at the foot of a chateau or a Roman basilica. It was a great way to spend a Sunday afternoon. But fishing? How fascinating could a French fishing trip be? Weren't all fish alike?

But Todd had asked me in front of the children, with their pleading puppy dog eyes and double-crossed fingers. How could I say no? I couldn't use Sam as an excuse not to go. He was two now and wouldn't have to be held. As soon as I nodded my head, they all started jumping up and down and singing, "We're going fish-ing, we're going fish-ing!" There was nothing more to do than to try to find my shoes and a new attitude.

We drove out into the country and finally came to a sign that read SALMONICULTURE DU CHÂTEAU DE ST-GENEST L'ENFANT (Salmon Farming of the Chateau of St. Genest, the Child). Chateau? I didn't see a chateau, just a little stucco house and a gravel parking lot set back among tall trees at the foot of a forested hill. There was a café table next to the house where two women sat, one old and one young, drinking wine and talking and enjoying the cheese and baguette laid out on a cloth. Two little blond girls in dresses chased a dog through the grass. As we got out of the car, the older woman stood to greet us.

I looked just beyond the house and couldn't believe what I saw. It was like stepping into a Monet painting. The blues and greens of the water swirled into the greens of the trees surrounding the pond and the deep blue of the sky. It was strange, but the pond was a perfect rectangle. I couldn't tell if the water was moving or if it was just a reflection of the leaves fluttering over it in the warm breeze. There was a bamboo grove on one side, just beyond the trees. I stared at it for a second and could just make out through the thick rows of bamboo the chateau on the hill.

"Bonjour, messieurs-dames," the elderly woman called.

Todd said hello and that this was our first visit. She gave us a little tour. "The fishing poles are over there," she said, pointing to a neat row of long bamboo poles (each at least three yards tall) leaning against a wall. "They already have the line on, of course, and the hook."

"Can we buy . . . uh"—what was the word for worms?— *"les vers?"* I asked, wiggling my pointer finger like a worm.

The woman looked horrified. "Worms? Certainly not! We use pâte—it is baguette dough, actually. Here, there is no charge," she said, handing us each a small ball. "They love it. We hand feed them corn and flour in the evening. You should see them—we just wade out and they come running to us. But they love the bread dough even more—that and the Volvic water. A Volvic stream feeds this pond, you know. It is actually the old reflecting pool for the chateau. It used to amuse the bourgeoisie and now it feeds us. Enjoy."

Sarah, Ben, and Sam each picked out a bamboo pole. Each one had a long line stretched out the length of the pole with the hook neatly and safely stuck into a thick rubber band at the opposite end. I helped Sam keep from knocking people with his pole as Ben and Sarah ran ahead to pick out a good place along the mossy bank.

It was like a picture postcard.

The children eagerly pinched off a piece of dough and pushed it onto the sharp hook and plopped it into the water. Within five minutes, Sarah felt a jerk on her line.

"Aaah!" yelped Sarah as she pulled a flopping fish out of the water. She panicked and threw her pole to Todd, sending the fish flying wildly through the air.

"Aaah!" cried Sam as the airborne fish nearly smacked him

in the face. Sam dropped his pole on the ground and hid be-hind me.

"Dad, no!" squealed Sarah. "It's struggling to breathe!" She held her hand over her mouth, horrified.

"Look how big it is, Sarah! You did great!" Todd said, and took the hook out of its mouth. The fish flipped and flopped wildly in his hand until he dropped it in the bucket of water.

"It's bleeding!" Sarah yelled. "I want to go home! I don't like this—it's mean!"

"Honey, what did you think this would be?" Todd said. "We're going to end up eating that fish—we're doing this to have fun, but also to have fish for supper."

"I want to go home."

"Sarah, you may not like it, but we just got here. I'm not go-ing to make everyone else pack up and go home."

Sarah stormed off to sulk, and I followed her. "Why don't you be in charge of handing out the bread dough?" I said. "I could use some help with Sam."

It turns out that they were a good pair. Sam thought fishing was scary too and preferred to walk back and forth along the bank, bending down to examine a leaf or a stick or to examine the fish in the pail. With Sarah close by, I didn't worry about him falling in. Ben, however, was so excited that I just knew he'd lean a little too far over the bank and end up soaked. He didn't, but his shirt did get wet from his constant reaching in the bucket and trying to catch the fish again with his bare hands. Sarah called him mean and a fish hater.

About an hour later we decided we had had enough fun, and took our bucket and poles back to the little house to pay.

"*Très bien!*" the old woman said to the children. "You make good fishermen. Here," she said, handing them pamphlets advertising the place. "Take them for your friends." Then she took the fish out of the bucket one by one, laid them on the counter, and hit them over the head with a broomstick. Sarah left the room.

"The cleaning is free," she said and proceeded to clean the first one lightning fast. She left its head on and popped it into a bag. Why did she do that? I didn't want the eyes looking at me as I cooked them.

"Could you take off the heads, please?" I asked.

The woman looked at me.

"If it's not too much trouble."

"Take off the heads? Why would you ask me to do that?"

"Uh . . . I don't like to see them," I said.

The lady stared at me. "No, I cannot do that. It would not be correct," she said, and hit the next one over the head with the broomstick. She mumbled to herself, "That would be . . . bar-baric."

So we went back to the car and stuck the bag of fish with their heads still on in the cooler in the trunk and headed home.

Madame Mallet was out in her yard when we pulled into the cul-de-sac.

"My fishermen have returned home!" she called as the kids got out of the car. "Show me your catch," she said to Ben. Sarah stood there with a fake smile. Sam ran over to Madame Mallet, gave her *bisoux,* and stuck a pamphlet in her hand. (He liked collecting pamphlets and had three of them.) Madame Mallet unfolded it as Ben showed her the fish.

"Oh, you'll have a good supper tonight," she said, and looked at the pamphlet. "What?" she said, glaring at Todd and me. "You took them to a fish farm? You call that real fishing?"

"We had heard good things about it, and thought it would be a nice way to introduce the children to . . ."

"A nice way? I don't know what to do with you go-go's. You know they build those fake fishing farms and people say they go fishing, but that's not real fishing! It's just a way to take people's money. It's just like the Grotte de Chien, over in Royat." The "Grotte de Chien" was a lava cave that tourists pay to explore. We'd never been there, but Madame Mallet had told me that it was named the "Dog Cave" because there was a crack in its floor that produced a low-lying layer of carbon dioxide gas that could kill a dog while leaving its owner perfectly fine, breathing the pure air above. There were also Roman ruins there and a mineral spring as well. "Oh, the go-go's like you," Madame Mallet continued, "they go there in throngs, in buses, and happily hand over their money, just to see an empty cave. It's robbery, I tell you, and the government should do something about it. But they won't as long as Chirac is in power. Oh, no, he probably approves of that kind of thing."

Madame Mallet had exhausted herself. She turned around and headed inside, mumbling about federal regulations and truth in labeling.

We went inside, and I fixed *truite amandine*. I got Todd to cut off the fish heads, and Katie followed him and the bag of heads all the way out to the trash can, meowing wildly.

Todd and I thought our fish was fantastic, but so is practically anything sautéed in butter and coated with almonds. The children enjoyed it too, except for Sarah, who now prefers unrecognizable fish rectangles from the freezer section of the grocery store. I never brought up the subject of the Salmoniculture du Château de St-Genest l'Enfant again with Madame Mallet. But it does make me laugh to think that Madame Mallet considers fishermen like us (*pêcheurs*) as sinners (*pécheurs*) after all.

23. Those Crazy Church People

Madame Mallet kept a Virgin Mary the size of a kidney bean in a brass capsule in the change compartment of her purse. When she took it out to show me, I thought it was a lipstick.

"My cousin Colette gave this to me. She's very Catholic, you know, and she knows I don't go to Mass anymore," said Madame Mallet. "She's always telling me that I should go," she said, and rolled her eyes. "It would be irritating except that she prays for me and I need all the help I can get.

"Anyway, she goes to Lourdes every few years and long ago she brought me this," she said, pulling out the capsule. "Here," she said, fumbling with it, "I'll show you." She opened it and dropped Mary into my palm.

"Oh, c'est beau," I said as I turned the tiny Mary with my fingers, examining her fine details—her pretty face, the folds of her gown, her pretty feet—so tiny.

"It's not that I'm not Christian, you know. I am Christian—well, mostly. I just don't like people telling me what I have to believe and what to do. And I don't agree with all that church stuff."

"No?"

"No. Perhaps I'm bound for the devil," she said. "How do I look with horns?" she asked, screwing up her face and making horns on her head with her fingers. "It might be just what I deserve—I haven't darkened the door over there for years," she said, nodding her head toward the village church. "But I know you go. All five of you, on Sunday evenings, the model Christian family," she said, with a hint of sarcasm. "In Royat, yes?"

I nodded.

"You know, I used to go right by that chapel every day when I was young. I had a job down in Royat at the thermal baths—until I got fed up. Too many rich whiners over there— 'Bring me this, girl. Bring me that.' Anyway, maybe you'll miss me up there in heaven. Do you think that you could play a little song on your harp for me? And how about throwing me down a little morsel of something every once in a while— maybe some *saucisson* and a good baguette."

"Okay." I laughed.

"Lest you think me terrible, I should tell you that I did do my First Communion, so maybe the good Lord will have mercy on me. But I have no interest in that church. Maybe you're not aware that after they rebuilt that church back in the 1850s, the vineyards all around it suffered a terrible blight. If that's not a bad omen, then I don't know what is. No, I'd rather play cards with the devil than join that dreary bunch."

I had seen that bunch filing out of the village *église,* and they didn't look so dreary to me—just old, like her. Every Sunday morning we would go to the outdoor market to get some exercise and a rotisserie chicken for lunch. It was a great market, packed with people no matter the season, with dozens of vendors with their tables and trailers full of cheeses and breads, fruits and vegetables, flowers, and linens, and a lady that sold seconds of Emile Henri pottery. There was even Chinese food and a pizza guy. The market wove all through the narrow village streets and wound up under the eves of the church. One of our favorite vendors, the cookie man, set up right there near the big front doors, with his trays of madeleines and biscotti. Next to him was the man with the pigeons and rabbits in cages. We always stopped there so Sam could pet the rabbits, Sarah could say that she thought it was cruel, and Ben could ask once again how they killed their rabbits and if the rabbits knew what was going to happen to them.

I had always wondered how it was to worship inside, with the noise of the crowds milling around outside and the shouts of the rotisserie chicken man. I had peeked inside the church before, during the week, just to take a look. No one was ever there, but it was always unlocked. Nobody took note of my coming or going, checked to see if I was stealing the statues or spitting in the holy water. No one stepped forward to introduce himself or to invite me to mass on Sunday. You'd think they'd want visitors, given the aging congregation.

And then one day my doorbell rang.

I figured it was Madame Mallet. Her cabbages were just coming off, and she had given me three in the last week and a half. My children hated cabbage, and I could tolerate only so much of it. So I put on my shoes and headed for the door, trying to decide whether I would try to refuse her politely or just accept it and hide it in the trash. To my surprise, instead of Madame Mallet and a cabbage at the door there stood two smiling old ladies in church clothes. One was tall and skinny and wore a hat and the other was short and round and held a stack of leaflets. Their smiling made me nervous, as it was not normal for French people, but I walked to the gate and shook their hands anyway, and the short one started talking at me really fast. I picked out a few words— something about the world and heaven and God.

Just then I saw Madame Mallet in her yard behind them, waving her arms at me. When she met my glance she started shaking her head no and then running her finger across her neck. She had done this before when a traveling salesman had come to my door. I had ignored her then too—I just didn't know yet how to politely get out of French conversations.

I butted in and told the ladies that I was sorry, but I did not speak French well. They didn't mind. The tall one joined in, and they both began to talk louder and faster. I did manage to understand that I was being invited to some sort of seminar for, as we would say at home, "the unchurched."

Madame Mallet threw up her arms at me and went back inside her house.

"*Merci,*" I said to the women, "*mais j'attends l'église,*" which at the time I thought meant "Thank you, but I attend church" but actually means "Thank you, but I'm waiting for the church."

They looked at each other nervously and started talking again. They started opening their leaflets and pointing to things and talking faster and faster.

"But I'm waiting for the church," I said. "In Royat. The *culte protestant.* It is near the *poste.*"

The short one handed me another leaflet.

They started talking at the same time, until finally I got desperate.

"But I love God too," I heard myself cry out.

The women stopped talking and looked at me.

I felt naked.

"Ah!" they both said with big smiles. "Then you'll come? It is Sunday morning, at ten a.m.," said the lady in the hat. "You can be our guest."

I didn't know what to say.

"How wonderful," said the tall lady to the short lady. "We've never brought a British lady before."

I smiled and said goodbye, and they walked away, talking excitedly. I felt guilty. They thought they had evangelized me, and I was going to be a no-show.

Would they remember where I lived?

The doorbell rang. Did they forget something?

It was Madame Mallet—no cabbages.

"Becky, what do you think you were doing, coming out here and talking to those crazy people?"

"No, they weren't crazy," I said, chuckling to myself. "They were just asking me to come to their church."

"Inviting you to church? Who goes around inviting people to church? That's ridiculous! Can't people lift their chins off the ground and see where the church is? We don't hide them, after all. Those people were pressuring you—that's what they were trying to do.

"What is happening to the Catholic church? I say if people want to go to church, they go. If we don't, leave us alone! But perhaps these women are not Catholic. In fact, I bet they're not. They must be members of some strange cult. I saw something on television about that, and it's quite dangerous.

"And what am I going to do with you, Rébecca, throwing your door wide open? My dear, you just can't do that here. You never know what people like that will do. What if they were robbers? I don't know about the United States, but in France you are not required to open your door for just anyone who rings your bell. If you insist on talking to them, at least do so from the safety of your balcony. That way, your front door stays locked, and you can leave them whenever you want."

"All right, I will," I said.

"I keep telling you that if you'd just keep the gate to your driveway closed, people wouldn't think you're always inviting them in, but you don't ever listen to me."

"Madame Mallet, as much as we come and go, it is too much trouble."

"And how long does it take out of your busy schedule to open a little gate?"

"You're right, Madame Mallet."

"You say that, but you're not going to start closing your gate, are you?"

"No," I said.

A week later, my doorbell rang. This time I followed Madame Mallet's advice and looked out the window.

There, standing by my gate, was a strange young man with an arm full of paintings and a bad case of bed head. Should I go out or not? All at once he threw down the entire pile of paintings onto the street. Then he picked up one with a sunflower on it and looked at it. He shouted something at it, waved his other hand around, and then straightened up. He nervously shifted his weight from foot to foot as he waited for me to answer the door.

I stayed at my window, wondering if my front door was locked. Then I saw a flicker of movement across the street. It was Madame Mallet, standing at her window with the curtain pulled back. She was waving her arms back and forth at me, like one of those people directing airplanes on the tarmac, trying to get my attention. When she saw that I saw her, she pointed down at him and gave me the two thumbs-up signal. Apparently the bed-headed man was safe.

I wasn't so sure. He did have paintings, which looked pretty good. Madame Mallet seemed to know him. I could go down and just look at them, and see what they cost. But wasn't it dangerous to open my door to someone who yells at paintings and throws things? How would she know if the last two screws holding his psyche together weren't about to pop loose? I nodded back to acknowledge her and looked down at him.

Our eyes met.

I jumped back from the window and crept down the stairs, my heart beating wildly, to check the lock on the door. When I got back to the window I saw that he had thrown the sunflower painting into my driveway, narrowly missing my car.

In two seconds, Madame Mallet marched out in his direction, yelling and wagging her finger. She stood over him as he gathered up his paintings and tied all of them in a stack with a strap. Then they began a polite conversation in the middle of the road. Finally he shook hands with her and walked back down the street. Madame Mallet turned toward her house, and I ran out to find out what happened.

"Madame Mallet," I called before she shut the door behind her.

"*Bonjour,* Rébecca," she said, and came to kiss me. "I saw you at the window. The paintings didn't interest you?"

"Yes, but that man—he was scary."

"That man? Oh, he's nothing to worry about." Madame Mallet laughed at me, probably thinking how funny it was that I was so frightened by the most commonplace things and so naive about truly dangerous things. "He comes by every few months, when his mother brings him home from the mental hospital for *les vacances.* I bought a painting from him a couple of years ago, and he always comes back when he's home. He'll yell and throw things around, but he won't hurt anyone."

"Oh," I said.

"But I'm glad to see that you're following my advice," she said, pointing up to my window. "You know—staying where it is safe. One never knows when those crazy church people might come back."

24. *Blessed Mary*

It may have been my imagination, but after the church ladies came to my door, Mary seemed to be following me around everywhere I went. Of course I expected to see her in the churches. She was the queen of all of them. There was the Romanesque Mary with her dour face, sitting stiffly on a throne on the altar and holding a miniature adult Jesus in her lap like a puppet—a sort of twelfth-century Charlie Mc-Carthy. I half expected her to say something to him and to see him whisper in her ear and dart his eyes from side to side. And there was the kinder and gentler Madonna wearing a crown and gazing upward in peaceful contemplation. And I still can't forget the Mary at Notre-Dame du Port. Not only was she young and beautiful, but she was practically laughing, as a chubby baby Jesus tried to nurse.

Driving around town, I started noticing her at every turn. I got on the autoroute and there she was, up on the hill above Vic-le-Compte, standing at least six meters high, a modern

Mother of God of white stone, stretching her arms out to all of us zooming past. I dropped off the kids at school, and she looked down at me from her pedestal on the playground. I ran to the market, and there she was beside my parking space, perched in an alcove above the Chinese restaurant.

And then she moved in with me. Actually, she was a gift from my American friend Jessie. Jessie's not Catholic—in fact, I'm not sure what she is—but Jessie had four Marys, all on little sconces and ledges around her French house, not to mention Jesus himself and a whole host of saints, which she had picked up from the flea market downtown. It seemed quite normal to me to walk into her house and see them all, chipped and broken, with their painted faces and pleading eyes. I almost forgot what her house used to look like before her love affair with religious iconography began, when all that adorned her walls were the van Goghs she had done up in oils on big canvases, the sketches she'd bought from her trips to Italy, and the black-and-white photos of her little girls.

I was there when her obsession began. A whole group of us mommies had left our families behind and run off to Paris for a weekend of flea marketing. It was going great. The tables at Les Puces de Vanve were loaded with treasures—pricier than back in Clermont, but the sheer volume of beautiful things was incredible. I had found a sugar bowl with curvy handles and was thumbing through a stack of monogrammed napkins when Jessie walked up with Jesus under her arm.

It was a little alarming.

"Can you believe what I've got?" Jessie said. "Isn't he beautiful? I'm gonna put him on my buffet."

"Wow," I said.

"He must have come right out of a church. He's just

like the one they have in Roche Blanche. Look at him. Isn't
he great?"

What could I say? I mean, he was pretty, and as her flea
market partner it was my duty to be supportive and get her to
go ahead and buy what she wanted to buy. I couldn't see putting him in my house, but Jessie was different about things like
that. She had this dark Spanish furniture that she got secondhand, and it just suited her style. Maybe a Jesus statue would
go with a Mediterranean theme like that. Besides, she had already paid for him and was quite happy with her purchase, so
I went along with everyone else and oohed and aahed.

We took the metro back to the hotel. I sat across from Jessie
while everybody was getting into a big conversation about
their husbands. I tried to participate, but I couldn't concentrate
with Jesus staring out at me from the paper bag between Jessie's
knees. There was no way I'd say anything in front of him.

Eventually Jessie noticed my loving glances at her Marys and
bought me one of my own. I was delighted. My Mary really
was pretty, old and beautifully chipped and imperfect. And she
was just the right size for me, about a foot tall—not too small
to be noticed and not so big that she took charge of the room.
But I just couldn't bring myself to put her on display.

"She'll be safer here," I told Jessie, closing Mary behind a
glass door of my *bibliothèque.* "You know, with the boys always
throwing things around. I wouldn't want her to get broken."
I was a Baptist, for heaven's sake. I couldn't have a statue of
Mary out for all to see.

For a couple of days I found myself standing at the glass
door, staring at her. Her nose and her chin were chipped just
slightly, and the blue of the sash drawn around her cream
gown was flaking off, like the flesh paint of her hands clasped

in prayer, the tiny worn fingertips revealing the ivory plaster underneath. There were no words rushing forth from her pale pink lips. She just stood there on that rock as a painted stream trickled by.

"You're too pretty to hide behind glass," I told her finally one day, and brought her into the fresh air, placing her prominently on our buffet beside the tall vase of dried delphiniums. The pink of the flowers reflected in her cheeks. She looked at home at last.

From her first breath of air, Mary started working on me, working herself into my dreams and daydreams. Ben would talk during dinner and I would catch myself looking at her over his head, or staring at her when I meant to be dusting. And it wasn't just because she was beautiful. I knew so little about her. French people seemed to know more. Mary's name was all over town, and the radio priest was constantly beseeching her. "Who are you?" I'd ask her inside my head, and she'd just stare back.

I got so absorbed in trying to figure out who I believed this woman was that before I knew it, I started turning the winter vacation of our second year in France into some sort of pilgrimage.

"Lourdes," I told Todd, showing him the picture in the *Michelin Green Guide*.

"Hmm," he said, scanning the picture over his cereal. "What's there? That sounds familiar."

"It's near the Pyrenees, and we've never been to that part of France. It's not too far, and it's supposed to be beautiful."

"Sounds great. I know I've heard of that. What's there?"

"Well," I hemmed, trying to find the right words. "It's sort of . . . a pilgrimage sight."

Todd stopped crunching his bran flakes.

"The story goes that back in the 1800s, Mary appeared there in a cave. To a poor shepherd girl named Bernadette. Eighteen times."

Todd started chewing again.

"She spoke to the girl and told her things, and there's this spring that just sprang up, and candles that wouldn't burn her. So now people come from everywhere—millions of them—"

"Millions? I don't think I want to be with millions . . ."

"Not in the winter. They go in the summer. It's probably a ghost town in the winter. All the books say that after Mont-Saint-Michel, it's the number one place people go in France, and I think that is reason to go in itself. I mean, why do they do that? There must be something there to see."

"All right, sounds like a plan," Todd said.

Our French friends were amazed.

"Lourdes?" exclaimed Jean-Claude with a gasp at a dinner party at his home. "Why in the world would you want to go there?"

"I just think it would be interesting," I stammered, dropping a stuffed mushroom on my lap. "I mean, millions of people make pilgrimages there, and I—"

"But you're not even Catholic. Pau, I could understand: it's a half hour away, right on the fringe of the Pyrenees, a beautiful resort town full of history, things to see. But Lourdes? Lourdes is . . . uh . . . Lourdes is . . ." Jean-Claude grimaced, searching for the right words.

"Jean-Claude," his wife, Mireille, scolded from the kitchen, "if she wants to go to Lourdes, she should go." I relaxed in my chair. I'd always liked Mireille.

"Don't you remember Cape Cod?" Mireille said, pointing the spatula at him.

Jean-Claude rolled his eyes.

"I always wanted to see Cape Cod. I was dying to get there. I had heard about it and seen pictures and everything. So we packed up and took this enormous trip, drove for hours, and what was there?" she asked. "Nothing. Just a lighthouse and shops and more shops. A tourist trap."

I looked at Mireille and took a gulp of my Kir Royale.

"Go," Mireille said. "If you don't, you'll always regret it."

"You think that was something? Wait until you tell Madame Mallet," Todd said on the way home. "I can just hear her: 'It's all a big racket.' Do you remember her lecture about 'La Grotte du Chien'?"

So I decided to get it over with. The next day Madame Mallet was out in her garden, pulling fistfuls of leeks out of the ground.

"Lourdes?" she said, smiling and shaking the dirt off her hands. "Are you going to bathe in the holy water?"

"There's holy water there?" Ben asked. "Cool!"

"Venez, venez," she said, waving us on inside her gate. "You liked my little Mary, but that's not all I've got from Lourdes. I'll show you." Ben followed us into her garage, and she led us up the stairs to her little bedroom. She opened a drawer and pulled out a long chain of beautiful purple stones with a gold cross.

"Colette got it the same time she brought me my petite Mary."

Monsieur Mallet appeared at the door. "You Protestants don't do the rosary, do you?" he asked.

"No," I said. "We—"

"I take it with me in my purse when I go out. It can't hurt, can it?" said Madame Mallet.

"No, and it is beautiful," I said, watching Ben finger the stones and the fine cross.

"What was the word for this?" Ben asked.

"Une croix," said Madame Mallet.

"Astrid, Benjamin knows what a cross is. He's asking about the rosary," said Monsieur Mallet. "There are many steps," he said. "First you do the sign of the cross like this," he said, demonstrating on his chest. "And then the apostle's creed—*Je crois en Dieu, le Père . . .'* and then *'Notre Père, qui es aux cieux.' "*

"Clément, he doesn't need to hear all that," said Madame Mallet. "Protestants don't say that."

"Oh, yes," I said. "We do say that—part of it." The Lord's Prayer wasn't part of every service back home at First Baptist, but now in our Episcopal service we said it every week, first in English and then in French. The French version was glued in the front of the prayer books, and I had it almost memorized. Huddling in our little stone chapel with all the other Americans and Brits and South Africans and saying the prayer together as best we could was one of my favorite parts of our service. Even with my bad accent it sounded beautiful. Saying it in French forced me to think about each word and reminded me that God was not American. I knew that years in the future, when France was only a memory, I'd try to recall it.

> *Notre Père, qui es aux cieux,*
> *Que ton nom soit sanctifié*
> *Que ton règne vienne . . .*

"But you don't have statues or music," said Monsieur Mallet.

"Yes, yes. We love music. But you're right. We don't usually have statues of Mary or Jesus or the saints. Just a cross."

"Just a cross?" barked Madame Mallet. "No Jesus? In a church? No Mary?"

"No," I got out, wracking my brain for how to say "stained glass."

"What are you people afraid of?"

"Well, uh . . . I love the statues in the churches here."

"You'll see plenty in Lourdes. And the holy water."

"Can I get in it?" Ben asked.

"I don't know about that," I said.

"I'm going to ask Dad," he said, and left us.

Madame Mallet leaned in close, and I tried not to breathe in her soup breath. "Take care while you're there, Rébecca. I'm serious. Whether you believe or not, bizarre things do happen there. I'll tell you this story. There was a woman that I worked with—very Catholic, this woman. But her husband? Now, he was a different story. Believed in nothing—never even took his First Communion. And he only liked his wife some of the time. A Communist—and that was the only thing that he loved—a downright hateful man. One day this man, he was in a terrible accident, paralyzed from the waist down, and months later he is finished with life, depressed, ready to end it all. His doctor was taking a group to Lourdes and asked him, 'Why don't you come along—even if you don't believe? It could be good for your morale to go there.' For some reason the man goes. And hup! He's in his wheelchair, taking the train to Lourdes.

"On the day he's to return, the train comes in. His wife searches for him, for the grumbling old man in the chair. And he's nowhere to be found. 'He's dead,' she says, and she runs from train car to train car, looking for him. And then a man taps her on the shoulder and says to her, 'Agnès, it is I.' And there he stands—not even using a cane. He's healed!"

"*Non!*"

"Yes, yes, it's true, I'm telling you, I know it's true. And so now this man spends three months every summer working there at the baths, helping others find what he found." Madame Mallet paused, and then took my arm. "I'm telling you, watch out. You never know what might happen in a place like that." Madame Mallet opened her gate for us. "And while you're there, take a moment to say a prayer for me, would you? Maybe you could even do something about this back of mine. I'm telling you, these doctors think they know so much. Four hundred francs later and it's worse than before," she said, and walked back into her garden.

The time came and we closed all our shutters, leaving my beautiful Mary there in the dark, and took off for Lourdes. As we drove through Toulouse, I told Todd about Madame Mallet's story.

He was quiet.

"Are you sure we should stop in Lourdes?" he finally asked.

"Yeah, why?"

"It just sounds like it would freak out the kids. You know—sick and dying people lined up, praying for miracles and lighting candles. And all this Mary stuff. The holy water . . ."

"It's kind of late to bring that up now. Look, no one is even going to be there. I didn't even make a hotel reservation because we're not going to need one. The guidebook says it's a ghost town in the winter. We'll walk around, see the sights, and go. If it's too much, we don't even have to stay."

"But I want to get in the water," Ben whined from the backseat.

"We'll at least see the water," I said. "Everything will be fine. Trust me."

As we neared Lourdes the next day, I was getting nervous. "How a city that plays host to five million tourists a year can have such small roads is beyond me," I said.

We turned a corner and in that instant there were cars everywhere, pulled off onto the grass. Old folks were pouring out of them, walking alongside the road.

"Who are all these people?" Todd asked. "We're not even in town yet."

"It must be a flea market or something," I said.

We turned another corner and it was as if a tidal wave of traffic blew right over us, sucking us into a small valley lined with towering hotels and hundreds of souvenir shops and cafés. We were stuck, sandwiched between huge exhaust-belching tour buses, and our windows were full of the buildings and the crowds—mostly old women, some in furs and some in simple housedresses and worn sweaters and coats. There were monks wearing robes of blue and brown, and nuns and priests, and troops of yellow-scarved tourists following guides carrying bright felt pennants on brass poles. It was like Christendom meets Dollywood. Everyone had shopping bags and cameras and candles of all sizes.

We took the first empty parking space we could find. It was in front of Le Musée Grévin de Lourdes, the official town wax museum.

This was not good.

"Cool! Can we go?" Ben and Sarah said in unison.

"No way," Todd and I said.

"I guess we'd better see if we can get a reservation in this *ghost town*," he said. He tried four or five different hotels, each time going in hopeful and coming out with a thumbs-down sign, as the kids and I sat in the car and stared at the wax museum. I don't like wax museums. In the window of this one was a glassy-eyed Bernadette sitting by a stream with a ridiculously clean gown, holding a still lamb in her arms. Its hind legs stuck out as though rigor mortis had set in.

Todd returned, shaking his head.

"I guess you weren't aware that today is the one hundred and fifty-eighth anniversary of the first vision of Bernadette. It's all booked—everything."

The kids started whining.

"But I want to touch the water," said Ben.

"I want to go swimming. You said there'd be a pool," Sarah said.

"If there's no hotel room, there's no pool," I said, trying to stay calm, and then turned to Todd. "And I guess you're not going to laugh at the irony that there is no room at the inn."

"No," Todd said.

So we took our disappointed children and waded into the ocean of old people, trying to keep track of the kids as they rode the crowd like a wave, washing out into the street sometimes and pushed into souvenir shops other times. We took a breather and stopped into one and I bought a little souvenir paperback called *Lourdes: From Vision to Pilgrimage*. Pushing my way through the shoppers, I couldn't help examining the merchandise. There were Marys of every size and every synthetic material known to man. There were plastic Marys, glow-in-the-dark greenish Marys, Madonnas with glittery crowns, and plastic Marys with screw-top crowns to fill with holy water.

There were Marys and Bernadettes on postcards, on polyester lace-trimmed plastic fans, in paperweights and on T-shirts. I half expected to turn the corner and see Hard Rock Lourdes, complete with framed relics and a Proud Mary Burger on the menu.

By the time we reached the basilica, an outside mass had just finished up, and we found ourselves swept into the current of blue-haired Italian women singing "Maria, Maria" as they headed down the hill. And when the women stopped walking, we turned around to find that we were standing right in front of the cave. There was a huge tiered candelabra inside, and a large life-size statue of Mary up high, right where she had appeared to Bernadette. Hundreds of visitors surrounded us, their voices buzzing.

"There it is! Look at all the crutches hanging from the ceiling," Ben said, jumping up in place to get a better view. "I want to go see it. Can I go?"

"Sure, but you have to get in line, honey," I said. There were hundreds behind the roping, waiting patiently in line to kiss the rock wall of the cave, offer their prayers, and touch the water.

Ben groaned and folded his arms in disgust. "It will take too long."

"Do you want to wait?" I said, hoping that he wouldn't.

"No," Ben sighed. "I guess not."

"At least we can see it," said Sarah. "That's better than nothing."

"Oh, shut up," said Ben.

"Ben, I'm just trying to make you feel better."

"Would you leave me alone?" he yelled.

I shushed them because people had started to stare. Sam started to squirm on Todd's shoulders, and I tried to pull him down as Todd videotaped with one hand and the kids continued bickering. And then my entire family was almost mowed down by a group of burly men in suits carrying a timber-size candle on their shoulders. The kids couldn't get over how big it was and started asking questions such as "How do you make a candle like that?" and "Where did they buy a candle like that?" and "How long will a candle like that burn, do you think?"

"Shhh," I ordered, looking at the people all around us. Their mouths were moving like robots', each one talking at the same time, each one gazing at the cave. What were they doing? It wasn't conversation—no one was listening. And then I saw their fingers moving.

It was the rosary. I was horrified. Here we were, tourists causing a ruckus in the middle of these hundreds of people praying. So we hurried our crew to the back and stood for a moment and listened to the chatter. Some folks were standing, others were in wheelchairs. Some had blank faces, a few with tears, some with smiles, some with eyes clenched shut, trying to block out the noise.

We decided to head on to Pau to spend the night. It wasn't right to stand and watch.

A few days later we were back in our own house with Mary watching us pull our suitcases onto the table and pile the dirty clothes on the floor. There was something lonely about her, this poor Mary, condemned to take up residence in a Baptist household, with no one adoring her and receiving no prayers, no rosary, no pilgrims at her feet. She needed something. I pulled out the plaster casts of my children's baby handprints and put the three at her feet. She's a mother, after all.

I loved looking at my Mary, though I still gave all my prayers to the Father, Son, and Holy Ghost. She stood there beside the pink delphiniums, a beautiful symbol of what it meant to be a servant, reminding me of our universal need to connect with what is holy, and bringing forth a prayer to my mind . . .

Notre Père, qui es aux cieux,
Que ton nom soit sanctifié,
Que ton règne vienne.
Que ta volonté soit faite
Sur la terre comme au ciel.
Donne-nous aujourd'hui
Notre pain de ce jour.
Pardonne-nous nos offenses,
Comme nous pardonnons aussi
À ceux qui nous ont offenses
Et ne nous soumets pas à la tentation,
Mais délivre-nous du mal.
Car c'est à toi qu'appartiennent le règne, la puissance et
la gloire,
Pour les siècles des siècles.
Amen.

25. *Corsica Man*

"The chicken came by to see you today," Madame Mallet called to me over her gate as I unpacked our groceries. "I'm sure you are heartbroken to have missed him."

"Oh, Madame Mallet, why do you call him that? I think he's a nice man."

"*Les poulets*—that's what we call *les gendarmes,* you know, the police. Did you know that he was a gendarme until he retired? Perhaps now you're not so impressed with him. It doesn't take much brainpower to be a chicken."

"I think he's nice."

"Think what you want," she said, taking the scrub brush to the lid of her garbage can, as the garbage men had done such a poor job at their bi-annual cleaning of it. "It matters little to me."

Le poulet, as Madame Mallet called him, lived around the corner and down another cul-de-sac, and we all liked him. We called him Corsica Man because he was from Corsica and because his real last name had so many syllables that we could never get it right. Months after we met him he told Todd that his first name was Santu, but by that point we had learned that it wasn't respectful to call a person by his *prénom*. Regardless, we had waited so long, a whole two and a half years, to ask him how to properly pronounce his last name that we just avoided calling him anything at all, except of course monsieur, which fortunately in France was perfectly acceptable. We didn't feel too bad. Our other neighbors couldn't say his last name either, calling him La Corse when he wasn't around. I don't think he would have cared—Corsica was the thing he loved most of all.

Corsica Man never wanted to retire in our little village, but since his wife, Marie-Hélène, had to care for her infirmed sister, he tried to make the best of it. As a former gendarme, he spent his days keeping his mind and body fit by lifting weights, walking, reading, and working on his English, which he had learned as a young soldier during the war. Marie-Hélène spoke only French and didn't care to learn a new language, so he had no one to practice with until we moved in. For forty-five years he had kept up his fluency by catching the occasional American movie in *VO, version originale,* at the *cinéma,* forcing himself to ignore the subtitles, and by reading Mike Hammer paperbacks and American police magazines. Sometimes he read them out loud, wondering if he still had the accent right.

It was amazing.

Hanging above the green couch in his living room was a yellowed certificate, his prized possession. He hung it there when he and his wife moved into their home fifteen years ago. She tried to get him to move it to their bedroom and replace it with a landscape or a pretty mirror, but he'd hear nothing of it. Every week he would wipe the dust off the frame with his big pointer finger and then put a little vinegar on a cloth to clean the glass. It was the extent of his housework, Marie Hélène would say, though she didn't mind. The ink of the big curly letters had faded, as had his youth, but it made him happy to look at it and remember when he was young, dark-headed, and muscular, with the girls flitting around him like birds.

"See," he said, showing it to Todd one afternoon, pointing proudly to the signature by the gold seal at the bottom. "William H. Smith, General, United States Army." The American military police had trained them, he explained, in Bordeaux after the war. "They were fine men," he said. "Taught me everything, to handle a gun, to walk my beat."

" 'Walk my beat'?" Todd said. "You've even got the lingo!"

"Lingo?"

"The right phrases, words."

"Oh, that is from Mike Hammer—you know of Mike Hammer—the books? I have every one."

Until we met Corsica Man, French policemen seemed all business and no talk. Occasionally I'd see them on their motorcycles, at the front of a marching mass of strikers (high school kids or doctors or garbage men), blowing their whistles to stop traffic so that those *en grève* could safely make their way down the street with their banners and posters. But I had never seen anyone walking a beat until we met Corsica Man. Though he was retired, he still considered himself on duty, watching over our *quartier* between the roundabout and the little stream that rushed through our neighborhood and ended with a trickle into a dozen garden plots a kilometer south.

No matter the weather, Corsica Man would be out in it, talking. He talked with the teenagers hanging out with their skateboards by the *collège* (middle school), the retired couples working in their gardens, the widows walking down to town for the day's groceries, and the young mothers pushing their strollers. Though his hair was thinning and white and his body not as muscular as it used to be, he always kept his dress neat. He especially liked the ladies.

And he liked us.

"You're speaking English!" he called to us the first time he heard us talking on the street. It shocked us all. As far as I knew, the only other person in our *quartier* who understood any English at all was Monsieur Mallet, and with Monsieur Mallet, you couldn't be sure what language you were getting. One afternoon I spent about three minutes trying to understand him as he repeated "Ees jauge boosh prazidon oo gahh?" which turned out to be "Is George Bush president or Gore?"

"What the hell are you doing in the Auvergne?" he asked, and Ben and Sarah grinned at each other. This guy cussed and was interesting—not the kind of person that would ask kids boring questions about their favorite subject at school.

We introduced ourselves, and he pointed to his house and explained that he had learned his English from serving alongside the Brits in World War II. "You Yanks don't speak English," he said, grinning. "You speak *sullang*," he said, "according to the Brits."

"It may be slang," Todd said, smiling, "but when we Yanks finally got here they were happy to hear it."

"Yes," he said, laughing. "You're damn right on that point. So how do you like this pretty weather?" he asked, pointing up at the dark clouds. "Oh, it's awful. I wouldn't live here at all, if it weren't for my wife," he said. And then he added in a whisper, "She's a Frenchy. And worse than that, she's an *auvergnate*, and you know how stubborn they are. So I am stuck here, in the cold and the ugly gray skies. As for me, I'm from La Corse. Do you know La Corse?"

Todd said that he had heard of it—an island in the Mediterranean between France and Italy. "It's part of France, isn't it?"

"En principe," said Corsica Man. "But only for two hundred years. We are our own people. That is certain. You must go there. It's the most beautiful place on earth."

We smiled.

"No, it really is," he said. "Really. And the smell? Like no other place—the maquis, the herbs. You breathe it and then you have to have it, the perfume of the air. How I miss it. And of course there is the sun and beaches and mountains. It is warm and *sauvage*—not dirty and gray with all of this dog shit everywhere."

Ben and Sarah looked at each other again.

"The people there, they laugh like you Yanks and are not afraid of pleasure—not like these stingy Auvergnats, staying at their house, trying to look poor. They're just a group of damn sheep. If I *had* to be a sheep, I would be one in La Corse. You know, in La Corse, the shepherds follow their sheep. They don't tell the sheep where to go. Oh, it's better to be a sheep in La Corse than a man in Auvergne.

"But, *tant pis*. We are here. Life goes on. You must come by for an aperitif sometime," he said.

. . .

THAT EVENING AT the dinner table Corsica Man was the subject of conversation.

"He sure does cuss a lot," Sarah said. "And I didn't really get what he was saying about sheep."

"Yeah," agreed Ben. "But I like him. He was just . . . nice."

As time went on, we got to know him better and the kids

began to look for him every time we went out. I would stop the car on the way to school, and we would shake hands through the window and talk. He would tell me that my French was improving, even though I didn't think it was, and he would talk to the kids. And then he would reach into his jacket pocket for a pencil and paper and ask me about English phrases that he hadn't understood in his Mike Hammer detective novels. "What does it mean, to be 'behind the eight ball'?" "What is it to 'let the cat out of the bag,' and what is a 'cock and bull story'—is that like bullshit?"

The next time I saw him, he was walking down the street with a little white dog in his arms.

"Her name is Coufou," he said, rubbing her fluffy head. "After the Egyptian pharaoh. My doctor said that I must walk, so I found a little girlfriend to walk with. Isn't she beautiful?" I nodded, as Sarah and Ben and Sam tried to pet her. "She was very expensive. She's a fine dog, really, a bichon frise. She has quite a pedigree. Her mother and father are both award-winning dogs."

From that day on Corsica Man was on the street not just for daily walks but all day long, carrying that dog. I'd leave in the morning to take the kids to school and he'd be standing at some lady's gate, holding Coufou and talking and laughing. I'd come back home and he'd be farther down the road, talking with another lady, still holding his baby. The dog's presence seemed to have even increased his attention from the ladies, and he was enjoying it. He liked them all, except for Madame Mallet.

The morning before one of our summer trips to the States, Todd walked back with him from the *boulangerie*. Corsica Man asked if we would send him a postcard, explaining that his wife collects *les couverts postales*. We sent the postcard right when we arrived.

A few days after our return to France, we had gone out shopping, and when we pulled in the driveway Madame Mallet came over with news.

"The chicken has been over three times this afternoon to see if your car is in the driveway," she said. "What is he bothering you about?"

"I don't know," I said. "Maybe he wants to talk about the postcard we sent him."

"You sent him one too?" Madame Mallet looked hurt. "Why would you do that? He's such an odd little man. What's his problem, a man like that, always muttering around and complaining about the weather and missing Corsica? I don't know why he doesn't move back. Except for all his lady friends. You know, Clément tells me that it takes him at least forty minutes to get out of Auchan, as he has to give *bisoux* to every single cashier. They all know him. He's a gigolo, I tell you, and I don't think his wife says anything about it. She must be as stupid as he is. He was a gendarme, you know—you don't have to be too smart to do that."

I gave Madame Mallet my standard scolding look, and she turned her back and stormed into her house. I felt kind of sorry for her. If Corsica Man would pay her the slightest bit of attention, she might like him as well as anyone else.

Later that day Corsica Man came by with a gift. I opened the wrapping and thanked him. "They're from Corsica," he said, pointing to the labels on the package of cigarettes and on the lighter. We exchanged kisses by the door. I could feel Madame Mallet's eyes watching us from her bedroom window.

"So what did he give you?" she asked me later, and I told her. "Why, you don't even smoke," she said. "Wouldn't he even bother to find out if you smoke before giving you a gift like that?"

"It's a nice souvenir," I said.

"If you want to keep a pack of cigarettes around for no reason I suppose you're right," she said, turning up her nose. "He's an odd man, you must admit."

• • •

A FEW MONTHS later, Corsica Man came again to our door to tell us personally his big news. He would soon be moving out of Auvergne and back to Corsica. He had had enough of the Auvergne gray winters and longed to live out the rest of his life where he belonged.

"I bet Coufou will like it," I said.

"*Non,* Coufou will be moving to Paris with my wife," he said.

What was he saying? They were getting a divorce? Did he want that? I didn't know what to say. I had met his wife once at the grocery store. She was a pretty lady, wearing a smart wool coat, her brown hair styled neatly in big curls, and pretty red lipstick on her lips. She had a mischievous air about her, like she could handle him.

"Paris is no place for a dog, or children or their parents either, but my wife wanted to take her, so she'll go with her."

It was a puzzle. A few weeks later Madame Mallet and I were chatting. "Did you hear that the chicken is moving back to The Great Corsica?" she asked, grinning.

"Yes," I said, hoping she had answers. "Do you know if he and his wife are divorcing?"

"What do you think? She's going to Paris and he's going to Corsica, so I guess it's so. If you want to know the truth about the whole thing, my husband saw him at Auchan, kissing all the cashiers goodbye for probably the third or fourth time, and one of them told Clément the real story. Apparently, one day he was handling the fruit too roughly—you know how that man would behave, picking up everything and squeezing it, like it was some girl—feeling it all and then putting it down, probably bruising it in the process. Some young manager scolded him about it, and he was so offended by this boy after being a customer for so many years that he made a pledge right then and there that he would never ever buy another thing from Auchan again, in any city, for as long as he lived. So maybe that started it. Where else would he get all the weird stuff those Corsicans eat?"

At that moment I caught a glance of Corsica Man himself, walking right toward us. This was bad—the two of them with me caught in the middle.

"*Bonjour, monsieur,*" I said and smiled slightly, embarrassed and hoping that he hadn't heard me gossiping about him.

"*Bonjour, Rébecca,*" he said cheerfully. He hadn't heard. We kissed each other, and then he turned to Madame Mallet. His smile flattened into a straight line. "*Bonjour, madame,*" he said curtly.

"*Bonjour, monsieur.*"

"Rébecca," he said, speaking in English. "I have come to say goodbye. I'm afraid we'll be leaving soon."

Madame Mallet stepped forward, saying in French, "Pardon, monsieur, but what is this that you don't have the decency to speak so that all can hear. They do speak some French in Corsica, don't they?"

"I'm so sorry, madame, of course we do," Corsica Man said in French, and then winked at me. I looked nervously at Madame Mallet.

"So I assume you're leaving today," she asked him.

"*Oui,*" he said.

"And what does your wife think about being swept away from the land of her youth to live in the wild?" Madame Mallet asked.

How sneaky! She knew that his wife wasn't moving with him to Corsica. I made a mental note of this tactic, as she was bound to use it on me as well.

"Oh, she's not going," Corsica Man said flatly. "She's moving to Paris."

"What? How sad to divorce at such a late stage in life."

"What is she talking about, the crazy woman?" Corsica Man said to me, grinning.

Madame Mallet cleared her throat. "In French, please, sir."

"I never said anyone was divorcing."

"You're not divorcing? What kind of marriage is that, please tell me? You, flying off to Corsica? And where will your wife go?"

"As I said, madame, she's going to Paris to live with our children and the loud grandchildren."

"And you're not accompanying her?"

"Me?" he asked, pointing to himself. "She's crazy," he said in English, elbowing me. "*Non, madame,* I'm way too old to spend my life in that crazy place. All the traffic and the noise and the people. What kind of a life is that?"

"Ah, I see, so you're going to Corsica, and what will you do there? Live like a single man? A gigolo?"

Did she say what I thought? Sure that I must have misunderstood, I signaled for a pause in the conversation and asked Corsica Man for a translation.

"A gigolo, you know, a . . . a pimp. Well, not exactly . . ."

"Oh, okay, okay," I said, nervous about where this conversation was headed. Corsica Man grinned.

"She's saying all this, Rébecca, because she knows that world. Who knows, maybe her husband is her pimp!" he said, and started giggling like a boy. "Though that may not explain how they could afford to feed themselves."

I had to laugh.

"What is he saying, Becky?" Madame Mallet asked.

"I don't think I can say, Madame Mallet."

She made a face at him and then continued. "So we know what you'll be doing in Corsica."

"Madame, I am too old, and my heart is too tired for that kind of play. But it will be a good life just the same. Better, I'd say, than to live with one's love beneath these gray skies."

Madame Mallet grunted in disgust. "But when it does get cold, at least there is someone to warm next to."

Corsica Man turned to me and said in English, "I don't think I want my mind to make a picture of that. Do you?"

Madame Mallet groaned, annoyed.

"I think I'll leave you two to speak in English. *Au revoir, Rébecca, monsieur,*" she said, and turned to close her gate.

"She's nuts!" Corsica Man said, and then gave me a kiss on both cheeks. "Give your family my regards. And come to La Corse before you move back. But be careful—once you get out of this shit and see La Corse, you'll never come back."

On our next vacation we wanted to go someplace warm. Everyone told us to go to Italy—to see the art in Florence, ride a gondola in Venice, and tour Rome. We decided to go to Corsica instead. We took the night ferry, and as we drove off the boat the next morning at sunrise, we rolled down our windows and smelled the maquis.

For a whole week we drove its winding roads and walked its paths through the mountains and along the beaches, stopping for the goats and sheep to wander across the road, followed by their shepherd—a laid-back-looking guy with a stick, every time. Whenever we passed through a village, we couldn't help looking over the *boule* courts, hoping to spot Corsica Man, even though we didn't really expect to find him. Ben said he might have seen him outside a little grocery store in Ajaccio, talking to some old ladies in front of the crates of grapes and apricots. But Todd said that he saw that guy and it wasn't him. His hair was too long and, being a former gendarme, Corsica Man always kept it regulation length.

On our first night back in our little village, I opened our bedroom window before getting under the covers. The air blew in, and I could have sworn I caught a whiff of maquis. Todd said it must have been the night breezes sweeping the last remnants of the scent out of the open suitcases on the floor. I lay there a few minutes, alternating between listening to the quiet and sniffing, hoping to catch just one more whiff of its perfume. But sleep came quickly, and I drifted back to Corsica in my dreams. We were at a beachside café in Ajaccio, sharing a table and an aperitif with Corsica Man and Mike Hammer and a laid-back shepherd with a stick. Behind us were hills full of maquis and thyme and rosemary, and the sea breezes swirled down through them like in a van Gogh painting, sweeping the perfume under our beach umbrella, around our heads, and out to the turquoise sea.

26.   11 Septembre

September 11, 2001, was a gorgeous day in France. It was our third French September, and I loved how the sun was so warm and yet there was a cool breeze that hinted at the approaching fall. I had left home for school an hour early, knowing that Sam would fall asleep in his car seat and I could enjoy a few moments with a good book before picking up the kids at four-thirty. Sure enough, Sam was snoring in the backseat when my cell phone rang.

It was Todd. His voice sounded strange. Had I heard what was going on in New York? I could hear his coworkers talking loudly in the background. He said they had a radio on, and something terrible had happened—a plane crash and maybe two, if what they heard was right. Had I heard anything? I told him I hadn't had the television on before I left the house. Was it an accident? An attack? What was happening to the world?

I pulled Sam into the stroller and walked briskly up to

188 · *French by Heart*

school. Outside the school gate, all the mothers were whispering: French, Spanish, Brazilian, American. Was it true? Someone heard that a tower was down. A tower, as huge as that, collapsed? How could that be? Had anyone survived? Someone said that our friend Debra had a brother and a sister-in-law who worked in the World Trade Center. Where was she?

We scanned the crowd and saw Adèle, waving at us, clearly shaken. She made her way to us.

"I can't believe it! I just saw Debra. It's terrible. Do you know?"

We nodded.

"She hadn't even heard. I can't believe I told her—I had no idea her brother worked there and I just told her, like it was some piece of news from somewhere far away. It was terrible. She turned white, and I said I would get her girls. I would never have told Debra like that if I had known." She started to cry. "What do I say to them?" she asked, and cleared her throat, trying to compose herself.

"Don't say anything," someone said. "Just get them home." We all wiped our eyes.

The gate swung open and the children started streaming out into the courtyard, skipping and laughing and chasing. They didn't know. Quickly, everyone whisked her children home instead of doing the usual lollygagging.

In the car I told the children what I knew. They were full of questions, mostly about their family back in the Carolinas and whether we were safe in France. We turned the corner to find Todd's car in the driveway and Monsieur Mallet, Madame Mallet, and Madame Fauriaux standing in the street in front of our house.

"Watch the news, watch the news," Monsieur Mallet said

in his thick accent, stepping forward as the leader of the group, armed with his translating calculator.

"I know," I said.

"The news, the news," he continued. *"Un attentat—à New York."*

"I know," I said in French, trying to get Sam out of his car seat.

"Deux airplanes," he said. *"Le World Trade Center."*

"Oui," I said, "I know."

I did know, but I had no idea.

"You people always thought it would never happen to you, kept nice and safe between your two oceans," Madame Mallet said, wagging her finger. "Now you are finding the pain with which the rest of the world is well acquainted. You will never be the same again. The most powerful country in the world, being brought down by a few thugs!"

People were dying. How could she go on like that?

"Astrid," Monsieur Mallet scolded, "this is not the time for that."

"Go inside, *ma chérie,* and watch the news," said Madame Fauriaux gently.

"Yes, Rébecca. And sit down. Have a drink, for your nerves," said Madame Mallet.

"Be with your family," Monsieur Mallet said, "and know that France stands with you. We stand with you."

I went inside and called my parents, just wanting to hear their voices. We clung to each other across the ocean, weeping for all the families touched by such horrible pain and sorrow. Later that evening I called Debra. Thankfully, her brother and sister-in-law had made it out in time, though there had been several terrifying hours before they found each other.

France did indeed stand with us. I could feel it everywhere I went. From my friends who called me, asking through tears if there was anything they could do, to the spectacled man at the newspaper stand, to the checkout clerk with the orange hair at the grocery store, everyone treated us with extra tenderness. Even Madame Mallet had changed by the very next day.

Like everyone else, we had been glued to the television, and as I tried to hold myself together and get the kids into the car for school, I heard her slippers behind me in the gravel. Her face was puffy and red.

"Bonjour, ma chérie," she said with a tremble in her voice. As we did our morning *bisou* I tried to swallow back emotion. I didn't want to start crying again. But she stayed right in my face and put her arms on my shoulders and I had to look at her. She had been watching the news into the night and again in the morning and had heard the horrible personal stories—the cell phone calls, the firsthand accounts, the pictures of the survivors walking through ash like live ghosts. With red-streaked eyes and tears she said, "We are with you, Rébecca, you know? We are all together."

They rang the bells at the Cathédrale Notre-Dame de l'Assomption downtown in honor of the victims, which someone said they hadn't done since the death of Charles de Gaulle. All of France went into *vigipirate* status, their version of Code Orange, I guess. They started bomb drills at the children's school, where all the American children went, and put up barriers inside the school gates. There were rumors of wild celebrations going on down the street at the kabob restaurant. Later we found out it had only been a rumor, nothing more, but still we felt uneasy. The U.S. Embassy in Paris kept e-mailing us paranoid letters warning us not to gather in large groups and to vary our daily routines. No one knew what would happen next.

Weeks later, calm eased tentatively back into life. Sarah, who was in sixth grade, was taking the stress well, though she complained that we no longer allowed her to leave campus unescorted to walk downtown for lunch like the rest of the kids. Ben, however, was still on watch. Every morning he would wake and ask for the daily report on what had happened in America and Afghanistan during the night. Had they caught Bin Laden? Were they bombing Tora Bora? Had any Americans been killed? He was still doing well in school, but there were more tears at home than normal. He had even gotten in a fight with some French fifth-graders who had been calling him Ben Laden. And his sleepwalking became an every-night occurrence.

"You should take him to a doctor about that," Madame Mallet said. "In France we have medicines for such things."

"But his father sleepwalked for years—he still does sometimes," I said.

"It seems to me, then, the answer is to take the two of them. It's never too late for proper health," she said.

"What could Benjamin be dreaming about that would cause him to sleepwalk?" asked Monsieur Mallet.

"Oh, I can tell you," I said. It was easy to know because of all of the yelling and running around. His dreams were played out in front of us, and he even could respond to our questions without ever waking up. "The last one was so sad," I said.

By the time we had heard the screaming and had made it to his room, Ben was sitting up in bed and yelling for his daddy into the imaginary walkie-talkie he held in his hand.

"Daddy! You have to do something!"

"I'm right here," Todd said, rubbing his back. "You're having a dream."

"No!" Ben yelled into his radio. "Do something! Help me!"

"Okay, honey. What do you need?"

"It's all broken up! I . . . I don't know what to do!" Ben cried, cupping his hands over his mouth.

"What's all broken up, son? What?"

"Can't you see it?" Ben angrily said, pointing at the floor. "It's the world! It's all broken up, and there's nowhere to land! I can't land! I can't come home!" Ben started sobbing.

"Ben, you're dreaming," Todd said. Ben's sobs turned to wailing.

"What do you need me to do, sweetheart?"

"You've got to fix it, Daddy. Please fix it. Please," Ben cried. "And they're all dead!"

"Who is?"

"All of them! Look! They're dead!"

"It's a dream, Ben," I said.

"I can't come back until you fix it!" he sobbed. "I don't want to be stuck out here. I want to come home!"

Finally, Ben wore himself out, lay down whimpering, and drifted back to sleep.

The Mallets were speechless.

"The poor dear!" said Madame Mallet. "Rébecca, why haven't you taken him to a doctor?"

Monsieur Mallet shook his head. "Dreams . . ." he said. "They tell the truth. His world is broken and it will never be the same. No one can fix it—that is the saddest part. Perhaps we don't properly appreciate how deeply children take in their environment, and how sensitive they are to the pain in the world."

"Or perhaps he just had a bad piece of fish for dinner," Madame Mallet said.

A few weeks later, I left Ben and Sarah at home and took Sam with me for a quick trip to the grocery store. When I came back, I found them leaving Monsieur Mallet at his gate and crossing the street back home.

"Was there something wrong?" I asked him after we greeted each other.

"Yes, there was, but it is fine now," he said, chuckling. "Benjamin had twisted a rubber band around and around his finger until it started turning blue. Neither he nor Sarah could get it off. Madame Mallet is on her Friday outing with Matilde, so they came to me for assistance. I cut it off for him."

"Oh, dear. Thank you so much for taking care of him."

"You are welcome, Rébecca," he said. "Perhaps I might need to reevaluate my theory—it appears that children are deep thinkers only some of the time. But I'm glad to do what I can. The pain of a finger I can handle—the pain of the world is another story."

27. New Year's with La Patriote

Two days after our third Christmas in France, Madame Mallet came over to our gate for a visit. We hadn't seen her for two weeks. My parents had come for a visit during that time, and I had wanted to introduce Madame Mallet to my mom. Mother and I had hung around the mailbox a few times, but Madame Mallet never came out. I was worried about her. I hadn't seen her niece Matilde's blue Opal or any other car parked by their house for the entire visit—no one on Christmas Day, even.

"So what did your grandparents think of their French grandchildren?" Madame Mallet asked Ben, putting her arms around him.

"I'm not French," Ben said, and unzipped his coat to show off his sweatshirt. It had a big American flag on the front. Mother had gotten it for him on sale at Old Navy. "I'm American," Ben said.

"And how patriotic," she said, smiling. "You know, when I

was young," she said, pulling him so close that he started to fidget, "I was quite a patriot too. And it wasn't as easy back in those days. They even made us learn German back then."

Ben stopped fidgeting. World War II was his favorite subject. Ever since he had watched a marathon of World War II movies on TCM, one of the only English-speaking channels on our satellite besides CNN, he couldn't find out enough about it.

"Not that we wanted to learn it," Madame Mallet said. "It was forced on us. They tried to teach me, but it's hard to force a mule like me. Oh, how I gave my teacher such fits! One day when he went out of the room, I went up to the chalkboard, and all the kids were cheering me on—I was that kind of girl—I'd do about anything. I drew a big German on the blackboard. He was big and fat, just like they were, you know, with their stomachs popping the buttons on their uniforms. And I wrote 'Schlerr' beside it—that's what we called them then, not exactly a compliment. The teacher came in and he said, 'Who did this?' But he knew who it was. He shouted, 'Astrid!' and I got five slaps with a ruler, but it was worth it."

"Wow!" Ben said.

"That interests you, huh? Try living beside a bunch of them—a whole troop of Germans. I lived with my grandmother, since my father was off in the mountains with the resistance and my mother had long since tired of him going to his Socialist meetings every night and had run off with some fellow that would pay her some attention."

Ben looked at me out of the corner of his eye, afraid that I might step in and end the conversation.

"They had commandeered the house next to Mamie's for an entire troop, and I had to listen to them drinking and singing every night. You know, those German drinking songs, and them swinging their beer around. One night I had had it up to here. I got out of bed and stood on a chair by the window and I sang '*La Marseillaise*' as loud as I could. But they were too drunk to care. My grandmother gave me a beating—that's for sure. You just couldn't go around doing things like that. But I was young. I didn't know anything."

"Madame Mallet, you should write those stories down," I said.

"Oh, I've done that already."

"You have?"

"Oh, yes. I believe that one should do that—write down all the events of one's life. Now, knowing my niece Matilde, my archives will probably end up over in Cournon at the landfill with the birds pooping on it and pages blowing in the wind, but at least my mind is clear. It's good for the psyche, I think—to empty it all, purge one's soul. Oh, I suppose I could be wrong about Matilde. Maybe she'll save it for little Spermatozoïde to read when he's grown, but I doubt it."

"That is really impressive," I said. "It's no small thing to write a memoir."

"I'm not so stupid, huh?" She smiled. "They're all organized—pictures too. I'll get out my archives when you come on New Year's."

So we were going to the Mallets' for New Year's? That could be fun. But would we have to go to the Roches' too? Last year, Alain and Pascale Roche and their two children, who live next to the Mallets, invited all of us over for New Year's, for the traditional *galette des Rois* (king's cake) and champagne. The Mallets always came, and Madame Fauriaux and sometimes her sister, and us too. It was fun, though a little nerve-wracking. We always felt a little like the rented entertainment. Most of the conversation centered around us, how we liked France, what were our favorite places and foods, and why wouldn't Sam speak French to them. Sam spent most of the afternoon (which often lasted three or four hours) on my lap with everyone staring at him, burying his head in my shoulder or knocking my champagne while I tried to take a sip. We'd try to shift the conversation, ask them about themselves, but it always circled back to us.

New Year's got closer and closer, and still there had been no invitation. Maybe the Roches had reconsidered. But what about the Mallets? Madame Mallet hadn't told us a time. Maybe she had changed her mind as well.

New Year's came, and I got dressed early, thinking that the Roches might come by, knock at my door, and apologize for the late notice. But around two p.m. I saw them in their driveway with another family, all dressed up in nice going-out-to-lunch clothes, laughing and talking with one another.

I looked over at the Mallets' house, so quiet and still. I walked around outside a little, knowing that she would hear the crunch of the gravel under my feet. I gave her plenty of time to make it down the stairs and come out, but she didn't.

The next day when the mailman buzzed in on his motorbike, I waited around at my box a little while, pulling weeds by the rose bush. Sure enough, I heard the lock on her garage door turn.

She pretended not to notice me.

"*Bonjour, Madame Mallet.*" I called and walked over.

"*Ah, bonjour, Madame Ramsey!*"

"*Bonne Année*," I said, kissing her.

"And *Bonne Année* to you. Were you sick?" she asked as Monsieur Mallet came out, and we exchanged kisses.

"Sick?"

"Yes. We found it very peculiar. You've kept your shutters closed too. 'Maybe she's depressed,' that's what I said. Clément thought you were upset. He said I must have done something."

"Upset? No."

Monsieur Mallet raised a shaky finger at me. "N-nervous breakdown?" he stuttered in English.

"No. Not at all."

"If you were not sick or upset, where were you yesterday?" Madame Mallet asked.

"Where was I?"

"Yes. Yesterday. Why didn't you come? I waited all day. I combed my hair and cleaned my house. But you never came."

"Was I supposed to come?"

"Of course you were. It was New Year's Day, wasn't it? I put on my best pants, and I had chocolates, and we sat on the couch and waited for the bell to ring. You didn't come. No one did. It was quite sad, really."

"But I didn't know."

"My dear, don't you remember? We said that we would celebrate on New Year's Day."

"Oh. Uh. When you didn't tell me the time, I, uh, thought we would go to the Roches' like we always do."

"Did you need a specific time to ring my bell? You don't need to go to the Roches' to wish me *Bonne Année*."

"I'm sorry, Madame Mallet. I kept waiting for the Roches, but I . . ."

"It seems that we can't depend on them. It was very unmannerly of them to end our tradition so recklessly."

Madame Mallet turned to Monsieur Mallet. "We can't blame Monsieur and Madame Ramsey for not coming. They're foreigners, after all. They can't help it. But those people, the Roches, they know how things work. And did they come over? No. They went off with friends. Loud friends at that." Madame Mallet looked back at me. "Do you know that I could hear them laughing in their driveway from the other end of the house? They didn't even give us as much as a knock on the door! Not even a simple hello and a *bisou* for the New Year, as one is required to do among neighbors and friends."

Oh. I was expected to go around and visit my neighbors on New Year's Day. I'd have to remember that for the future.

Just then Alain Roche rounded the corner in his van.

"Hey!" Madame Mallet yelled to the back of his van as it passed by, wagging her finger at him. Alain didn't notice.

"See?" she said. "Nothing. Poorly raised, that's what those people are."

Madame Mallet sighed and put her hand on mine. "Anyway, I'm glad you're not mad at me. Clément had said to me, didn't you, Clément, he said to me, 'You've probably done something, old woman.' Humph. See! I didn't do a thing."

"You're right as always, Astrid," Monsieur Mallet said.

"We must make up for the confusion. Come tonight at seven."

So I went home and called Todd and told him to leave work early. We had to get it right this time.

So promptly at seven p.m., the five of us, freshly scrubbed and dressed, knocked on the Mallets' door. They were dressed up too. I had noticed Monsieur Mallet's second trip to the grocery store after lunch, as well as the arrival of Madame Mallet's hairdresser, carrying in his suitcase and hair dryer.

We had cake and champagne, and she had instructed Clément to buy juice boxes for the children.

"You'll have to open them yourselves," she said. "I called Matilde and she suggested I buy them, but I have no idea how these things work. Little Spermatozöide drinks nothing from a glass."

After our dessert, she cleared away the coffee table. Apparently the program for the evening was first to talk about current events (Iraq, Chirac, Bush, and how he was so homely next to Clinton, whom she found extremely attractive, and how it wasn't Clinton's fault that women fell in love with him.) This was to be followed by important events in her childhood, youth, young adulthood, adulthood, and old age. She had brought out their archives and put them on the table. These turned out to be mostly her archives: photos, mementos, her communion gown, and a notebook full of stories, which jogged her memory and got her started.

"No, war is not something to hope for, unless there is no other way around it. It's better for the young than the old. They don't know what is happening. But the old, we know. See this young girl?" she said, pointing to a sepia-toned photo of herself. "That's the only picture you see. We didn't have time to loll about, smiling and taking pictures then. I was about sixteen there. The next year, my father went into hiding with the Maquis, and that's when I went to live with the Queen of Sheba—my aunt with the café.

"That woman worked me harder there than I ever worked in my life. And never paid me one centime. We were all there—me, an aunt, and another uncle, who lived in Marseilles, until you Americans bombed it to pieces and there was no place fit to live anymore. I was pretty quick on a bicycle, and so my aunt would send me four or five kilometers away to pick up this and that, take bills and payments to and from people. She had a car, but the Germans would take it if she used it, and anyway there was no gas available.

"And my bicycle—it was a fine one. My father had paid for it, since I left my aunt's bicycle in an alley while I was taking a bill up the stairs and someone had stolen it. Oh, were they mad! I had a little boyfriend in the same building, and spent a little more time there than was necessary, but I didn't tell them that. Anyway, he bought it on the black market. So I was riding this beautiful bicycle down a road—the first day I had it—it was a beautiful day, and I was riding along farmland—that's all there was in that part of the country. There were huge old olive trees that lined the road. Then I came upon this column of German soldiers that was marching down the other side of the road, and I stayed to my side, and then I heard an airplane coming from behind. It was real low, and started shooting! Oh, I remember the sound of the bullets ripping through these great old trees, big pieces cracking and falling everywhere. I jumped my bike into a ditch off the road. I was at the foot of this big tree and this farmer woman ran over there. She had been working in the fields, and she had run over there for shelter. She was scared to death, praying to God and saying that we were all going to die, and holding a basket over her head and praying, 'Our Father, protect us. Our Father . . .' I was young and stupid, and I thought it was funny, seeing her with that basket on her head, yelling and praying, 'Sainte Maria, Sainte Maria, save us.'

"When the plane was gone I got up. The Germans were all dead, lying all over the road, and my bike was ruined. I was furious. I knew my father would kill me for spoiling my bike on the very first day.

"I had no idea what could have happened to me. A beautiful memory of war, huh?"

"Was it the Americans, or the English?"

"Oh, I don't know. English, I think. But you Americans, you gave me enough trouble," she said, winking.

"Astrid," Monsieur Mallet interrupted, "you're boring them with all your stories."

"Humph," Madame Mallet grunted.

"No, no. It's very interesting," we said.

"Maybe you should take over, since you know so much," Madame Mallet said, putting the photo album in Monsieur Mallet's lap.

"You want to see something interesting, take a look at this," Monsieur Mallet said, opening the photo album. "That was my first deux cheveaux," he said. "Now that was a great car."

Madame Mallet watched as he turned the page. She couldn't resist.

"And take a look at this," she said, grabbing the album. She turned the page and showed Todd something so disturbing that he couldn't put a sentence together for the rest of the evening. I didn't see whatever it was, but given the stunned look on his face, it must have been bad. It was still bothering him after we put the kids to bed.

"Ugh! I can't get it out of my head."

"What was it? I just got a glance, but it just looked like Madame Mallet on a towel at the beach."

"It wasn't the beach. I can tell you every detail. She cauterized the image to my brain. It was someone's backyard, there was a tree on the left hand side, a dog and a car on the right, and Madame Mallet was on a blanket."

"She said it was Bastille Day, wasn't it? So what's the big deal?"

"One word."

I waited.

"Topless."

"No!"

"Yes. I saw it—them!"

"No!"

"Yes! I . . . I'd pop out my eyeballs and dunk them in boiling water if I could. And get this: she said to me, 'Not bad for thirty-nine years old, huh?'"

"No," I said, and laughed.

"And did you see what she was holding in her hand? A little French flag. I'll never be able to look at the Tricolore again without seeing Madame Mallet and her . . ."

"Todd," I said.

"She's a patriot," he said, making a face. "You've got to give her that."

28. Grant Takes on France

Grant Tomas was a down-home Carolina boy who Todd and I had known back in our college days. He had been a business major then and a good friend, but we were surprised when he ended up doing contract work for Michelin. We just couldn't picture it, Grant working in other cultures, eating something besides chicken tenders and his ubiquitous honey mustard. He spoke only English, but somehow he always got along fine. Everybody loved him.

On his first trip to Clermont, Todd met him at the airport and brought him to our house before dropping him off at the hotel. We showed him around the house. He couldn't get over the gravel floor in the wine cellar and the lack of closets. He also didn't understand the yard.

"Todd, big guy. You're falling down on the job. What's with all the dirt? This place needs mulch something awful."

"The French don't do mulch, Grant. They don't mind the color of dirt."

"Oh, yeah?" he said, and shook his head.

We went inside and he joined me in the kitchen. "Becky, I bet you just can't wait to get home to a decent-size kitchen. You got what, three cabinets?"

"Four," I said. "But I'm in no hurry. I like it here. You get used to it."

"Yeah, well, you've just been away too long. In a year or so, y'all will move back home and Todd'll buy you some big house in Crawford Creek and you're going to walk in that kitchen and say, 'This is Nirvana, baby! What was I thinking?' "

We laughed. When it was time to leave for the hotel, Todd said, "You know, they have breakfast at the hotel, so you can eat there before I pick you up for work. It's a nice spread, with coffee and some great French pastries. Yogurt, juice."

Grant made a face. "Yogurt, for breakfast? Naw. Don't worry about me, big guy. There'll be a 7-Eleven by the hotel. I'll just get me a Pop Tart and a Diet Mountain Dew. I'll be fine."

We looked at each other. Was he joking?

"Grant, there are no 7-Elevens in France. And no Pop Tarts."

Sarah joined in. "And no Diet Mountain Dew."

"Yeah? What do these people eat?"

"Pastries," Todd said. "Coffee. Yogurt. Juice."

"I'll just bag breakfast then. I packed some snacks in my suitcase."

• • •

THE NEXT DAY, Todd brought him home for dinner. I asked Grant how things were going. "Okay, I guess. But what is the deal with hotel rooms here? I got this tiny room. There's barely enough space to turn around in without bumping into the bed, and they've got no shower curtain on the tub. What are you supposed to do to keep everything from getting wet? It was crazy, man. I got in the shower and was washing my hair, and I couldn't see and knocked the hose to the sprayer off the hook. The thing went wild. It started jumping and leaping around like a snake, soaking the place. Then I slipped and it was still squirting all over, getting the whole bed wet, the carpet. Everything got soaked.

"I tried to explain it to the maid lady, but I think I scared her. She didn't speak a word of English. So she got the manager up there in my room and then that lady started fussing at me. I don't know what she was saying. The three of us were all around my bed, and I'm pointing at the water on the bed. I didn't want them to think I was weird or something, that I had peed all over it. So I said, 'NO PEE-PEE. NO PEE-PEE,' and finally they both just left the room, shaking their heads, talking French to each other. Then the manager looked back at me and said, 'Something something something, *voilà.*' French people seem to love that word *voilà*. They're always saying it. I'm pretty sure it means 'get lost,' because I always hear it after I've stood there trying to understand them for a while and they get mad and decide they're done with me. Anyway, I think I'm going to keep a low profile from now on."

. . .

SO GRANT CAME for dinner every night that week, with a couple exceptions for business dinners out, at which Todd accompanied him. When he was at our house, I tried to make him feel comfortable, keeping the TV on the satellite CNN International station and letting him use the computer to e-mail home. I tried to fix food that I thought he would eat, while still sneaking in a few French dishes here and there.

One night I decided to give him a real treat. I had finally learned to make my favorite French dessert, *tarte aux framboises,* raspberry tart, an egg custard in a pastry shell, topped with luscious raspberries and a light glaze. It would be perfect. Who didn't like raspberries? I picked the raspberries right off our bushes, washing them carefully so as not to bruise the fruit. I baked the pastry shell, filled it with homemade custard, and placed each berry on top one by one so that it looked like the *tartes* at the patisserie. Then I drizzled on a light glaze. It was gorgeous.

We had pot roast for dinner, fresh vegetables, and, of course, lots of bread from the bakery. At the end of the meal I brought out the tart. My family clapped. Grant looked at it skeptically.

"What's in it?"

Todd explained. The kids begged for their servings as Grant looked on.

"Can I serve you some, Grant?" I asked.

"Sorry," he said. "No, I don't eat eggy tart."

"That's okay, Mr. Grant," Ben said. "That'll just mean more for us."

• • •

THE NEXT WEEKEND Grant wanted to go to Normandy and invited us to come along. Todd thought it was a good idea. We hadn't been yet and wanted to visit my grandfather's grave and tour around the battlefields and museums. We left right after dinner.

Grant wanted to drive.

"Grant, why don't you just let me drive?" Todd said. "I'm used to the roads and the signs and I know the way. You can just take a nap."

Grant was firm. We had been so nice to host him and he wanted to return the favor by doing all the driving. So we buckled ourselves in and left Clermont. Grant had a map, and Todd had highlighted the route. It wouldn't be a difficult trip. We'd take the autoroute north, and bypass Paris all together. It would take about six hours.

Todd seemed confident. I, on the other hand, wasn't so sure about this. It wasn't Grant I was worried about. A six-hour drive with someone else in the car to witness my children's behavior? I sat in the back with the kids, passing out juice boxes and trying to keep everyone from whining. Soon we came to our first tollbooth.

"Here's the money," Todd said, handing it to Grant.

"Naw, let me get it," Grant said, reaching into his wallet. "I need some change anyway."

The man in the toll booth gave him change, two bills.

"No, I don't want bills," Grant said, as if the man spoke English. "I want change."

The man made a face.

"Monsieur," the man said, pointing to the bills in Grant's hand. "You gave me twenty euros."

"Nooo," Grant said loudly. "I . . ." he said, pointing to himself, "waaaaant chaaaaaynge."

Was this foreigner crazy? The man ignored him.

"You know," Grant said. "Liiiiittle moneeeey?" he pretended to count out change in his hands.

The tollbooth man slammed his window shut and turned his back.

"Man. What's wrong with these people?" Grant said, and drove on.

Todd and I looked at each other. Ben and Sarah grinned at me and shook their heads.

Within an hour the kids fell asleep and I leaned back and drifted off. A couple hours later all the talking in the front woke me up. Something was going on. I sat up, rubbed my eyes, and to my shock, right outside my window as clear as day was the Eiffel Tower, all lit up in lights!

"The Eiffel Tower?" I said, half awake.

I rubbed my eyes and looked again. There it was, right across the street.

"I thought we weren't going near Paris," I said.

Todd looked back at me. I knew that look. He closed his eyes for a moment and went back to reading the map to Grant.

Grant was gripping the steering wheel, staring ahead, trying to read a sign.

.   .   .

IN SPITE OF the detour, it turned out to be a great trip. We went to the cemetery in Colleville-sur-Mer, where my grandfather was buried. A guide took us out in a golf cart to see his grave. I had been there only once before, the time my family went when I was in college. The guide put wet sand in the letters on his cross so his name would stand out in our pictures, and when he was done he radioed back to the office. They turned on a recording of taps, and all over the cemetery, old men and their wives stopped what they were doing and saluted the American flag. Even though I had experienced this on my first trip there, it still made me cry.

Grant's dad had been there on D-Day, so he took lots of pictures. We toured the beaches and museums and stayed in a hotel with decent-size rooms, for Grant's sake. There were no shower incidents. As Todd drove us home, Grant slept in the passenger seat.

By the time Grant left a few days later, he had become like an uncle to our kids. They loved having him around. Ben would take him back to his room to show him Lego castles he had built or something he had drawn. Being a neat freak, Grant couldn't help cleaning things up while he was back there. "Buddy, let's get these clothes off the floor," I heard him say. He was a good influence.

• • •

THEN GRANT LEFT, and we had our first family dinner without him. Though I had enjoyed his company, it was kind of nice to get back to normal life. We all came to the table and sat down to say grace. Sarah volunteered to pray.

"Dear God," she said. "Thank you for this day and for this food. And please help Grant find his way home to where he belongs. Amen."

29. Jeanne d'Arc and the Baptists

Some might be surprised that we, a family of Baptists, became Joan of Arc groupies. By our third year in France, our obsession with her had reached a fever pitch.

It had started at the very beginning of our French life, just days after our arrival. On Todd's first day of work, Yves Bacconet, Todd's *chef,* invited us to his home in Riom, a neighboring city, the following Sunday for lunch. So we went, not sure of what to bring as a gift or what to expect. We settled on flowers, steering clear of chrysanthemums, as a friend had warned us that in France they were only for funerals, and we gave our children a lecture about proper table manners and the importance of not making faces at strange-looking food.

Lunch turned out to be a pleasure. Yves and his wife were so kind to speak mostly in English, since our heads were still spinning from the move and the newness of everything. We sat at the table for two and a half hours. Thankfully, Sam took a nap. For the most part, Sarah and Ben hung in well, though not as well as the three Bacconet children, who turned into zombies the moment the hors d'oeuvres were brought out and stayed that way through the cheese course. Finally, Monsieur Bacconet pushed his wiry body away from the table and suggested we go on a walking tour of the town. "We can . . . how do you say? Stretch our legs?" he said. "We must show you the fine history of our little city."

He didn't need to try to impress me. I was so amazed with everything I had seen that day, I could hardly speak. It was our sixth day in France, and there we were, eating Sunday lunch with a French family in their fifteenth-century house. I hardly believed it and tried not to gush too much about how beautiful it was: the stone staircase, the keyhole openings in the outer walls, which Yves explained were for shooting arrows through, the buffet in their *salle de séjour,* and the huge tapestry above it. Yves's wife, Eloise, said that it was a family piece, handed down since the seventeenth century. It was all so elegant—the way the entire family greeted us at the front door, all dressed up, and the little boys kissed us on both cheeks. And the meal—so simple and beautifully presented, served in the sunshine of the inner courtyard with the breeze blowing around the scent of mint from the huge terra cotta pots. There was a beautiful linen tablecloth, a quiche served cold and a beef stew made with fresh peas, followed by fruit, brioche, *mousse au chocolat,* a tray of five cheeses with more bread, and then tiny cups of coffee, the smell of which swirled in heady ribbons around me.

And then this, to walk through their narrow streets past black stone buildings with carved faces looking down at us. And to discover that Joan of Arc, whom I always thought was a legend, was a real person. Yves told us that she had sent a letter to the citizens of Riom and had plucked a hair from her head and sunk it into the beeswax seal.

"No one talks about it anymore, but it used to be the pride of the city," he said. "Not because of its age, as it was only five hundred years old, but because it was a first-class relic, an actual part of the body of a saint. It even survived the revolution—you know, when mobs stormed the streets destroying everything," he said. "But then it vanished, only a century ago. It's very sad."

"You're boring them, Yves," Eloise said, smiling.

"Oh, no," Todd and I said in unison. They had no idea, but Yves was casting a spell that would enchant us for the next four years.

"What happened to it?" I asked.

"No one knows."

There was a moment of silence.

"So she wrote to the people of Riom? For what?" Todd asked.

"For supplies. Arrows, saltpeter, that kind of thing," Yves said, pointing to a copy of her letter chiseled into a stone plaque on the wall at the *mairie,* the town hall. "It was one of only three letters she had signed. She dictated the letter of course. Jeanne d'Arc was only a simple farm girl. What makes the loss even more, uh . . . *humiliant* is that the mayor wrote back, you see, promising the things, but they were never sent."

"Oh," Todd and I said.

Yves shrugged his shoulders and smiled. "Such a story. She had the angels of God, but not Riom."

And so began our family's interest in Joan of Arc, the peasant girl who loved God so much that her friends teased her, who one day began to hear God's angels talking to her, and later was asked to do the impossible: restore the dauphin, the rightful heir to the French throne, to power. We were all amazed that we could actually visit the places in the story, and started making short Joan of Arc pilgrimages during almost every vacation. On our first year's trip to Paris, we stopped off at Orléans, the site of Joan's first battle, the gateway to loyal France, which the English had surrounded. In the Loire Valley the next year, we did the tourist thing and saw the fine châteaux of Chambord and Chenonceaux, with their gilded mirrors and manicured gardens, but saved a day to drive an extra hour west to walk among the ruins at Chinon, the ancient chateau where Joan of Arc first met Charles VII.

We were the only tourists at Chinon, except for a vanload of mentally handicapped men and women, who wandered around after us, giggling at our English. They walked with us to the great hall and mimicked our excitement when we saw that the huge fireplace was still there. Sarah's book had a drawing of that very fireplace, where Charles VII had mingled among the crowd, disguised as just another guest, wanting to test Joan.

"She said, 'It's you,' and Charles said that he wasn't, but she knew that God had told her right," Sarah recounted. "And finally he believed her. He had to. You just don't mess with people doing what God told them to, if you know what's good for you."

As we walked back to the parking lot, a woman with Down's syndrome and a choppy haircut followed us to the bathroom. She pointed to the book Sarah carried with Joan of Arc on the cover. *"Jeanne d'Arc,"* she said in a hoarse voice. *"Je l'aime"* (I love her), she said, and hugged herself.

The next chapter of Joan's life, however, deserved more than a side trip. During our third year in France we traveled to the site where Joan enjoyed the finest moment of her life. It was in Reims, a city northeast of Paris in champagne country, at the Cathédrale Notre-Dame de Reims, where Joan escorted Charles VII down the aisle and watched him be anointed with a drop of holy oil from a sacred vial one thousand years old, dating from the baptism of Clovis, the first Christian king of France. Nearly every king of France was crowned in that cathedral. It was a must-see.

On a brisk blue-sky Saturday in February the five of us crowded into my little Honda and drove the four hours northeast to Reims. We followed the signs marked ÉGLISE through the city, wondering if we had the right Reims, smelling the diesel fumes and passing the coin laundries and the magazine stands and the wine shops and graffiti. I scanned the sky for the double spires I had seen in a book, but there was nothing on the horizon. Then we made a turn and saw it. Everyone gasped.

The Cathédrale Notre-Dame de Reims rose out of its cobblestone circle in the middle of the city like a gothic giant trapped in a time-warp bubble. Outside the circle was the twentieth century—young mothers carrying their shopping bags and hurrying their children along, a group of old men talking in front of the *tabac,* and shopkeepers standing by their doors with their aprons on, chatting in the sunshine. But on the cobblestone island there was only one sign of life, an old bent-over man pacing in front of the huge cathedral doors. As we left the car and stepped onto the cobblestones, I could see that he was as skinny as a rail, dressed in rags and talking to himself.

He looked like the crooked man from the nursery rhyme—the one that walked a crooked mile and found a crooked sixpence beside a crooked stile. But this man had not been so lucky. He had only a rusty child's beach chair, which he would fold and then unfold, alternating between sitting on it and talking to it. In front of the chair he had stacked little cards in piles, which he would rearrange and then pick up and start all over.

We approached slowly, since we were all trying to take in the bright blue sky and the hugeness of the limestone giant looming over us. After my experience with the one-armed bloody drunk man in Clermont, I was less focused on this UNESCO world heritage site and more concerned with the scary man pacing between us and the cathedral doors. What was he going to do? He saw us and unfolded himself from his tiny chair and shuffled toward us, looking into our faces and mumbling something. His clothes were dirty and tattered and his gray beard matted in tangles. He had only a few teeth, and I couldn't understand anything he said as I hurried the children along. Todd pulled a few francs from his pockets, handed them to him, and walked on.

"*Non, non,*" the man barked out, following us.

Wasn't it enough?

"*Melyrllnasootch yeysoo,*" he yelled.

"Keep walking," I told the kids, hustling them toward the huge doors of the church. I glanced over my shoulder and jumped as he lunged for Todd's arm. Todd turned to face him, looking like a giant next to the man's frail, crooked frame. The man thrust a small playing card at him and muttered angrily.

"Merci," Todd said and swept it into his pocket as I hurried the children through the huge wooden doors.

We were in.

Dust danced in the beams of light streaming through the stained glass. There was so much to take in: the hugeness of the place, the long walk to the altar, the brilliant windows, the musty smell. But the kids were only interested in one thing: the card in Todd's pocket. It was pink on the back and worn at the corners and bent by the man's nervous shuffling. Todd turned it over and there was Jesus, barefooted and standing in a white robe on cobblestones, his right hand raised peacefully and left hand touching his heart, sending beams of pink and white light radiating out to the card's worn edges.

"We should keep it," Ben whispered, and we nodded and followed him and Sarah up to the altar.

After we finished our tour and readied ourselves by the huge wooden doors to face the card man again, an old lady in a wool coat approached us and politely asked if we had any questions. "Did you see the Smiling Angel?" she asked. "It's on the left portal, near that door," she said, pointing. "It's the only one ever made of its kind, smiling like that."

"Is that near the man, uh—"

"You mustn't worry about Jean-Baptiste," she interrupted. "He likes to stay close to the angel. It's his favorite."

We nervously opened the door and were relieved to find the card man paying us no attention, preferring to concentrate on stacking his cards. The angel was indeed beautiful, looking down on us with a gentle smile. He had curly hair and stretched one foot into the air, as if he were about to step off his stone roost and fly a loop around us. As everyone examined him, I kept watch on the card man, who continued talking to his chair and shuffling his Jesus cards, in the angel's shadow.

"I wish they would do something about people like that, hanging out at the churches where they know they can get money from the tourists," I said to Todd as we walked back to the car.

"But who would give out the cards?" Ben said. "I think it's a good job for somebody like that."

I got in the car, more than a little ashamed of myself. Ben was right. When it comes to God's work, not everyone can be Joan of Arc.

30. *Daffodils*

A week before America started bombing Iraq, Madame Mallet came over for a visit.

"At this moment, I must say that I am ashamed of the French," she said. "We French talk and talk, but we don't really do anything. In fact, my fear now with Iraq is that we'll do the same thing that happened in France in 1939. We were so afraid of death after losing an entire generation of sons in World War I that we'll roll over and do nothing as we did when Hitler moved in." I was beginning to think that Madame Mallet was sounding kind of reasonable, but then she continued. "Just one big, big bomb, Rébecca. That's all I want."

"You don't mean that," I said.

"I do. Look what has happened to your country. Don't forget about September eleventh. Those people have absolutely no fear of killing us all," she continued. "In fact, if they do, they get seventy-nine virgins as reward! Only for the men, of course. What do the women get? Nothing! Not that one could find seventy-nine men who are virgins anyway."

I had to laugh.

"Well, it appears that you're going to get your bombs," I said. "I hope it's over soon."

"I do too," Madame Mallet said, taking a serious tone. "I've been through war, and it's not much fun."

Two days after the bombing started, Madame Mallet came to my door with a huge bouquet of daffodils.

"For a true *américaine* from a true *française*," she said with a grin and a mock curtsy.

"Thank you, Madame Mallet! They're beautiful!"

"You like daffodils?"

"Oh, yes. And there're so many!"

"I'm glad they please you." Madame Mallet paused. "I hope my countrymen are not giving you too hard a time, being American."

"No, Madame Mallet. We're fine."

"Are you sure?"

"Yes," I said. "But I wish people would stop asking me about the war. They think that all Americans agree and that we want to take over the world. Last night at a restaurant we were waiting to be seated and a man at the bar said that we could come in for a meal only if we promised not to bomb him."

"Ha! And what did you say?"

"Todd said that we wouldn't bomb him as long as he behaved himself. It was funny."

"Oh, I'd be careful about things like that. Not all French people are as tolerant as I am."

Tolerant? Madame Mallet?

"Thank you again for giving me the flowers. That was nice of you."

"Oh, don't get so excited about it. They would have died eventually in the ground anyway," she said, turning around and taking a careful step off the porch.

I put the daffodils in a big vase on our dinner table. Until then, I had never noticed how bad daffodils smelled—like a greenhouse, slightly rotten. Sam held his nose through his entire dinner and Todd complained. But I kept them on the table until they wilted, a few days later.

31. Marie-France Rousseau, Maîtresse Extraordinaire

Marie-France Rousseau didn't look much like a preschool teacher. To me she looked more like she belonged in a lab coat, examining gunshot wounds and pushing some poor soul back into his drawer down in the morgue.

I'd drive by her in the mornings as she walked to work, leaning forward in a precarious angle, smoking a cigarette. She was tall and very thin, with short brown wavy hair and not much makeup. Her redheaded son was always struggling to keep up with her, the heavy *cartable* (backpack) on his back slinging from side to side. She carried only a purse.

Madame Rousseau wore black and sometimes gray for variety. What was she doing dressing like that? Preschool teachers weren't supposed to wear black. Back in South Carolina they wore sweaters with the alphabet on them or cats or schoolhouses with apples and bells. Preschool teachers were soft and smiley. They were sopranos or maybe altos—not tenors with an emphysema hack like Madame Rousseau.

The first time I met her it was a Saturday and open house at École Saint-Pierre, the festive day when prospective students and their families were invited to visit, examine the school, and talk with the teachers. Madame Besson, the directrice, had requested that some of us foreign moms attend. If other foreigners came, she had said, we could answer their questions in a positive way and give them tours of the school. She had put out two tables on the courtyard, and some potted plants I had never seen before. Three French ladies sat at the long table and drank coffee, smoked, and talked with one another. I sat by myself at my little table behind the sign that said PROGRAMME INTERNATIONALE, looking at my watch and praying that no one would show up. In three years, I had been inside the building only a couple of times. I had no idea where anything was.

I had ten minutes left on my shift when a Brazilian family presented themselves to me at my table. They spoke Portuguese, not English. We tried charades, and I gave the woman my handout even though she couldn't read it. The man and woman looked nervously at each other and then tried to speak in French. We listened so hard to each other that it hurt, trying desperately to find the French underneath our accents. Finally one of the ladies at the other table had pity on us and took over.

She had just left with them on a tour when Marie-France Rousseau walked through the gates, wearing a black trench coat and smoking a cigarette.

"Marie-France," one of the French ladies said. She winked at the other ladies at the table and continued, "You came. What love you must have for the school, for the children."

Marie-France rolled her eyes, puffed her cigarette, and said out of the corner of her mouth, "I love them Monday through Friday, and this week I guess I love them on Saturday too."

It was a mystery to me at first, but the children loved her like crazy. She told them all to call her Marie-France, and she asked us mothers to call her that too, for simplicity. I had seen this group of mothers daily for three years, and I only knew one by her first name. We all loved Marie-France. Even my reluctant Sam adored her, and Sam hated French school.

When he turned two, we started him in Madame Charbonnier's class of *Toute Petit Section.* The first day I dressed him in his new clothes and he went in happily, having no idea what was about to happen to him. The next morning he kicked me in the stomach and tried to claw his way out of Madame Charbonnier's door. I walked out of the courtyard, still hearing him screaming behind me, trying not to cry and repeating to myself how good school would be for him once he got used to it. At eleven-thirty pickup time, Madame Charbonnier handed me back my red-faced son. "He cried all morning. He kept on saying the word 'mygo,' and my English is not very good. I tried to look it up in my dictionary, but I didn't know how to spell it." I explained to her that he was saying, "My go," two-year-old talk for "Get me out of here!" At the end of the year Madame Charbonnier wrote in his little report card:

"Samuel speaks neither French nor English. He likes to play alone or with the American friend in our class and is not interested in our proposed activities. Perhaps when he gets bigger he will like to work with a group of children."

Not exactly a glowing report. Thankfully with Marie-France, things had begun to change. I stopped having to fight him every morning in the *garderie,* the madhouse holding room where children chase one another, squeal, wrestle, and throw fits as they await the beginning of school. Most of the French moms or dads knew what was good for them and stayed out of there, giving their goodbye *bisoux* at the door. But we foreign moms, being in need of adult conversation we could understand, hung around and talked as our children either joined in the chase or clung to us, whining and bargaining for a day at home.

But when Marie-France entered the room, her charges flocked to her like little chicks. Sam would stay at arm's distance, but she always noticed him.

"Bonjour, Samuel. Ça va?" she would say, and he would nod and give her a shy half smile. She spoke French relentlessly with him and the other foreign children, even though someone said that she knew a good bit of English. Marie-France talked with them in a dry, adult way, as if they understood everything she said. It amused her, and it worked. Eventually they'd start understanding and even answer back. The other *maternelle* teachers seemed to see the foreign children as a hassle. Marie-France thought they were interesting and would talk about their personalities and idiosyncrasies if asked. She understood Sam almost as well as we did, how he wanted so much to be big, that he was extremely *tétu*—stubborn—and that more than anything else he hated being laughed at. She would tell me stories of his interactions on the playground with little Florian and Antoine, and how when he turned three he started pretending that he didn't understand her when it came time to go to the potty.

Sam didn't care for the morning break to *"faire pi-pi,"* in which the entire class was walked down to the *toilette,* a small room with a bench and a row of six tiny porcelain toilets, no stalls, no doors. Children were to sit on the bench to wait while their classmates went *pi-pi* in front of them, and then places were exchanged. It was very practical and was seen by the children as just as routine as undressing down to their underwear for their afternoon nap. As much as I had worked with him, Sam was not yet *propre* (potty trained) and wore pull-ups to school.

One cold damp Tuesday I was driving him home from school when I asked him if he would like to have a hot bath at home. He said that he wouldn't need one since a man at school had already given him a shower.

I tried not to overreact.

"You had a shower? At school?"

"Uh-huh. Enrique gave me one. I didn't like it."

I raced right home and called my friend Mary Ann. She had never heard of showers at school. I called my French friend Camille. She had never heard of showers at school. I examined Sam's privates and asked questions about touching. "No," he said, playing with a Matchbox car. "He just squirted water at me."

The next morning I tried not to look hysterical and calmly asked Marie-France about it. She explained that Sam had soiled his diaper and of course he needed to be thoroughly cleaned. Enrique was the assistant who took care of that kind of thing.

Sam potty trained shortly after that.

Spring came of our fourth year in France and a note was sent home that the class would be going on a *sortie* to the farm. Chaperones were needed. This was my chance. I had wanted to go to the farm with Madame Charbonnier's class, but she wouldn't let me go because I had been too late in signing up. Two days after the notes went home, she said that she had already appointed the chaperones. Maybe she was worried about having space for me on the bus, I thought, and I told her that I would be happy to drive myself and meet them there, that surely she couldn't have too much help taking a class of two-year-olds to a farm. "No, Madame Ramsey," she said. "That is not necessary, and neither is it appropriate. Perhaps next time."

I wasn't going to make the same mistake this time around. The morning after the note came home, I raced the children to school and made sure I was first in line to volunteer. Marie-France wrote my name on her clipboard and asked Samuel why the American mommies were always so eager to trade off their peaceful hours at home to chase other people's children around a farmyard. While Sam tried to determine whether he had just been praised or scolded, Marie-France assigned me my charges. There was Odette, a docile little French girl who wouldn't run away from me, my Samuel, of course, and Steven, a new little American boy who was currently in the clawing-at-the-door stage. I didn't ask Marie-France if Steven's mother, Cheryl, had wanted to go. It would have been nice of me, but there was no way I was missing this trip again. Everybody said it was the best one. Cheryl probably couldn't go anyway, on account of her baby. She could get someone to babysit, but she probably wouldn't do that, being new in town. I pledged to my guilty conscience to make sure Steven had a good time.

I avoided talking with Cheryl about the field trip for a whole week. Not that she and I could have had a long conversation about it anyway. She always had her hands full, trying to juggle her sweet baby boy and the diaper bag and pry Steven off her legs in the *garderie*. He was almost as good a kicker as Sam and had a scream that really carried.

Tuesday was the big day. I packed lunches for Sam and me and made sure we wore old clothes and mud shoes. We drove to school a half hour early so that I could find a good parking place. Normally I parked illegally like everyone else for drop-off, but for the field trip I needed to find a space for all day. About a half mile away I parked near the van Cheryl had brought over from the States. She had the baby in the stroller and had started down the street toward school, but where was Steven? Usually they played a kind of tug-of-war as they walked, with Steven occasionally breaking away and running for the car, but not today. And then I saw him stepping out from the other side of the stroller, walking like a normal boy, holding his mother's hand.

"Hey, Steven!" Sam called, and Steven turned around.

He had something black across his eyes. What was it? It looked like a blindfold. When we got closer, I saw the holes cut out for his eyes.

"Hey! You're Batman!" Sam said.

Steven let go of his mother and jumped ahead a few feet. Cheryl rolled her eyes at me.

"Steven is Super Boy today, Sam," Cheryl said.

Sam jumped ahead to catch up with him.

"I have no idea where the mask idea came from, but I'm not fighting it," Cheryl whispered to me. "Since he put that thing on after breakfast he has not whined or cried one single time about going to school."

"Wow," I said. "Whatever works."

This was not going to work.

The French kids would mob him and want a turn, and there was no way that the teachers in the *garderie* would allow him to wear that mask. "It is a distraction to learning," they would say.

I was right, at least partly. As soon as we walked in the *garderie,* the French kids mobbed him. The boys and girls closed in around him, speaking French at him and wanting a turn with the mask. Surprisingly, Steven liked the attention. He even smiled at them. When Jean-Baptiste snuck up behind him and tried to pull it off, Steven leapt out of the crowd like a Power Ranger, arms posed to fight. "Up, up, and away!" he yelled, and struck a pose. Until then I had never heard him utter one word in front of the French kids. They looked at one another and laughed and ran after him. Steven was the It boy of the *garderie*.

When Marie-France arrived, I took the baby from Cheryl and she went to try to talk with Marie-France. I watched her point out Steven, still running around the room in his mask. Marie-France said something, shrugged her shoulders, and they talked some more, ending their conversation with a nod to me.

"I could hardly understand that woman, but I did get that she put Steven with you for today," Cheryl told me. "I'm so glad. I would have gone. Mary Ann said she'd take Michael, but Marie-France said she had all her volunteers. I don't understand it. How can you have too many volunteers for a field trip? But, whatever, it looks like he'll be okay. You'll probably think I packed him too much lunch, but he's pretty picky so it's not like he'll eat the snack that they bring. Oh, and Steven gets hay fever, so here's some Kleenex. I'd give him his Benadryl, but he'd sleep all day."

"He'll be fine," I said. "What did Marie-France say about the mask?" I asked.

"Oh, yeah. I did get that part. She said if it works, why not?"

Steven didn't even cry when it came time for the mommies to leave. He held Sam's hand as our class walked the city block to the bus, and I held hands with little Odette. She wasn't quite sure what to make of me. I tried to make small talk, telling her she had a pretty jacket.

She looked at me with big eyes.

"Do you like school?" I asked.

She nodded and started nervously sucking her thumb.

We got on the bus, and I sat with her in the seat in front of the boys. Fifteen minutes into the ride through the countryside, I asked her if she liked field trips.

"You talk funny," she said.

"It is because I'm not French," I said.

"Odette," Marie-France said from the seat beside us. "Did you know that Sam's mommy is from the United States?"

Odette nodded. "That's where McDo's comes from. I went there once for Salomé's birthday party. Mommy says Americans eat too many hamburgers and that is why they are so fat."

"Odette," Marie-France said. "Are all Americans fat?"

Odette looked me up and down. Then she looked out the window.

I laughed. "We do eat other things, Odette."

"*Oui,*" said Marie-France and winked at me. "There's always Filet-O-Fish."

I laughed. I asked Marie-France about an article I had tried to read in the paper, something about fishermen protesting in McDonald's. "Apparently McDonald's uses frozen fish fillets from Canada instead of local French fish," she said. "So they brought in truckloads of fresh fish and dumped them in Mc-Donald's restaurants all over France."

"Wow," I said.

"They're very serious," she said.

She asked me if McDonald's in France was the same as the McDonald's back in the States, and I said that in the States they don't put out tablecloths for Sunday morning brunch, and neither could one order a Croque McDo there or have a beer with dinner. "Why not?" she asked, and I explained that it was really a restaurant for children, not adults.

"Ah," she said. "My son had his ninth birthday party there, but since I dropped him off, I did not try the food."

That didn't surprise me. I had never seen any parents at McDonald's parties in France. It was always just the children, screaming from their Orangina high, hitting one another with the free balloons fastened to plastic sticks and running laps through the play space.

"Does it make you feel at home, to go there here?" she asked.

"No, not really. I never liked McDonald's much in the States," I said. "And though my children see it as a little taste of home, I don't care for it here either." I had plenty of reasons to dislike French McDo's, in spite of the food being better. I told her about my last visit to McDo, when a four-year-old in the ball pit called me a whore (*putain*), all because I wagged my finger at him for using my Sam for target practice. "And French people never understand me there," I said. "To be understood, you have to speak the McDonald's vocabulary with a fake French accent."

Marie-France thought this was interesting. "How do you mean?"

"*Je voudrais un* BEEG MOCK, *une boite de six* NEW-GAY [nuggets], *et un* OM-BUH-GUH," I said. Marie-France laughed, deep and throaty.

We got to the farm and filed out of the bus. As the children ran around like wild ponies in the morning sunshine, the farmer and his female crew guided us over to a little shed lined with picnic benches. We sat the children down, and the women started serving us from the table in the center of the circle. There was hot coffee and mulled wine for the adults and pitchers of creamy milk for the children. To eat, there were giant loaves of *pain de compagne* (country bread), a huge wheel of cheese, large jars of homemade raspberry confiture, and Nutella, the chocolate hazelnut spread to which my children had become addicted. Most of the French kids asked for a big wedge of cheese with their bread, while nearly all of the foreign children ended up with chocolate on their faces. As I sipped my coffee and talked with a few other mothers I knew, I looked around for Marie-France. There she was, behind the bus. The edge of her trench coat stuck out, as well as an elbow.

Odette saw me looking. "She's having her snack," she said. "It is a cigarette."

The day was glorious. The children ran through the fields and picked up chicks and rabbits and threw poopy hay on one another. I took my three to the dairy barn, and the farmer showed them how to milk the cow into a bucket. Before I could say anything, he passed the bucket around for a taste. All of them took a sip, getting white foam on their upper lip. "It tastes like hot chocolate without the chocolate," said Sam. I looked at Steven grinning under his white mustache and thought about antibacterial hand wash. His mask drooped on one side, and he still had chocolate on his cheek.

He was having a great time. Odette took seconds from the milk bucket and had chicken poop on her shoes (a chicken had sat on her feet during lunch), but she didn't seem scared of me anymore.

"Madame, I have to go *pi-pi,*" she said to me as we walked to sit on the tractor.

I asked Marie-France where the *toilettes* were. She laughed.

"Oh, there aren't any *toilettes,*" she said. "Just use the field behind the shed."

I tried not to look shocked. "Oh, okay," I said nonchalantly, and started walking Odette to the shed. How were we going to do this? I had easily adapted to the French habit of letting little boys go *pi-pi* behind bushes in the park. Sam called it "going pee-pee in the woods," though there were never any woods and sometimes not any bushes. It was very convenient. But with a girl? I had never learned how to accomplish the goal myself without getting wet in the process. It was annoying. Even at many tourist sites there were never any toilets with seats, only the two-footprints-and-a-hole Turkish toilets. I always ended up taking my pants entirely off and felt like an animal. Sarah had had the same problem with the Turkish toilets on the school playground. I needed to learn how to do this, I decided, for Odette and for all of us. I would ask Marie-France.

It could have been very embarrassing. It could have been awkward. But with Marie-France it was very matter-of-fact and very useful.

"You put the child with her back to your chest so that you are both facing the same direction. Then you lift the child up under her knees, so that her bottom is hanging between your legs. Then she goes *pi-pi.*"

I looked doubtful.

Odette looked scared.

"Odette," Marie-France said, "would you like me to take you?"

Odette nodded a big nod. We were both relieved. And I waited to go *pi-pi* until I got home.

The farm trip was such a success that I couldn't wait for the next *sortie*. I had heard that Marie-France's class always went on a hike around the Puy de Dôme in May. I wasn't sure about taking a group of preschoolers to hike up the side of an extinct volcano, but as long as Marie-France was leading the trip, I'd go along for the ride, if I could sign up in time. The kids were sure to enjoy frolicking in the sunshine, and if anybody needed to go *pi-pi,* I was ready, willing, and able.

32. Grandmère Bonnabry

Considering that we practically lived with Madame Mallet, I wasn't sure about spending my vacation with another old French lady, particularly one that I'd never even met.

"I promise," insisted my friend Mary Ann. "It'll be just like spending the weekend at your grandma's house." Mary Ann always had ridiculous luck with vacations. She and her husband would just pack up their kids and run off to some ancient city without any reservations or plans and always bump into the greatest bed-and-breakfast, owned by a professional tour guide host or master chef. "Even better," she went on, "there's an entire apartment upstairs with a television and games for the kids, so you wouldn't have to worry about bothering anyone. And the owner is great. The first night we were there, there was a family already in the upstairs apartment, so she squeezed us into the bedroom downstairs. We had to share her bathroom, and Lauren got a stomach bug and we were in there all night long. I tried to apologize the next morning, and she told me not to worry about it, that she had no trouble at all going *pi-pi* in the backyard."

"That's accommodating," I said. I still wasn't sure. We had never stayed in a *chambre d'hôte* before, choosing instead to stay in big hotel chains, where no one at breakfast could figure out that it was our kids who were up dancing around at six a.m.

"You *have* to go," Mary Ann said. "Not only is the Dordogne valley the most gorgeous place on earth, with all its medieval châteaus and forests, but it's the land of truffles and foie gras. The food is *incredible*. And you'll love Madame Bonnabry. She'll bring you slippers and hot tea if you want it, and she'll want to talk to the children. She *loves* children. She's a typical grandma, really."

Okay. That settled it. After Madame Mallet's constant spying and backhanded compliments, a lovey-dovey grandma would be a refreshing change. I made the reservation.

It was raining, a soft, constant rain like it does during the entire month of April, when we arrived in the medieval town of Domme after lunch. The sky was dark, and the grass almost glowed bright green. We pulled up next to an uninteresting gray row house, and I opened my umbrella and ran to the front door to make sure we had the right place. The door opened, and out stepped the tallest French woman I had ever seen.

"Madame Ramsey?" she asked. I nodded.

"Bonjour, madame. Venez, venez." Later, she told us that she was seventy-five, but she moved like a young person, confident with lots of arm swaying. She had hazel eyes, and her hair looked a little odd. Her dye job hadn't worked very well; in the dim light of her hallway, her shade of brown looked a lit-

tle green. She wore gray slacks and a cardigan sweater and shocked us with her white sneakers. I had never seen a French woman in white sneakers.

"I was worried about you," she said. "It's a little tricky finding this place, and with the rain. Oh, what beautiful children," she said, grasping Ben's wet head in her hands and then Sarah's. "Tell me your names, children."

Ben and Sarah smiled and meekly said their names the French way. "And they speak good French too. And they look so intelligent. What beautiful eyes." Madame Bonnabry caught a glance of Sam hiding behind my leg. "Oh, but where is the littlest one?" she said, pretending not to see him.

"What is his name?" she whispered. I told her.

"Where is Samuel? Samuel?" Sam peeked out. "I see you. What dimples you have. Why, all three of you have them. Where do they get their beautiful dimples?" I could feel myself blushing as Madame Bonnabry surveyed Todd's face and mine. "Ah, it's your mother who's given them to you."

"I love children," she continued, pulling our suitcases out of our hands and placing them in a neat row by the stairs. "I raised four of my own and raised seven others too—some with Down's syndrome, some that had been abused or abandoned. We'd have thirteen at the table. What a joy that was."

Todd and I looked at each other. Was this lady for real?

We took off our raincoats and she gave us a tour of our apartment and the public rooms of her house. The stairs smelled old, like my grandma's house, and had dark brown wallpaper with pink flowers. The apartment upstairs was neatly furnished—with odd-size pictures scattered all over the walls, embroidered tablecloths on the tables, thin blue duvets on the beds. It was clean and private. In a little side room there was a bookcase neatly stacked with games. Sarah pulled one out, and Ben and Sam whipped open the cover and started taking the pieces out. "Gently, children," Madame Bonnabry softly scolded. She pulled up a chair and directed the children to have a seat and began giving instructions. She was sweet and affirming but made sure the dice didn't fall on the floor and that the children sat up straight.

As she played with the kids, I had a look around. In the bathroom there were stacks of mismatched towels and shag rugs on the linoleum. In the corner there was a shower that looked like a space capsule but with saloon doors. Madame Bonnabry looked over her shoulder and saw me examining the toilet. It had a plug. An electric toilet? "This *toilette* is very energy efficient—and good for the environment. We must always consider that, you know." This was no ordinary grandma, in spite of the crocheted cover on the extra toilet paper.

"I suppose you want to settle in and then go see the town. Domme is well known. I'll be serving tea at four-thirty if you would like to come. Perhaps hot chocolate for the children." We nodded. Yes, this was going to work out just fine.

At 4:29 we arrived back at the house after a soggy walking tour of Domme. My heart sank upon hearing a male voice coming from the *salle de séjour.* I was glad to visit with Madame Bonnabry, but not some stranger. Would we have to sit with him at breakfast too? I got so tired of being examined and evaluated as an American, even if people were nice. Making small talk with a complete stranger in French was brutal.

"There you are—and there is my little friend," Madame Bonnabry said, bending down to poke Sam in the belly. Sam whined a fake whine and grinned behind my leg. We nodded to the stranger, a handsome man in his mid-fifties, sitting on the couch. My heart sank again to see the large round table in the corner, set with a lace tablecloth and china. How were my kids going to make it through tea and two breakfasts without breaking anything? Didn't these people ever do plastic?

Madame Bonnabry introduced us to Monsieur Courtois, a friend of her son's and now a close friend of her own. "This dear man lives in Paris but comes to see me often," she said with her hands on his shoulders. He smiled and patted her hands with his rough hands as she continued, "He and his wife spoil me, never forgetting a birthday or a holiday. After my divorce a year and a half ago, he helped me move to Domme to get away from that man. After fifty-three years, I just couldn't take it any longer. He helped me find this *chambre d'hôte* to run. He has a weekend house in Sarlat, nearby."

"But it is my pleasure, all my pleasure," he said.

Madame Bonnabry patted him on the arm and then tucked the children into their chairs at the table. I watched as she took over. She pushed in Ben's chair, and I quickly found a seat by Sam's side. Immediately he reached across his plate for a piece of cake in the middle of the table and knocked a knife onto the floor. Before I could get it, Madame Bonnabry swept in and picked it up. Then she lifted Sam up and tried to slip a small pillow from the couch onto his chair.

"I used to do a lot of business in the States," the man said to Todd in perfect English. "Where are you from?"

"No pillow," Sam said, trying to pull it out from under himself.

"Leave it alone, Sam," I said, already beginning to sweat.

"Would you care for some coffee? Or tea? Tea is really better for us, now isn't it?" Madame Bonnabry asked.

This was going to be work. I smiled at Madame Bonnabry and stuffed the pillow farther under Sam, and said that yes, Todd and I would love some tea. The teakettle whistled, and Madame Bonnabry went to the kitchen.

"We're from North and South Carolina," Todd said. The man had been through South Carolina, yes, he had some customers in Charleston, he believed. Their conversation faded into the background as I tried to manage the children.

"Mom, would you fix my hot chocolate?" Ben asked. "Is that what this is for?" he said, precariously picking up the porcelain bowl Madame Bonnabry had put in front of him.

"I guess so," I said. It had no handle, so it wasn't a mug. Was he supposed to drink out of it? It seemed familiar; maybe I had seen advertisements with kids drinking from bowls like those. But what if it wasn't? What would she say, seeing my children drinking from bowls? I glanced at Sam. He had stuffed so much cake into his mouth that he had to put his little index finger to his lips to keep pieces from falling out. Suddenly his eyes widened, a signal that he was about to cough or throw up. "Here," I said, pouring him some water from the crystal pitcher. "Why do you put so much in your mouth at one time?" I looked around for extra napkins for him to spit it into. There weren't any.

"Mom, can I have tea?" Sarah asked. "She gave me a bowl like Ben's, but I think I'd like tea. With milk. Do you think that would be okay?"

I picked up the napkin off the floor where Sam had knocked it, grabbed Ben's and Sarah's, and helped Sam hold his crystal water goblet. "Don't you dare throw up," I said.

"Mom, is that okay?"

"Sarah, just ask her."

"Would you make my chocolate?" Ben asked me.

"Can't you ask her?" Sarah said. "I don't want to ask her."

"No," I said loudly, and Todd and Monsieur Courtois looked up from Todd's map of the Dordogne. I smiled weakly and reached for a thermos of what I hoped was warm milk. "Your French is better than mine," I whispered to Sarah. "You ask her."

"But Mom," Sarah whined.

Ben handed me his bowl and then reached for the plastic carton of *chocolat,* squeezing it. The lid flew off and poof, a thin cloud of chocolate dust rose from the carton and drifted down upon the freshly pressed tablecloth.

Madame Bonnabry came back in with a silver tray with tea poured for Todd and me. She put the china cup and saucer in front of me. At that exact moment, Sam grabbed another piece of cake and stuffed it into his mouth. I tried to grab him, and in his effort to get away, he slipped off his pillow and chair, sending his china plate flying toward me and his chair banging onto the wooden floor. Amazingly, I caught the plate midair with my right hand.

Madame Bonnabry jumped for the chair like a basketball player. She righted it and fixed the pillow, and Sam climbed up to reach for more cake.

"Honey," Todd said, "is Rocamadour that place you were talking about, you know, that château and church that the Johnsons told us about?"

"Mom," Sarah whispered, pointing to my teacup.

"Uh, yes, I think."

Madame Bonnabry put Sam back in his chair, and I asked her for Sarah's tea. Ben was slurping his hot chocolate when Monsieur Courtois bid us a pleasant evening.

"You must see Sarlat while you're here. Here is my address," he said, scribbling it on a card and handing it to Todd. "Perhaps we can have an aperitif."

Todd started going on about how we'd love to do that. What was he doing? Getting us committed to yet another table, set with crystal and alcohol and maybe some pistachios and pâté. Was he completely clueless?

We said our goodbyes to Monsieur Courtois, and Madame Bonnabry walked him to the door.

I groaned at Todd.

"What?" he said, dumbfounded. "What is it?"

I shook my head in frustration.

"You don't look so good," he said, patting my shoulder. "And you're sweating. Are you getting sick?"

Just as I was about to let him have it, Madame Bonnabry walked in.

"He is a very important man in Paris, you know, but he always takes time to check on me when he comes for the weekend to Sarlat," Madame Bonnabry said. "When my son died, he became especially dear to me."

"Did your son die recently?" Todd asked. He doesn't mind asking those kinds of questions. I kept telling him how all the books said that the French like to keep family things private, but he just came out and asked. So far no one had ever seemed offended.

"Yes, I'm afraid it has been almost five months ago. It is really a very sad story."

The children were fidgeting in their chairs, so I sent them upstairs to play, with a stern warning about running and jumping on the beds.

Madame Bonnabry continued, "He was a wonderful boy."

I smiled to myself that she still thought of him as a boy, though he must have been in his fifties. "He was an activist, very well known. He had begun to speak out about the harmful effects of big business on the human spirit and had received many death threats. He died in a car accident. He had so much left to say." Madame Bonnabry's eyes began to well up with tears. "He was a poet, you know," she said, took a deep breath and smiled proudly. "He had five books of poetry published. We were all quite proud of him."

"And you have other children?" I said.

"Yes, one of my boys is a wine steward in Marseille, a very important one, very well known. People from all over France seek his advice. And there is my oldest—he owns a computer business in Lyon and has thirty-five people working for him. Oh, he's quite intelligent. But his wife—she's an idiot. She has one of the top twenty-five fortunes in France, and she is very smart, but she knows nothing about caring for their children. She hires a large staff to care for the house and children, and do you know what she gave my son for his fiftieth birthday?" I shook my head. "A three-hundred-year-old terra-cotta pot! Imagine that." Madame Bonnabry shook her head in disbelief. "It's just incredible. And you should see the state of her garden."

Madame Bonnabry went on to tell us more about her life story, how she started out working as a teacher and then became a mother and devoted her time to raising her children. Then she went back to school and ran a bookstore, as well as running a home for children. Then she changed tracks and opened up a *chambre d'hôte* near Paris in Dreux, before her divorce. Her *chambre d'hôte* was rated the top in her area. As she spoke I began to hear the boys racing across the floor upstairs. I hoped she didn't notice.

"It sounds like your wild horses need a *fessée,*" she said quite seriously, looking up at the ceiling. Usually the word *fesse* made me laugh, but not today. *Fesse* was the word for "buttock," making *fessée* a "buttocker"—the French word for "spanking."

"I, uh—I'll tell them to stop," I said, feeling my face flush.

I ran up the stairs and put a stop to the racing and dressed everyone in jackets for our night out. She was supposed to be a lovey-dovey grandma. Didn't she understand that children can only be quiet and still for so long?

We found the tourism office and loaded up on brochures for things that would keep us out of that house, and then went to a park and let the kids run crazy. I ran my mouth about how Madame Bonnabry was just expecting way too much of our children and how unreasonable it was to have china on the table for them. Then we found a pizza place for dinner where we could relax. They still had breakable plates and glasses on the table, but they let us sit in the back and there was a jukebox playing that would drown out all the noise we made. I ate slowly, not wanting to hurry back to the room.

She was waiting for us when we returned, just like Madame Mallet did at home, wanting to know where we went and what we did. Then she insisted on bringing us bottles of water and slippers she thought might fit us, as well as pointing us to her library of books, which we were welcome to peruse. Then she went to lock the front door and left us for bed.

I stayed in her library and studied her collection, which was quite a strange mix for a grandma. Besides the dozens of tour books on Domme and Sarlat and La Dordogne, there was a shelf full of nutrition books, as well as *Comment comprendre votre horoscope,* books on personality types, and a book by Brigitte Bardot called *The Sixth Sense of Animals.* There were books about extrasensory perception, and two others that I pulled out and looked at: *Les 111 energies cosmiques et la loi du karma* and *Hypnose et télépathie.*

The next morning the children woke early, as they always do on vacation, and started dancing. We tried to get them to stop, but then they'd start again, sitting on the bed and insisting that they were just dancing quietly while sitting. There was virtually nothing we could threaten them with—no toys to take away, and only music videos and boring news and interview programs on the little black-and-white television. I was considering giving out *fessées* when suddenly there was a knock at the door.

Everyone froze, and before I could get to the door, Madame Bonnabry unlocked it with a key, stuck her head in, and shushed us like a librarian. "*There is a young lady downstairs who came in very late last night, after a long voyage. She needs to sleep. I'll serve breakfast at eight-thirty.*" Then she closed the door. What were we going to do for two and a half hours? I was ready right then to pack up and leave for our drive through the Dordogne. "Let's at least stay for breakfast," Todd said. "Don't take this so personally. The walls must be thin."

It was still dark outside, so we played twenty questions, I spy, and tic-tac-toe until eight-thirty finally came. I had read the children the riot act, and they were on their best behavior. Madame Bonnabry came to the table with coffee for Todd and me, tea for Sarah, and *chocolat chaud* for the boys. "I hope you like the bread this morning. I bought it at the market. They use a grain that was from Egypt that people used one thousand years ago in this region that they are beginning to use again."

This time she went around pushing our chairs closer to the table and then sat down with us. She cooed over the children as if nothing had happened. "How are my wild horses this morning?" she asked. Ben smiled sheepishly. "Tell me about yourself," she said, and Ben told her that he liked to draw and play soccer, and that he was in CE2—third grade. She told him that she was sure that he was very athletic, that you could tell by looking at him that he was fast. I waited for her to scold him about the upstairs races, but she didn't.

"You know, you are very lucky to have parents who take you places, to see the world. When I was a child in Poland, my parents ran a boardinghouse and people from all over would come through, and I would learn from them. But then the war came."

"You're from Poland?" Todd asked.

"Oh, yes. My grandparents had a farm outside of town and grew wheat and had several animals that they kept only to entertain the children. When the Germans moved in, they commandeered all the animals from farms in the area for food, and one day they saw my sister and I riding our pig around the farm. Just like a horse! Ah, we'd have so much fun. That pig was faster than the soldiers were," she said, laughing. "And the sight of the pig running with two little girls on its back made them all fall down, it was so funny."

We all laughed.

"Those soldiers told my grandfather, 'That is the funniest sight we've seen for a while. You get to keep the pig.'"

We sat there and talked a long time over breakfast. I even

relaxed and stopped watching the children for manners. By our second cup of coffee, she had even pulled out a book of her son's poetry and stood up from her chair to read one of his poems. She read it with great feeling, pausing at the right times and using inflection for effect.

"That was beautiful," Todd said.

"Yes, it was," she said. "We all need more poetry in our lives. And it brings me peace to think of him."

It was touching for her to let us into her life like that. I had been so petty to dislike her for reprimanding my children, for embarrassing me. I was sad to pack our bags, and I lingered in the hallway before we left.

Maybe she sensed that, for whatever reason, I needed her approval. As Todd packed the trunk and the children "helped" him, she told me that she thought we were good parents, that our children looked at us with admiration. I thanked her for telling me and said that it was difficult to tell how one was doing at the job. She clutched my hand and said my children were beautiful and *bien élevés*—well brought up.

As I made my way to the car, I sensed she needed something too, that our visit wasn't properly finished. "Have you ever heard of face readings?" she asked. She explained that it was the study of how face shape reveals personality and that she had some ideas about career choices that might be suitable for our children. "Perhaps it is my mission, to guide and educate," she said.

"With Benjamin it is easy. He has the face of the artist. One can tell by the shape of his face that he is very intelligent. As for Sarah, that gap between her front teeth means power. I don't know her well enough to say more, but I can say that whatever she does she will do with great power. As for Sam, it is too early to tell. You just have to make sure that this wild horse doesn't run in the road."

We gave her *bisoux,* and she asked us to please come again.

I'm afraid we never went back, though Mary Ann made a trip and came back with news. Madame Bonnabry was closing the doors to her *chambre d'hôte* and taking retirement at the age of seventy-seven. Apparently, some young snobby Parisians complained to the tourism office that during their stay they had been forced to share the bathroom with the owner, and so the tourism office took her *chambre d'hôte* off its list. Not to worry, she told Mary Ann, she had plenty of interests to fill her life. In all of Domme there was not one tearoom, and she was thinking that that might just be her next adventure. After all, she loved being with people, and she could set a pretty table. Perhaps they could even have occasional poetry readings. People need more poetry in their lives, and she had five great books in mind.

33. *Closest and Dearest*

Up until our big confrontation, the only time I had ever made Madame Mallet cry was when she came over for cake and ice cream to celebrate her seventy-fifth birthday. "You've given me a beautiful memory to dream about," she said as we kissed her goodnight. "I'll sleep like a baby."

She let the tears trickle down her face, dabbing at them once they reached her chin. I handed her a tissue and we smiled together, basking in the warm glow of shared friendship.

I had no idea that just three weeks later her eyes would spurt out tears like water guns and our friendship would be teetering on the edge of destruction.

It was a silly thing that started it all. I'm not a teenager anymore, and it embarrasses me that I was bothered by it, but I was.

I had just turned the key in my mailbox when I saw Madame Mallet giving me the once-over from Madame Fauriaux's yard. *Am I not fully dressed?* I wondered, checking myself. It was those jeans. I had asked Todd if they made me look fat, and he had said that they didn't, but I still wasn't sure. *Maybe it's my bad posture,* I thought, straightening up. I really needed to work on not slumping my shoulders. Madame Mallet marched toward me on a mission to tell me whatever it was, staring disapprovingly at my stomach.

"Watch out, there," she said, and wagged her finger at my tummy. "You're getting a little belly."

I sucked it in, floored by her uninvited reproach.

"Madame Mallet," I said, "that's not nice to say."

"It is something that's easily remedied, Rébecca," she assured me, and began to instruct me on the most effective exercises for the tummy region.

This was too incredible. For three years I had put up with her rude comments on my parenting, my clothing, my children's clothing, my automobiles, and the way I cooked, cleaned, and put out the trash. But to comment on my *body?* My own mother didn't do that.

Todd walked up, clueless as to what was going on. They exchanged kisses and small talk as I stood there glaring at the ground. After a few awkward moments of silence, Madame Mallet went back to her yard.

"You won't believe what that witch said to me," I said to Todd, not caring about my volume. She couldn't understand English anyway, and I was furious.

For the next few days I avoided her.

"Give me a week to cool off, and I can start taking it again," I said to Todd. When the mailman buzzed down our street on his motorbike, I stayed by the window until Madame Mallet had collected her mail and shut the door behind her. When we were going somewhere and needed to get to the car and she was in her garden, I started a conversation with one of the kids before we opened the door and continued it outside while we got into the car, pretending not to notice her.

For days she piddled about in her garden, waiting for me. Once she even started a fire in a metal bucket in her driveway. Sarah walked over to ask her what she was doing. "I'm burning my lover's letters before Monsieur Mallet finds out," she said, tempting me to go talk to her. I wasn't ready.

Then came winter vacation and our trip to the Alps.

Todd loaded the car with our suitcases. Madame Mallet was out there, waiting to give us the standard *avant le voyage* interrogation/lecture. She would begin by wanting us to show her exactly on the map where we were going so that she, who had never actually driven a car, could point out the quickest route. This was always followed by a short discourse on the products and sights of that region, of which she was well aware, even though she had not ever been there herself. Finally, she would warn us about the rules of the autoroute and would ask my husband, the tire designer, whether his tires were properly inflated. After kisses all around, she would stand at our gate and wave and watch us leave. Most often, when we returned five minutes later for the camera or our passports, she'd still be there.

It was time for the lecture. She was outside and ready, and I was stalling.

"Would you go out there and get in the car?" Todd said. He was always grouchy before a trip.

"Okay, if you're sure that you're ready," I said. "I'd like to skip you-know-who's lecture."

We headed to the car and called the kids over. Madame Mallet had been talking to Ben, but I saw her look at me as I opened the car door.

"Oh, the video camera, I forgot," said Todd and left me there, stranded. I hated him.

Madame Mallet saw her chance. I couldn't escape.

"Is everything okay, Rébecca?" she asked.

"No," I said, surprised at myself. "Everything's not okay."

Apparently I was going to tell her how I felt. The children jumped into the car and shut the doors, staring at both of us with big eyes.

"What's the problem, *ma chérie*?" she said, putting her hand on my arm. "What's wrong?"

That was it. She asked, so I told her. "You . . . you hurt my feelings."

Madame Mallet's hands flew up to her mouth. Her face wrinkled into a tight red ball, and her eyes flooded with tears.

"But, but," she stammered, "you should've told me, you should've said . . ."

"I did, Madame Mallet, I did! I said 'That's not nice to say.' "

"But I didn't know!"

"But I told you!"

"Oh, *ma chérie,* my sweet Rébecca." At this point, her jets started firing, getting me wet. She looked so childlike there, covering her eyes with her hands and then pulling them back to show me her tears.

I glanced at the porch and saw a flicker of movement. It was Todd, hiding behind the door, scared to come out.

"My Rébecca, I've always said that you are a beautiful woman. You are. You mustn't listen to me. I didn't want to hurt you. I was just talking, trying to have something to say. Why, look at me—I have just as big a stomach as you do. Please don't be mad."

"It's okay, Madame Mallet. It's okay." Why did she have to be so pitiful? She started me crying too.

"It's over then?" she asked. "It's done? We love each other, don't we?"

"Yes, we love each other."

"You know, it is rare that I cry like this. It's rare. Really," she said, dabbing at her eyes with a handkerchief. "I would never want to hurt you."

"It's over, Madame Mallet. I should have told you sooner."

The front door opened and Todd peeked out.

"Is everything okay?" he asked.

"Don't be afraid, *mon chéri*. You can come out. You know, I don't cry very often," she said, showing him the tears on her face. "We're friends again. You know, Rébecca, I told my husband after our conversation the other morning that maybe I had been naughty. I could tell by what you said to your husband that you weren't happy with me."

"Oh yes?"

"Yes, you talk really fast when you're angry. I may not know English, but I'm an expert at people."

The day after vacation, I told my friend Jessie about it and asked her not to tell anyone, on account of the belly part being so embarrassing. Jessie went straight home and told her husband, Henry, who was German and understood European people.

At a wine and cheese party the next weekend, Henry stopped me by the assorted nuts. "Jessie told me the latest Madame Mallet story. What are you so bothered about?" he asked, reaching for a cashew. "Don't you know that Madame Mallet paid you the *biggest* compliment?"

"Huh?" I said, feeling my face flush. People began to gather.

"She *loves* you, Becky! Don't you know that?"

"Well, I . . ."

"What's this about?" said Cynthia, a beautiful British friend of mine who looks just like Claudia Schiffer. "Another Madame Mallet story? Oh, I want to hear this—that woman is incredible."

"Madame Mallet told Becky that she was getting fat," Jessie said, "and Henry was just explaining that actually she was paying her quite a compliment."

"She didn't exactly say *that*," I said.

"But you're not getting fat," Cynthia assured me. "I can't believe she said that. You're in great shape. I've been thinking that you've lost weight, if anything."

I was dying. The whole corner of our room, all the women and all their husbands, were focused on my body, evaluating me for weight gain.

"Don't you see?" Henry said. "You are such a close friend to her that she can be rude to you. You've made it. French people are only rude like that to their closest and dearest friends."

"None of my French friends has ever told me that I'm fat," Jessie said, wistfully.

"She didn't say that I was *fat* exactly—just that I was getting a . . . a belly."

"Anyway, celebrate it," Henry said, and took another sip of his Bordeaux.

34. A Home for the Greatest Show on Earth

I had no decorating style of my own until Ben hit fourth grade and had to do a class project on snakes. It was a group project, so for about a month Ben and his buddy Jean-Marie walked home with their classmate Édouard and they worked on it at his kitchen table.

Édouard lived with his parents and five brothers and sisters in what his mother called their city house, a first-floor apartment in a three-hundred-year-old building. The first time I went to pick him up, it changed my life.

I had met Édouard's mother at the school courtyard. My French friend Camille said she was nice but a little *BCBG*—*bon chic, bon genre*—the label the French had for the preppy French women descended from nobility. Their children were easy to pick out on the playground; the girls wore smocked dresses and Mary Janes, and the boys wore knickers and leather shoes with long socks. The mothers were easily identifiable as well—very classic, very proper, with their hair in a bun or brushed neatly or tucked under a padded headband that coordinated with their clothes. But Édouard's mother was different. With her headband and wool skirts Madame de Thiolas wore crazy necklaces—beautiful tangles of wire and colored glass. And matching earrings that bobbed. And she smoked. In my limited experience, *BCBGs* didn't do that in public.

The first time I went to pick up Ben I buzzed the intercom but I couldn't get the door to open. Madame de Thiolas called out directions on how to open it, but I still couldn't get it, probably because I was still unnerved from trying to squeeze my little Honda through the narrow road that twisted into her parking lot. Finally she came out and opened the door for me, holding her cigarette with one hand and holding back her dog with the other.

She was very polite and formal, and welcomed me into her salon. *What a fire hazard,* I thought at first glance at all the paintings and chairs and stacks of boxes and books. Then my eyes adjusted in the dim light and I saw how stunningly beautiful the room was. There were tables loaded with stacks of books and collections of shells and magnifying glasses and three upholstered chairs and a red velvet canapé, none of which matched but somehow went together. The walls were upholstered in a blue damask and were completely covered with framed and unframed paintings—some that the children had done, and some they hadn't—big landscapes and a half-dressed woman that looked suspiciously like a younger Madame de Thiolas, and one of a dead bird hanging upside down. Taffeta drapes hung from the high ceiling to the Turkish rug on the floor, and there were bookshelves crowded with books and sculptures and stacks of magazines and a set of little metal soldiers that someone was in the middle of painting. Madame de Thiolas cleared some papers off the canapé and invited me to sit down.

"Your home is so beautiful," I said.

"Thank you," she said, puffing her smoke away from me, as the dog settled by her feet. "It's a little crowded during the week, especially with my work, but we have our country house to spread out on the weekends. I would love to have room for a studio of my own, but here the children can walk to school and Pierre to work. One cannot have everything, and this suits us well."

"So you're an artist?" I asked.

"No, not an artist. An artisan, really. The paintings are my husband's hobby. I create light fixtures. And sometimes jewelry. Whatever I can make with wire and glass."

She must have made the chandelier, a big fixture of wire curlicues and pink glass teardrops. It was gorgeous.

"I've never seen anything like that."

"No, I make what I like. I suppose it is the French way to surround oneself with the things one loves. I couldn't live any differently."

"It is so elegant, but so warm."

"Thank you. You know, when I was young my father took me to Connecticut on business and one family entertained us in their home. It was a grand home, but I must say that it was too perfect for my taste—too stiff, too sterile. Everything matched—even the artwork! Is that the American way?"

"Well, uh, I don't know . . ."

"That would stifle me—to lock myself into such a formula. I didn't understand it. What if you found something you loved but it didn't fit? What are you supposed to do—abandon it? No, I couldn't live like that."

That was just how I felt in my house—locked in. Locked in by a chair I had bought at Service Merchandise. I bought it because it had an ottoman and it was on sale, and now it was holding me hostage with its overstuffed arms to a room full of mauve and sage green. I hated mauve and sage green. But I couldn't go as far as Madame de Thiolas—maybe it was American, but I liked things to match. It started me thinking. What did I like? What did I like? Then I saw it.

I was picking the kids up from school the first time I noticed it. It shocked me so that I lost track of where my legs were going and stepped right into a pile of dog poop.

"Gross, Mom! Your shoe!" Ben shouted.

"Oh, yeah," I said, scraping my feet against the curb, my eyes still stuck on the five-foot-tall circus poster plastered to the electrical box beside our parking space. I was love struck. It was the most beautiful thing I had ever seen, an advertisement for Cirque Medrano, with painted animals that seemed to look me over with their hypnotizing eyes. They were so odd and magical that I could almost hear the carousel music, plinking and tinkling like from a hand-cranked toy. It played faintly in my ears at first, and as I stared at the animals, the music soon drowned out the chatty banter of my kids and the sound of the dry leaves skittering across the sidewalk and whirling around us like a little tornado.

"Right, Mom? Mom?" Sarah's faint voice echoed in the distance. I blinked back to reality.

"Give me a sec, honey," I said, pointing to the poster. "What do you think of that?"

"Cool," Ben and Sarah said in unison, and then they started arguing about who jinxed whom first.

The five bewitching faces called me back, pulling me into their world, and I stood there in my dirty shoes, looking at them peeking out at me from behind a brilliant yellow taffeta curtain. The colors, I thought, those were the colors I liked— those were the colors I wanted around me, deep hues that don't have the blood drained out of them. And the animals—how fun! I wanted—I needed—more fun around me. The stunningly blue elephant, her forehead and trunk bejeweled and painted in swirls of gold and red like an indigo sari. The golden eyes of the bear, and his goofy pink-lipped smile. The zebra with his shiny black mohawk. What personalities! The zebra was clearly the con artist, and the shy tiger? He was crouched in the corner, nervously holding the curtain up to his mouth, as if he hoped I wouldn't notice him. The camel didn't care if I looked at him at all. He was too busy sending puffs of smoke swirling from the cigarette in the brass holder he held tight to his teeth. Yes, in that red velvet fez, he had that mysterious bad boy look. His charm was working on me.

"Can we go there, Mom?" Ben begged. "To the circus? Please?"

"No, I don't think so," I said. We'd been to a circus in Clermont before, and I had no intention of going back. It had been a one-ring show under a striped red and yellow tent at Place de Premier Mai with a tightrope walker who looked just like Matt Lauer and a weary troop of animals that needed a couple of vitamins with their coffee. Of course, they did have a group of housecats with frilly collars jumping through hoops, and I was impressed at that. But overall, it left us stoop-shouldered and depressed. But the idea of a circus? Now, that was another thing. I've always loved it—the concept of a world where people wear feathers and walk through the air on strings while the animals wear clothes and dance the jitterbug. An upside-down world.

My three children weren't so fascinated, just sitting there in the open car, their stomachs growling, while I stared at the poster and pointed out all the details, so I took them home. Thankfully, the poster started popping up everywhere. Todd saw it and loved it, though not as much as I did. It was just a circus poster to him, not a symbol of my newfound freedom. My kids started saying that they liked the poster too, if only to save themselves from another tirade on its beauty. Every day for two weeks we found it all over town. If I was having a hard day and someone cut me off in traffic, I could see that poster and I'd feel better. A big loud "Ha!" would burst out of my mouth, scaring onlookers or passersby. If I was walking a city street and lugging bags of groceries while trying to keep Sam from stepping in dog poop, I could see the poster and the bags would feel lighter and the poop piles would seem fewer and farther between. If the kids were arguing, I could say, "Hey, look," and point to the poster at an intersection or on a wall, and they would stop and laugh and then start arguing about which animal was the coolest or which had the best eyes.

Soon I became so attached to the poster that I started worrying about losing it; a circus wouldn't stay in town forever. One Sunday I read in the paper that Cirque Medrano had its final matinee show that very afternoon. They were leaving already? What would I do? Men with buckets and brushes would be papering over my gorgeous posters any day now, I thought. My only option was to find one to keep for myself, for our family. I would rip it right off the street corner and bring it into our home. Why not?

Todd went along with me and packed the children into the car. Surely there was one, a little loose around the edges that needed a home. We tried corner after corner. Todd would slow the car and I would jump out, run up to the poster, and pull at it. But every time it wouldn't budge, or it ripped into little shreds in my fingers. Meanwhile, Ben sat in the backseat, saying that everyone was staring and thinking we were the Doofus family. After about six or seven tries, we gave up.

"Why don't I just drive over to the circus and see if they would sell me one?" asked Todd. Why didn't I think of that? Of course they would have one. Why, I bet they'd even give him one, free advertising and all. Todd dropped the kids and me off at the house and left for the circus.

"You children have the best daddy there is," I said to the kids as I searched my walls for the perfect empty spot for my new poster.

When I heard the car in the driveway, I sat down in the armchair I hated and tried to look calm. *He probably couldn't get one. Don't get excited.*

"Hel-lo-o," Todd called.

"Did you get it?" I called out in a thin voice.

"They didn't have that one," Todd said, quickly adding, "but I brought you another one that's pretty cool."

My heart dropped. I had seen them all. The one with the line of elephants. The one with the mermaid with the square-shaped head and the skinny clown with a fishing pole. They were just ordinary circus posters—not like mine. Mine came with the sound of tinkling music and the smell of cotton candy and sawdust.

Todd walked into the kitchen with a notebook-size poster in his hand. "I'm sorry," he said with sad eyes, handing me the mermaid one. "This was all they had."

Of course I thanked him and tried to be gracious. I said I would keep trying. I was sure I could find one on the street.

Then one Saturday I was stopped at a busy intersection when I caught a glimpse of something familiar on a wall to my right. There it was—my big poster with all their faces— in perfect condition, no less, and with the edges loose and curling over. I pulled over and left my lights blinking, not caring about the people staring at me or the honks of cars whizzing by. I pulled on an edge. It loosened just a bit. An old man with a purse walked up behind me and started talking at me and wagging his finger. I ignored him. He persisted, saying something about public property.

"*Excusez-moi,*" I said, scaring him with my accent. He hurried across traffic and kept watch on me from the other side of the street. I tugged uselessly at the poster. It wouldn't budge. It was over. I had to stop pulling on it and, with everyone watching from their cars, turn around and walk back to my car.

On Sunday, Todd brought the big kids home from the skating rink. Sarah came racing into the house. "Sit down on the couch!" she said. Ben followed close behind with a silly grin on his face.

"Close your eyes! I'll tell you when to open them!" he said, out of breath. Sam and I sat down, and I closed my eyes. I could hear my husband's footsteps on the stairs and Sarah and Ben laughing.

"Okay," Todd said, "you can look now."

I opened my eyes and there was my husband standing behind my big beautiful poster. My dear golden-eyed animals were life-size!

"What do you think?" he asked. "I pulled it off where you saw it yesterday on N9. You must have loosened it for me."

I knew then and there that I would love that man until the end of my life.

So I bought a piece of plywood from Bricomarché, painted it a bright blue, decoupaged my poster to it, and propped it on the landing of my stairs. It wasn't sticky anymore, but you could still see the wide brush marks from the glue. I liked it like that, looking as though someone had just taken one of those wallpaper brooms and brushed it on, like a billboard.

And though I didn't put it out for the purpose of startling people, that did seem to be its effect. My American friend Kate blew into the house one day, all aflutter over a series of chicken recipes her mother had sent from home. "I'm going to get them copied and pass them out to all the expats," she said as she headed up the stairs. "What with mad cow disease and the lack here of cream of chicken or mushroom soup, planning meals has just gotten impossible for everyone."

I was climbing the stairs ahead of her, saying something about how that was very nice of her, when I heard her give out a little gasp. It was my fault. I hadn't warned her, and just at the moment when she had glanced up from her loafers, she was nose to nose with a brightly painted tiger. Kate grabbed for the stair railing, as if the troop of life-size animals might trample her in their stampede down the stairs.

"Oh. Guess I didn't tell you about my latest project," I said.

"Wow," she said, reaching out her hand to touch the shiny surface of the poster.

"What do you think?" I asked. "I know it's kind of wacky, but I had seen it for months around town and just fell in love with it. I liked their faces." For a slight moment I felt a tinge of embarrassment. What was I doing, hanging up a weird poster like that in my house? Kate's house was so tasteful, very Pottery Barn. Very Traditional Home.

"It's really . . . interesting," she said, searching for words. "Where did you get it?"

"Off a fuse box in town," I said.

"You're kidding! You just peeled it right off, right in public?"

I nodded and then returned her to the safer conversation of chicken and fish, where she was more comfortable. She probably thought I was nuts, but I loved my poster. And I didn't feel held hostage anymore. The poster might be a little crazy, but it was me.

. . .

JUST A FEW weeks later we were taking a trip and got stuck in a traffic jam in a town called Brives. It was hot, and the car was barely moving when Todd pointed across the street to a double-sided sign stapled around a phone pole. It was an ad for the Guignols, the famous papier-mâché-headed hand puppets that entertain children in parks all over France. It had the same wild colors as my poster, and I'd always loved the puppets' big noses and the pom-pom buttons down their shirts.

"Why don't you go get it?" Todd urged, grabbing my knee and daring me with a raised eyebrow.

I looked at the endless line of cars in front and behind us, all filled with bored people with nothing to look at.

"Uh, I don't know," I said.

"What's the problem? You chicken?" Todd said. "I know you want it. Look, the date's on the bottom. It finished last week. Why not take it?"

"Yeah, Mom. Go get it!" Sarah said, and then Ben piped up, leading them all in a chant, "Go, Mom! Go, Mom!"

So I opened the door and made a break for it. I ran in front of the car and had to climb over a waist-high metal barrier to get to it, but pulling it down was a cinch.

As I ran back to the car with the newest prize for our home, I looked at my crazy family. The kids were all laughing and waving their arms in a Rocky Balboa victory pose, following the example of my head cheerleader, rooting me on. I loved every one of them. My heart was racing, the air smelled sweet, like cotton candy, and I knew that our life was the greatest show on earth.

35. *Birds*

Gypsy was an annoying black bird, the family pet of the Roches, who lived across the street next to the Mallets. The Roches were always taking in wild animals and enjoying their company. Once they caught a rabbit and popped him right into a hutch in the backyard, and they kept a large toad named Hoquet (Hiccup) imprisoned in a garden pond on the right side of their house. They did add a gurgling fountain and some water plants to make him feel at home, but who knows if he was really happy there. The bird, however, seemed to love life with the Roches. They made sure to keep birdseed sprinkled on the concrete posts of their gate, and they talked to him and conducted daily bird-training sessions.

I admit, I never tried to like that bird. Every time I wanted to sweep my balcony or put Sam in the swing we tied to the cherry tree, Gypsy would fly around my head or peck at my shoes or poop on my railing. The first time he flew in to visit me, Alain and Pascale and the children were out having Sunday lunch on their picnic table. "Look, he wants to meet you," Alain called from across the street. I tried to smile and resisted the temptation to swat at him.

"He's pretty," I called back.

"You should hear him sing," Alain said, and went back to the cheese course.

Gypsy wouldn't leave me alone. I turned my back to the street. "Get!" I said to the bird. Gypsy tried to land on my shoulder. I couldn't take it and went inside.

I've never liked birds. It's probably my mother's fault. Every time she would read that line from Dr. Seuss, "There's a bird in your ear, I fear," she would wiggle her pointer finger at my ear. Her fingernail felt like a little beak on a bird trying to flit into my head and make a nest in my brain.

About a week and a half later, Gypsy stopped coming by. The Roches looked for him for days. Alain asked if I had seen him, and as I said no, that I hadn't, I tried to force my eye not to twitch. I didn't need to feel bad about it. One whack with a broom doesn't kill a bird, does it? He did fly away. I was just training Gypsy to leave me alone, not trying to assassinate him. Anyway, they still had their toad and rabbit.

Birds were a big thing in France. Lots of people had them in cages, and nearly everybody fed the wild ones. There was a bird lady at Place de Jaude just like the one in *Mary Poppins*. Every day she would come and sit on a bench outside of C&A with an armload of baguettes stacked up like kindling. Birds came from miles around, lighting on her hat and her shoulders, and all morning she broke off pieces and scattered them to the flocks at her feet. It wasn't just her. On the way to school the children and I had to constantly tromp through baguette crumbs that people threw down from their windows for the pigeons. For a long while I wondered why they did that. The bread got all soggy in the rain, and as far as I could see the only reward people got was streets and balconies covered with poop. It was a terrible problem at the cathedral. Every year they had to hire crews to scrub Jesus' head and shoulders and clean up the gargoyles and all the saints.

Just around the corner from our house on allée des Cerisiers, one of the houses had a tin-roofed shack in the front yard. Anyone could see into it since the front was all chicken wire, and it was full of pigeons and doves. I didn't know why, but I found that I couldn't resist looking in there every time I took a walk. I used to stop and stare, until one of the owners caught me. They started coming out and standing in their yard until I went away. Even after that day I still stopped, but I always made up a reason—I bent down to tie Sam's shoes or had a drink from my water bottle. I just couldn't pass by without looking and listening to the slap and flap of their wings and the cooing and warbling of their voices.

I asked Madame Mallet about them, hoping they were being raised as pets and not destined for a stew or the spit, flavored with *beurre* and *herbes de Provence*.

"Of course they will be eaten," she said, shaking her head at my ignorance. "Anyway, doves aren't anything to get excited about. They're just pigeons with white feathers." Then Madame Mallet paused and said, "By the way, where exactly are you going on those walks of yours?"

"Nowhere. I just walk for the exercise and to see the birds."

"Oh," she said, disappointed. "I thought you might have a French boyfriend, but since it lasts only thirty-five minutes, I wasn't so sure."

· · ·

WHEN SARAH TURNED thirteen, I took her on a girls' weekend to Paris. I hoped that we could make some good memories to help us weather the teenage years. On the four-hour train trip we drank *chocolat chaud* and made a list of all the things we wanted to do. Eating of course was a priority, as was hitting the flea markets, but we also wanted to include a little bit of culture. We'd start by touring the Cathédrale de Notre Dame. Without Sam along this time, we wouldn't have to rush.

Paris was as outlandishly beautiful as always, with its Gothic architecture, crowded sidewalk cafés, wrought-iron balconies overflowing with flowers, and streets bustling with stylish Parisians talking on their cell phones and tourists with their fanny packs gazing up at the sights.

It was Halloween back home in the States, but it was Toussaint (All Saints) weekend in France, the time when families all over the country take off from work and school and gather together to remember their dear departed loved ones. The church was packed with throngs of tourists as well as faithful parishioners who had come to say a prayer and light a candle in memory of their relatives. We squeezed in and were swept around the church with the crowd. We struggled to see above the masses. Disappointed, we left to have a picnic lunch at a small park on the cathedral grounds.

In the shadow of the church towering over us like a stone giant with its gargoyles and flying buttresses, we ate our baguette sandwiches and talked, throwing bits of bread to the tiny wrens at our feet. They pecked at them hungrily.

A ponytailed man in a black turtleneck on a nearby bench watched us feeding the birds as he smoked. After a few minutes he spoke up.

"They'll eat from your hand if you wish. I can show you if you want."

Sarah looked at me with pleading eyes, and I handed the man a piece of my sandwich.

"You hold your hand steady and you mustn't look at them. Just continue talking, but quietly, while offering the bread. Like this, see?" He pinched a scrap of crust and lowered it in front of him. He looked at us and in a quiet monotone said, "They'll see it. If you are patient, they'll come."

We tore at our bread and nervously held it out, forcing ourselves to stare down at our feet. It was hard to be still, wanting to look, wanting to coax them or call to them. But in less than a minute, out of the corner of my eye, I spied one and then two tiny wrens hovering around Sarah's hand. Darting between her fingers, they took little pecks.

My fingers tingled in anticipation. I steadied my hand and took a slow, deep breath. There was absolute stillness. As crowds of people walked by, just ten feet away, I focused on the shadow of the swaying trees lapping at my feet like a wave. Finally I felt the flutter of feathers brush my hand.

It was then that I realized what the fascination with birds was all about. Part of it was their cooing and warbling and the fluttering of their wings. But the rest was just pure beauty. In spite of being cynics, the French, whether in Paris or the countryside, were addicted to raw beauty and innocence and would put up with poop to get it. And what could be more beautiful—small feathery beings that swoop down out of the sky, land on a cherry branch, and send the petals falling like snow. And in the city, with the bustle of people, noise of the garbage trucks, and honking of the cars, it was nice to hear a songbird or the cooing of a pigeon on the windowsill.

After Sarah and I got home from Paris I took another look at the cathedral downtown and told Todd I had changed my perspective.

"If you don't look too closely," I said, "the pigeon poop on Jesus' head could be a lacy prayer shawl."

Todd made a face. "Beck, I think we've stayed in France a little too long."

36.   *Pride Goeth*

The most embarrassing moment of my life happened on a Friday night in the *Chansons et Poésies* aisle of a French bookstore. I crept home and promised God that I would start reading the Bible again. I knew the verse in Proverbs about pride going before the fall, but until that night I didn't know God meant it literally.

Only a week before, I was feeling pretty good about my family and myself.

"Why, we're practically French," I bragged to Todd, who was watching TV.

He gave me a look.

"I'm serious. Look at what you're watching," I said, pointing to the French documentary on the wonderful world of mushrooms. No one would argue with me. While many of our expat friends were passing around videotapes of *Friends* and *Law and Order* that somebody's brother had sent them, we were perfectly content with our French entertainment and French life.

And that wasn't all. With the recent exodus of several experienced American expats, I had become one of the "old hands." The new people were always calling me. I would take them to the grocery store and show them what is detergent and what is cat litter, comfort them, and assure them that their children would eventually stop throwing up before school and that, with time, life would feel more normal. I helped make hair appointments and doctor's appointments— speaking on the phone, no less, the most difficult form of communication. My French was flowing like crazy. And my children's French was much better than mine.

"They speak with no accent," said our friend Gaston. It was indeed amazing. Sometimes when Ben and Sarah were playing with the neighbor kids, I'd leave the doors to the balcony open just so I could hear them talking with each other. And I loved seeing them in their Wednesday-afternoon sports classes. I'd sit on the sidelines, watching my debonair son leap and touché in his white fencing uniform. And then I'd drive over to Sarah's track and field class and watch her throw *le javelot* and see her consult with her coach.

"We're making it," I said to Todd. "Doesn't that strike you? Can you believe it?"

Todd broke away from the mushroom show and stared at me.

"We're living and working—okay, I'm living and you're working—and going about our normal life in a whole different country and language, and it's no big deal. But it is."

"Yes, it's incredible," Todd said, looking back to the TV.

"Why don't we go out Friday night and celebrate," I said. "With the kids—really celebrate. Go out to eat and to the bookstore like we used to at home."

Todd gave me a nod, and I started planning. We'd have to flip-flop our regular recipe for a Friday night out, since people eat late, but it could still work. The kids would love to pick out a couple of books, and I could get that textbook for my French class. I started picturing the five of us laughing and talking and raising our glasses in a toast to our own success. I would wear my black dress pants, and I might even put on a scarf—French women always wore scarves. And my black jacket—they always wore black. This was going to be great.

Friday night came, and it wasn't starting out well. Sam missed his nap and was cranky, so I filled him full of the macaroni and cheese that someone had sent me from home and *pain au lait* and tried to soothe him. "We're going out with Daddy to see some books. Won't that be fun?" Sam looked unimpressed. "And then we'll go out for crêpes. Wouldn't you like a chocolate crêpe?"

At the mention of one of his favorite treats, Sam leapt at me with his macaroni and cheese hands, smearing orange goo all over my black jacket. So much for the French black. I'd have to wear my Lands' End red field coat, but no problem. At least I wouldn't be wearing white tennis shoes. You can always tell an American by white tennis shoes.

The big bookstore downtown, Les Volcans, was packed. The narrow rooms snaked into other narrow rooms, going up a few steps and then down a few steps, the tall shelves of books arranged like a maze for skinny people. The thin young women were dressed to impress, with their high heels and short little skirts and stylish leather blazers belted at their tiny waists. Their heels tapped against the linoleum as they moved gracefully through the store. They would stop for a moment, purse their lips as they surveyed the shelf for the book in question, and then bend down like a dancer to grasp it with their pretty hands. The older women moved elegantly through the aisles as well in their long wool coats with matching purses and shoes. The men came in various sizes and stood in front of the shelves and tables of books, turning the pages quietly. There were couples standing very close to each other, pointing out pictures or passages and then murmuring quietly. Even the children's section was fairly quiet, as mothers leaned over the tables, showing their children the brightly colored pages. Occasionally the children would speak, whispering in their cute baby French about the pig on the page that was carrying an umbrella or asking *Maman* when she would be finished and they could all walk home.

I might have marched in confidently, but, standing there in my big red field jacket and clunky black clogs among all these beautiful people, I felt like a frumpy giant. I had intended to speak French to my children for the evening, but what was I thinking? They'd probably say "Huh?" loudly and then, "What are you doing that for?" Even if they didn't say anything, it wouldn't be a good idea. Though I hated that it was true, I knew very well that my French only drew attention to the fact that I wasn't French. It'd be better to just whisper in English. So I whispered. Everyone in the room turned to stare. Even in a whisper my words sounded so harsh and rough next to the silky French sounds that curlicued out of their mouths. I tried to add a little lilt to my southern accent, but it just made me sound fake.

"Beck, do you mind taking Sam for a minute?" Todd asked loudly, not noticing the stares.

"Sure," I said, ready to negotiate a swapping-off agreement. Before I could say anything, he had disappeared through the rows of shelving.

That's okay, I thought, refusing to be disappointed. *We'll just go over to the children's books.*

"No! I don't want to go!" Sam said, trying to twist his hand out of mine. "I wanna wun awound."

"No, Sam, you can't run," I whispered, but he was off. He wormed his way around two old people, and by the time I caught up with him he was all the way to *Littérature.*

He set up a little course to do his running. Within ten steps or so there was a ramp, a carousel of paperbacks that he could spin, and a set of steps low enough for jumping. He quickly completed his circuit, landing on the linoleum with a proud "Ha!"

Adults were giggling.

"Sam," I called in a strained whisper. "Stop it, Sam!"

"Daddy," he said loudly. "Where are you, Daddy?" I followed him, trying to shush him, but he thought that was quite funny—me running after him, sounding like a train.

The next trip around I grabbed him by the hood. By this point we had an audience of several people fascinated with this cute little boy speaking English.

Sam laughed loudly. "Let's go again! Again!"

"No, Sam," I said, my whisper straining. "They have a rule here that you can't run. You have to stop that." Sam made a face. "Let's go look at the children's books, okay? I bet we can find one with dragons and castles."

"No! I don't want castles. I want to stay here and look for Daddy."

If we hadn't have been in *Littérature,* I probably would have given in and let him wander. I could have stood there and skimmed through anything in *Voyages* or *Cuisine et Vins,* but *Littérature?* None of these books had any pictures in them— just millions of pages of miles of French words.

I grabbed Sam's arm and pulled. "Let's go, Sam. Let's find Daddy."

"No!" Sam yelled, leaning away from me and wriggling his arm out of his coat.

"Samuel Ross, do what Mommy said."

Sam had wriggled his arm out and I almost lost my balance, holding tight to the empty sleeve as Sam swung away from me.

"I wanna see Daddy."

"You stop that right now," I said, and dragged him by his arm across two aisles toward *Jeunesse.* He was crying and fussing loudly all the way through *Santé* and *Bien-être.* Finally I pulled him to his feet. Sam shook out of my hands and began to walk to the children's section.

That's when it happened. He threw himself prostrate on the floor in front of my feet and I tripped. It wasn't just any trip—I was airborne. As I flew through the air, life began moving in slow motion. My clogs remained earthbound—I saw them on the floor. There I was, in my black socks with the threadbare toes, gliding through the air like Superman, or rather, Humiliated Woman. As I flew, I could feel my backpack purse gaining on me, like some short sidekick, rising up on my back and then flying over my head. I could hear the tinkling of centimes spilling onto the linoleum. Finally gravity won out, and I slid into home plate—right into a low shelf of *chansons et poésies.*

This could not be happening, I begged, lying on the cold floor.

It was.

I was on the ground, and Sam was behind me, screaming, freaked out that he had brought Mommy down. And hurrying over to him was a cute little brunette in a short plaid skirt and sparkly pantyhose.

"Samuel!" I said. I knew he wasn't hurt. I had cleared him by half a meter at least.

"Is he hurt?" the clerk asked with her beautiful French words. "Come, sit down," she said to him, pulling a stool out from another aisle. Meanwhile I was still in a heap on the floor, surrounded by my clogs, my purse, and a dozen or so centimes scattered around me. I got to my feet up as gracefully as I could. The crowd dispersed as I stuck my exposed toes back in my clogs.

I put him on the stool. He sat there with his eyes closed, screaming. It upset him, toppling his mother like a tree. Todd and the kids heard the screaming and appeared.

Todd saw the look on my face and picked Sam up.

"What . . . ?" he asked.

"We've got to get out of here," I said, teeth clenched, staring at the ground in utter embarrassment as we wound our way to the exit.

"But we can't leave yet. I have to buy this *répertoire.*" Ben said, handing me the little notebook. "Madame Fayolle said I have to have it Monday, and she'll be mad . . ."

"Okay, okay," Todd said, eyeing me nervously. We got in

line behind a dozen French people. I adjusted my purse and tried to focus on the floor tiles as Todd calmed Sam.

"What happened, Mom?" Sarah asked.

"Shhh."

"What's wrong, Mom?" Ben asked.

"Shhh."

"What's wrong with Mom?" they asked Todd.

"You want to know what's wrong? I'll tell you," I said. "Your little brother threw a fit and fell at my feet, and I tripped and flew through the air right over him and landed on the floor in front of everyone."

Sarah tried not to laugh right away, but Ben couldn't help it, and once he started, Sarah couldn't hold it anymore. The giggles burst out in spurts, and when she swallowed them, they burst out again. Todd pulled them aside and chastised them for laughing at their mother's misfortune.

By the time we reached the front of the line, Sam had stopped crying but Sarah began hiccuping.

"*Ça fait huit francs cinquante, s'il vous plaît,*" said the clerk. I fingered through my change and paid her.

"*Non, madame, ça fait huit francs cinquante,*" she repeated.

I looked at the change I had given her. "*C'est pas correct?*" I asked in my best accent.

"Oh, you're foreign," she said, breaking into flawless English. "Here, this coin is worth only two francs, not five," she said, not caring to lower her voice as she picked through my change. She smiled at me as if I were cute and showed me a five-franc coin from her register. "See, this one is a five franc. It is much larger than the two franc."

I sunk into the linoleum and found her a five-franc piece.

"Enjoy your vacation here," she said. "We don't get many

tourists in the Auvergne. And don't worry about your accent. You'd have to practically live here to lose it."

Needless to say, it was a short evening. We ended up picking up a couple of pizzas to eat in the safety of our own home. After the kids went to bed, I nursed my bruised ego with a bowl of popcorn and a *West Wing* video my parents had sent me. "So I guess I'm not practically French," I told Todd, trying to laugh.

But at least I didn't wear white tennis shoes.

37. My Friends, the Disenchanted

When my friend Camille started up a *club cinéma* our last year
in France and asked me to join, I was thrilled. I could just imagine sitting with a bunch of French ladies in someone's living
room, drinking café and sharing secrets. Camille and her husband invited us over to dinner, and I told her how much I was
looking forward to it.

Her husband, Léon, spoke up. "Yes, we will give you a good
education in French films."

We? What was he talking about? Wasn't this a ladies' club?

"Uh . . ." I said, "I thought it was just for women."

"Why, no! Of course it is for men and ladies too," he said.
"Becky, in France, everything we do is bisexual."

It would have struck me as funnier if I hadn't been so disappointed. A movie club for couples? With the husbands around,
how was I going to get to know anyone? That was the whole
reason I had said yes. It sure wasn't the movies. I had loved *Le
fabuleux destin d'Amélie Poulain,* a charming film about a quirky,

innocent girl in Paris who decides to straighten out the lives of everyone around her and falls in love with a man she barely knows. But from what I had heard, that movie was the exception to the rule. Everybody knew French films were depressing. And now husbands too? Husbands would ruin everything. No one would really open up and share anything personal. So much for finding my French friend.

Not that Camille wasn't my friend. She was, and she was wonderful, open and kind and willing to do anything for me, but Camille didn't count as completely French. She had lived in the States for five years and was an English professor. I wanted to make a real French friend, on my own. We had been in France for three years, and it still hadn't happened.

Back when we were still new to France, I thought I was doing just fine in the friend department. I had started meeting other moms at school, and I was hopeful. That is, until I talked with Virginie. Virginie was another French friend who had lived in the States for a few years. She and I had met each other at the Kensington Farm pool back in South Carolina when Ben had one of his freak accidents. We had both been big and pregnant—well, I was big and pregnant, she still looked like French aristocracy, even in her purple maternity bathing suit. Ben pushed his foot through a pool light and started screaming and bleeding all over the concrete, and I started to pass out. Luckily Virginie was trained as a nurse and could doctor Ben's foot and hold both of our hands.

Virginie moved home to Clermont-Ferrand the same summer that we moved there, and she decided to take me under her wing.

"What you must do, Becky, in order to survive here and even enjoy life is to get involved with women apart from the school—like a tennis group or an art class. That's the only way to really work on your French and to make friends. There's no other way."

"Oh, I'm making friends," I had said. "You know, Thisbé's mom, Raphael's mom. We talk on the playground all the time."

"No, that's not what I mean. They're not your friends," Virginie said.

I didn't know what to say.

"Do you know their first names?" she asked.

"We haven't gotten around to that yet." What was with Virginie? Everyone knew, certainly she did, that French people have a thing about first names. Yes, the moms called me madame, like I called them, but we had only known each other a few months. Our friendship would bloom with time.

"Becky, I'm sure they do want to talk with you, but don't think that they are your friends. It is different here. In the States, you're friends with most everyone you talk to regularly. But— and this is a big but, no one ever wants to go farther than that. I can tell you that many times I'd meet someone, maybe at Cottonwood, and they'd say, 'I'll call you. Maybe we can get together.' I would stay at home, waiting for their call. No one ever called. After a while I did make two real friends, but it wasn't easy. In France when we make friends, we're friends for life. We don't run around introducing ourselves to everyone and calling that friendship."

I wondered, with all her talk, were Virginie and I friends? It didn't sound likely.

A few weeks later Club Cinéma began. The plan was for each of the ten couples to take a month to host. I had Todd volunteer us for April, so I'd have plenty of time to watch everyone else and learn how to do it. We'd all meet at the theater for the film, which the host couple would pick, and then go afterward to the host couple's home to talk about it and eat. So we went for the first time. The movie was *Embrassez qui vous voudrez (Kiss Who You Want)*. It was horrible, with an unlikable cast of characters who go on vacation and have meaningless relationships in all sorts of revolting combinations. The last straw was the coupling of the boy with the old woman. When it was all over, I didn't know whether to try to throw up or take a bath. Even Léon and Camille were a little surprised. "I guess you wouldn't see that back in Greer," Léon said.

"No, we wouldn't," Todd said. I tried to smile.

Todd wanted to make good use of our babysitter—to leave then and sneak off to a restaurant to cheer ourselves up, but I refused. I was going to make friends if it killed me.

Claire and Frédéric's city apartment was all lit up with candles, and there was soft music playing. It was nearly ten-thirty, but their children were dressed up and walking around with silver trays of hors d'oeuvres. The babysitter was pouring the wine.

Todd paired up with a guy he knew from work, and I stood safely next to him and surveyed the crowd. After a few awkward moments, Camille took me around to meet people. I made myself say *enchantée* when I shook their hands, even though it sounded a little frou-frou. I recognized several ladies from school, among them, Margot. Ben was in class with her daughter Anne-Marie. Luckily she didn't ask me about what I thought of the movie. We talked about our children as Gabrielle joined us.

"You have a daughter in *sixième*, don't you?" Margot asked. "How is it to have an *ado*?"

"*Un ado—un adolescent*—a teenager," Gabrielle translated

for me. I knew the word, actually, but pretended I didn't to be polite.

"Ah. When she was little I never imagined the day that she would leave me, but now that she is behaving like a teenager, after a few more years I'll be ready to kick her out the door."

No one laughed. I was horrified. They didn't get it. I was joking—mostly.

"Oh," Margot said, looking sad.

"Oh, I'm sorry," said Gabrielle. "That does happen with some children."

"When it comes to my children I have been so lucky," Margot said.

"She has," Gabrielle added. "Her girls are exceptionally well behaved."

I smiled weakly. I knew her girls—her youngest had been tormenting my Sam in *maternelle* since school began, and Ben was always complaining about whiny Anne-Marie.

There was an uncomfortable silent moment, and Margot went to get a cup of tea. Gabrielle went to refill her wineglass. I stood there by myself, trying to appear at ease.

Claire came up to me. She looked exquisite in her pearls, even without much makeup. "So what did you think of the movie?"

I wasn't sure how to answer. I couldn't tell her how I really felt. As hosts, she and her husband had picked out the movie.

"Uh . . . it was a little much for me."

"Hmm, yes, you Americans have a different sensibility when it comes to films. It was a little strong, I suppose, to get the point across. Could you follow it? I know they were speaking quickly."

"I got most of it, I think."

"So your French lessons must be going well."

"Okay, I guess. Sometimes it is better than others. It's funny, simple things trip me up. Like the difference between *pleuvoir* and *pleurer.*" I was sure that Claire would think this was amusing. My American friends and I were always laughing about how we mix up the words for "to rain" and "to cry." "I'm always saying 'The clouds are heavy and I think it might cry,' or 'Why are you raining?' "

Claire looked at me blankly. "That problem is easily remedied. It is just a matter of memorization," she said, and began a lengthy lecture on the conjugation of the irregular verb *pleuvoir.* I was dying. Didn't these people ever laugh at themselves? Where was their sense of humor?

After another thirty minutes of milling about, people began arranging themselves to discuss the film. Oh, what a beautiful film, they said, going on about how masterfully the director used exaggeration. "It so beautifully showed the futility of life," said Margot's husband. Everyone nodded and agreed. Todd and I didn't say anything.

After a few minutes, I decided to risk asking a question. "But I didn't understand the part about the architect."

"Architect?" People buzzed. "Who was the architect?"

"There was no architect in the film," Gabrielle said. "At least, I don't remember one."

I felt my face flush. "There wasn't?"

"No, there was a real estate broker, though," Camille said. "Maybe you're asking about the real estate broker married to Elisabeth. You know, the man who has an affair with his transsexual assistant?"

"No, I was talking about the man who tried to commit suicide."

"Oh, no. He wasn't an architect. I don't think they stated his profession."

The stream of conversation ran off without me, off to the subject of suicide as an artistic tool in film.

A few minutes later the large group dissolved into little groups again. Todd and I were whispering, planning our exit, when Adèle, the woman with the Chinese husband, came over to talk with me. She insisted on speaking English. I wasn't sure whether or not to take it as an insult. But we had a nice talk about the PTA at school and how she rides a bike to the school. She said that after living in China with her husband, she just didn't understand why the French didn't make it easier for people to ride bicycles. I realized I was destined to be friends only with disenchanted French people. Finally, at midnight, we made our excuses and left. The next morning we were still depressed.

Over the year the films never got much better. Maybe I just didn't understand them, but I tried. We continued to attend each month, and each time I'd come home, flip open my calendar, and shudder at how fast April was approaching. I looked to the circled date with both anticipation and dread.

April came.

We had to pick a movie. There were suggestions made. All the ladies at school were talking about the French film just out—one of a tragic love, beautiful in its sadness and misery. Choice number two was *The Magdalene Sisters,* in which young girls are abused by nuns. Thank goodness for choice number three: *Monsieur Schmidt,* with Jack Nicholson and Kathy Bates. I wondered if anyone besides us would want to see Jack Nicholson and Kathy Bates, but it was our turn, so we got to pick.

Camille did make a point to tell me that Frédéric had told her that he and Claire hoped we didn't choose *About Schmidt,* not because it was American, of course, but because American films translated into French were never as funny as they were in English. Also, there were whispers that if we didn't choose choice one, there were two couples who planned to go see it anyway and then come to our house for refreshments, in order to be polite. I couldn't believe it! After we had sat through all their depressing French movies. That decided it. We chose *About Schmidt.* With the way the movie club was going, I couldn't take sitting through another tragedy.

The next job was to write the e-mail invitation. I knew people would be curious—could the American lady write good French?—so I worked on it like crazy. I looked up the spelling of each word, even the ones I was sure of, making certain I had all the accents right. I gave it to my friend Cathy, who had a French husband, for proofreading. I also took it to my tutor, just in case. I tweaked it and tweaked it. Finally I held my breath and clicked on "Send."

The rest of the week I spent cleaning my house, buying new wineglasses, and checking my e-mail every few minutes. No one RSVP'd. Didn't the French do that? *RSVP* is French, after all.

We went to the theater. No one was there. Five minutes after the starting time, we were still waiting for someone to show up. Finally Camille came in with Claire. "Didn't people get my e-mail?" I asked.

"Maybe they didn't understand your joke," said Camille.

"My joke?"

"Yes, you know, all the crazy symbols and smiley faces. You know, all the nonsense words."

"What nonsense words?"

Camille looked at me. "Uh-oh."

"Do you have a French keyboard?" she asked.

"No," I said. What difference would that make?

"How do you put in the accents?"

"I insert them from the symbols directory."

"That's it! Every time you inserted an accent, French e-mail turned it into gobbledygook. How funny." Camille laughed.

"I was wondering about all the smiley faces. I thought it was a joke," Claire said, laughing.

This was not starting well.

Surprisingly, the evening didn't go too badly. We had eleven people, and the ones that could speak English did so since it was at our house. They didn't drink any wine, but they did have hot tea and ate up all the food. We didn't talk much about the film, but we talked lots of politics, which made me nervous, even though I agreed with a good measure of what they said.

"What, is America like a big bully now?" Claire asked me by the table of food. "They think that because they rescued us back in World War II that we have no right to have our own opinion about how to deal with Iraq?"

I had to agree. But then her husband started going on about how George Bush should be tried as a criminal, and I excused myself to the kitchen to make coffee. I didn't vote for him, but he was president of my country. I could say what I wanted to about him, but I didn't care to hear Claire's husband doing it.

Margot said she had a headache and went home early, but most everyone else stayed until after midnight. I met a really nice new lady named Élise, who taught English at the university. I told her we were moving back come summertime, and she offered me her son's outgrown books on tape to help my kids keep their French. And I had a chance to talk with Camille about her upcoming move. She and her family were headed to Toulouse, where she and Léon would teach at the university.

• • •

BEFORE CAMILLE LEFT, she started a hiking club, this time just for women. It was mostly English teachers like her. My friend Mary Ann and I went along and tried to pretend that we were in shape. Every time the French ladies stopped to pick mushrooms or comment on a plant, we would chug-a-lug our water or massage our feet. Finally, after three and a half hours on the trail, the group stopped for lunch. It was a little embarrassing. They brought out salads, hard-boiled eggs, cheese, and fresh baguettes, and even had little paper cups for coffee at the end. Mary Ann and I had brought peanut butter sandwiches, Cheetos, chocolate chip cookies, and Diet Coke. None of them knew what Cheetos were, but after I passed them around, they were hooked. We told them where to find them in Auchan, and Élise said they'd be perfect with aperitifs.

Looking back, I feel pretty foolish. I had fallen in love with France and thought a real French friend would be proof that France loved me back. So, it wasn't to be. So what? What did it matter if all my French friends were the disenchanted ones, the ones who complained about the lack of bike lanes and the dog poop, the ones who appreciated smiling and the ability to be a little optimistic every now and then, even though it made them look naive?

Anyway, I still had Madame Mallet.

38. Jamais la Première Cigarette!

Ben got his first pack of cigarettes in a birthday treat bag when his friend Mathieu turned six. I went to pick him up from the party, and he was hiding up in a cherry tree, smoking away with four other rough-looking first-graders. The cigarettes were candy, of course, but it still unnerved me.

When Ben got to fourth grade, Madame Fayolle requested that each of her students bring five boxes of matches to school. Todd joked that it must be time for his indoctrination into the tobacco arts. When Ben got home I asked him what the matches were for. His eyes got big. "Mom, it's so fun. You won't believe how much fun it is to light a bunch of matches. I had such a great time. The teacher showed us how to do it, and I was really good at it."

"What were the burned-off matchsticks for?" I asked.

"Oh, I don't know. I think we're going to build houses with them—maybe."

When Todd got home, I told him about our son's new passion. "Don't they have Popsicle sticks in this country?" he said, and hid our matches behind the flour canister.

Since we'd moved to France I had tried to get used to the smoke. It was everywhere—in the malls, in my hair, in the cafés, in my coat, even in Dr. Allezard's waiting room. Still, it always surprised me when June Cleaver types from school would offer me a cigarette at the park.

But what really bothered me was seeing so many kids smoking. I'd walk by the middle and high school, and they'd be running out of the school gate on breaks between classes, masses of preteens and teenagers crowding the sidewalk and spilling out into the bus lane, puffing away. Maybe it was the teacher in me, but I had to fight the urge to march up to them, pull the cigarettes out of their mouths, and stomp the things out with my shoe. Instead, I had to try to navigate my stroller through the crowds of them, as they laughed and shrieked and flirted, waving their cigarettes around as they gestured wildly with their hands. Their burning cigarettes were right at Sam's eye level, and as far as I could tell, they didn't notice or care that they might drop ashes on my sweetheart's little head. "Hey! *Faites-attention!*" I'd say loudly, and they'd move slightly, or stare at me with that blank teenage look.

When Sarah graduated from *école primaire* and entered *sixième,* sixth grade, she complained about them like a teacher's pet. "They smell bad, Mom," she said. "I guess they don't know what they're doing to their lungs. Or maybe French people don't care."

But apparently some French people cared. In late September of her seventh grade year, Sarah came home with a project assignment and said she needed poster board. "It's called

'Jamais la Première Cigarette,' you know, 'Never the First Cigarette.' Isabelle is having us do it. Everybody has to make these storyboards for a commercial against smoking. Kids all over France are going to send them in, and Isabelle says we get to go on a train to Paris near Christmastime and vote on the best one," Sarah said. "The winner gets to have theirs made into a real commercial to go on TV."

Isabelle was Sarah's young, pretty French teacher. She had never taught before, and the rumor was that she was supposed to go to law school but changed her mind. While she reconsidered her life's plan, the directrice of the international program at the school, Madame Pradine, had snagged her as her assistant. Madame Pradine was a smart lady. Lately she had been given more and more responsibilities overseeing several international schools. She knew Isabelle could easily run the program at one little school.

But originally Madame Pradine hadn't intended on putting Isabelle in the classroom. It was just how things worked out. Apparently, once our international students got to *sixième,* Madame Cousart, the ancient French teacher who had taught at the school for decades, refused to admit them into her classes. We parents complained, and Madame Pradine had us in for a conference. "Trust me," she said, "if Madame Cousart says that she does not want your children there, it is better that they are not there." We looked at each other in disbelief. We had heard that some of the French teachers were less than enthusiastic about having our children in their classes, but no one had ever directly admitted it. Madame Pradine added in English, "She is mean."

So Isabelle volunteered. "Madame Cousart is unjust," she said, and with the drive and enthusiasm of a defense attorney,

Isabelle took on the task of perfecting the grammar and oral expression of her eleven pupils. She would prove to Madame Cousart that her international students could finish her class at least as equally prepared as their French counterparts—maybe even more so. She worked them hard, drilling them and piling on extra homework, berating her students when they didn't show the proper work ethic.

But was she the right person to lead this particular project? After hearing Sarah's retelling of her antismoking lesson, I had my doubts. As far as I can tell, this was how it went:

"So, people, the title of this project is *Jamais la Première Cigarette.*' Can anyone share with us why we should not smoke?"

The three American children started talking at once, sharing what they learned in school back in the States about how smoking fills up your lungs with black gook and how cigarettes are addictive and cause lung cancer. Someone told about how their great-uncle had to have his throat cut open and voice box removed and now at Christmas get-togethers he talks through this little thing attached to his throat. Then Sarah said that smoking makes you smell bad and is a disgusting habit. Someone else said that she would never ever take even one puff, because you could get addicted and have to spend your money on cigarettes the rest of your life. At this point Isabelle had to interrupt.

"I don't think that one puff will make you an addict."

"That is what my grandmother said."

"That is ridiculous," Isabelle said. "One cigarette is just one cigarette. It will not overcome you with a deep hunger to smoke."

"My grandmother said it will."

"No, that is not correct. She just doesn't want you to start smoking—that is why she said that. In fact, I think that smoking one cigarette is good for you. You should all try it, just so you know what it is like."

"But Isabelle, isn't this project called 'Jamais la Première Cigarette'? Doesn't that mean never to try it the first time?"

"That is a little unrealistic, don't you think? I smoke, and my lungs are just fine. But I do it only socially. It is a whole other thing, to smoke *socially,* you know—with friends when you go out, at a soirée. Smoking in that way is certainly not an addiction. It is just a social thing to do—out of politeness. For enjoyment. But a smoking habit? Now, that is another thing all together. You should never become addicted," Isabelle said. "Addiction is not attractive. Not at all."

. . .

SO SARAH WORKED on her project, making up a storyboard about two birds talking on a branch of a tree, ending with one of the birds dropping dead and falling to the ground. I thought she had a good chance of winning, given that the French love a tragic ending. But, sadly, hers didn't make the final cut. She wasn't too disappointed. She still got to go to Paris.

In early December I drove to the train station near midnight to pick Sarah up from the school trip. Sarah came out wearing a T-shirt with the words "Jamais la Première Cigarette!" printed on it, buzzing on adrenaline and Haribou candy. She talked the whole way home.

"You wouldn't believe the finalists," she said. "There was one with a boy and girl in bed with their clothes off. All you see is clothes on the floor, but you hear their voices talking the whole time. He is saying, 'Oh, come on and try it. I wouldn't do anything to hurt you,' and she's saying, 'No, I made a promise that I wouldn't,' and 'I'm too young.' But he keeps trying to persuade her. It finally ends with the words on the screen Jamais la Première Cigarette! Do you get it? He is trying to get her to smoke. Not do you-know-what. Do you get it?"

I nodded and swallowed hard and tried to remain calm.

"But the funniest thing was this strange man that came up to us on the metro ride to the Gare de Lyon. We were wearing our T-shirts and eating our McDonald's food—we had picked up dinner on the way to the metro since we had to hurry—and I know you're gonna tell me that you're not supposed to eat on the metro, but Isabelle said it was okay, that people do it all the time. Anyway, this old homeless-looking guy came up and he read our T-shirts and started lecturing us that cigarettes weren't really bad for you and if we really wanted to be healthy we'd stop eating bags full of hamburgers. Isabelle got in a big argument with him and finally we got off the train. She got really mad." Sarah took a breath. "So how was your day?"

So that was Sarah's antismoking education, her indoctrination in the tobacco arts. I might have worried more about it, but I didn't have time. The end-of-school carnival was coming up and I had promised Camille that I would help her get donations for the grab bags. So far all we had gotten from people was a box of licorice candy, two hundred plastic whistles from the party store, and one hundred and seventy-three ashtrays. Ben said we ought to add matches, but I thought that was going a bit too far.

39. *Au Revoir*

Three weeks before our move back to South Carolina, Monsieur Giraud called us and asked if he could bring over some prospective renters. I straightened the house and told Madame Mallet, knowing that she would want to be at her window to get a good look at them. It was a cute young French couple, carrying a baby. They drove a big white van. Madame Mallet would have something to say about that.

The next day she saw me getting out of my car and stormed out her gate.

"I just got off the phone with Madame Giraud. We are blindsided. Four children, plus the baby and one more on the way. Six little urchins! Rébecca, what will we do? I figured when I saw the van that we were in for it. I'm furious! How could the Girauds do this to us? If we weren't so old we'd sell this place and move off where we could get some peace and quiet."

A good part of me was doing the Snoopy dance inside my

head. Now she'd appreciate us. She thought we were loud. Just wait—six children.

"You are taking the swing set, aren't you?" she asked, pointing her finger at me. "Imagine the noise they could make with that."

"Yes, we're selling it to our moving agent," I said. I had been happy to sell it to Théo, the nice man from the international moving company. Thanks to him, our move was a breeze. As my French movers packed up all our treasures, I relived the memories of our four years in France. They crated up the piano and I thought of Monsieur Rougé. They circled around my huge circus poster, debating how to pack it, and I thought of the man on the street with the purse, fussing at me as I tugged at the poster's corners. They lugged my buffet down the stairs, and I envisioned Madame Bernard tethered with rope, her heels scraping on the tile. Then they wrapped my Mary up in bubble wrap, along with the tons of junk I had carried home from flea markets—plates and teapots and linens. I loved it all so much—there were countless stories in those moving boxes, precious memories of our life in the Auvergne.

So much had changed in the four years. My children had blossomed and grown. Todd and I had added crow's feet and some gray hair. Corsica Man was gone, Place de Jaude was all torn up so a tramway could be put in, and Auberge du Fleur, our favorite restaurant, had changed management. They wouldn't let us substitute crème brûlée for the *tarte aux pommes* anymore, and it just wasn't as good.

Before we left, we took a family drive to get a last look at our favorite places. Our old apartment still looked the same, with the tiny overgrown front yard and ceramic bugs by the front door, but we hardly recognized the house across the street. The wishing well, lush lawn, and rose topiaries were gone, replaced by crabgrass and Little Tykes plastic toys littering the yard. I wondered about the *soupe* man. Had he died? Or moved in with his children?

Though I was sad, really sad, to leave beautiful France, I must admit I was ready to say good-bye. We had been saying it for months. Sarah's best friends had moved away the year before, and she could hardly wait for American middle school. Ben's class threw him a party, signed their names on his shirt, and gave him a beach towel that looked like a French flag. He didn't want to move and had been sleepwalking up a storm, and he still hoped Todd would come home from work and say that he had changed his mind about going back to South Carolina. Sam didn't know what to think about moving. He just wanted to be sure that he didn't get left behind. His teacher, Marie-France, organized a little class party for him. On his last day of school all his classmates brought French and American flags they had made at home with paper and tape and sticks, a flag bouquet for his new room in South Carolina. I bit my lip and tried not to cry. Marie-France gave him a little book about volcanoes and wrote in it that she hoped that one day our family would come back to visit her. As I read it, I had to bite my lip again and pinch my arm as well.

I had dreaded saying good-bye to my neighbors, particularly Madame Mallet, and hoped that presents might help. I bought Madame Fauriaux a breakfast cup and saucer to add to her collection and finally decided on a silver champagne bucket and a small framed picture of our family for the Mallets. She went crazy over the picture and put it on her television in their little living room. She accepted the champagne bucket in typical Madame Mallet fashion.

"A champagne bucket," she had said, looking it over. "It looks very nice. It's a pity we hardly drink champagne anymore."

I laughed. Oh, well, she'd keep it anyway, and maybe it would bring her nice memories. Later, as the movers were packing, I took her a small wooden suitcase of oil paints that weren't allowed in the shipping container. "Could you use them?" I asked, knowing she liked painting cement lawn bunnies and turtles to put in her garden.

"Oh, thank you, Rébecca—yes, I would love them. Are you sure?" she asked, and I nodded. Forget the champagne bucket. This was the perfect present for her. "Thank you. I'll be sure not to say anything to Madame Fauriaux."

I looked at her, puzzled.

"You know, that she got one present and I got three."

"I appreciate that, Madame Mallet. Thank you."

"And I certainly won't tell the Roches, given your severed relationship."

"I appreciate that too," I said, and changed the subject. I was not proud of what had recently occurred between Alain and me. A year earlier I had felt a notable distance between the Roches and us. Had we offended them? Pascale no longer stopped to talk with me, and Alain's hellos were forced and curt.

Alain had come over about a week before the move, as Madame Mallet and I were talking at her gate. "And how is the Ramsey family? Are you ready to go back home to George Bush?"

I made a face at Alain. He continued, "Were you able to buy everything you wanted from France to take back to America?"

I ignored his comment. He always teased me whenever I brought home an old chair or table from a secondhand shop, saying that we foreigners were trying to rob France of all its treasures.

"I will be sad to leave," I said.

"Sad? What could you miss?" Alain said, still smiling. "You always socialize with the Americans, so it's not like you're leaving behind lots of friends. You eat your American food and do your American things. What could be different back home?"

Madame Mallet looked worried, but she didn't say anything.

"Alain, that is not fair," I said, not sure if he was joking.

"Oh, but it is true. I wonder, have you ever had French people to your house?"

Ah, that was the problem. We were about to move without ever having them over, though they had entertained us every New Year's Day. It was my fault. I knew we should have done it, but I never could bring myself to follow through. With Madame Mallet across the street always nosing around in my business, I always felt watched and judged. I had had other French friends as guests, but I couldn't bring myself to invite in all my neighbors to look over my things and evaluate us as human beings. But still, I should have made myself do it to be polite.

"That is enough, Alain," I said with a smile, excusing myself.

"Ah, you haven't then, have you?"

"That's enough, Alain," I said, and walked inside my house.

. . .

THE DAY BEFORE moving day, Madame Mallet and Madame Fauriaux came over with a gift. It was a beautiful Haviland china footed dish with a wreath of tiny blue flowers painted on it. I thanked them and kissed them and served them cake and tea. We laughed and enjoyed memories, retelling old stories we knew by heart. They reminisced about how nervous they were when they first heard that a family of Americans was moving into the neighborhood, and I recalled how nervous I was sitting at the table with them at our first New Year's get-together.

"We could hardly get you to say a word." Madame Mallet laughed. There was a comfortable moment of quiet, and then Madame Mallet said, "Don't you worry about Alain Roche. He is an idiot and doesn't understand the real world."

Madame Fauriaux nodded sweetly. "He's just jealous of you, Rébecca. He'll never be a rich American and he wishes he could."

"But we're not rich," I said. "We aren't—far from it."

"You are to us," said Madame Mallet.

"You have made me rich," I said, knowing that I sounded sappy, but meaning it with all my heart. "This life has made me rich. I'll never forget it."

"Young lady, we'll have no sad good-byes," Madame Mallet said. "We will write to each other and you will come for visits, since I am too old and broken down to make the trip to America."

I promised we would.

SIX MONTHS LATER it was almost New Year's, and though we were settled among our French things in our new house back in Kensington Farm, we felt somewhat lost. We had no plans for New Year's Eve, except Todd's plan to smell up the house with collards and black-eyed peas, and the boys' plan to set off fireworks in the cul-de-sac with the neighborhood kids. As I walked to the mailbox I thought of my neighbors back on allée des Cerisiers. Had the Roches invited everybody over again for champagne and *galette des Rois*? Did they like the new people in our house? Why had it taken me so long to write Madame Mallet? I had put it off and put it off, finally managing to get a letter in the mail the second week of December.

Then I saw the envelope and the stamp. It was Madame Mallet's handwriting.

She was her same old self. It made me miss her. She had written me back right away, spending most of the five-page letter complaining about the new neighbors, how very Catholic they were, and how every Wednesday after school the mother taught catechism at their house to a group of fifteen "urchins." "We are devastated! Last week when the pope was sick," she wrote, "that woman held them there an extra hour for more singing and prayers. It made me so mad that I got out my leaf blower and tried to drown them all out." She drew a little devil with horns in the margin. Then she went on to say that they never talk to her and that the wife keeps the sheets in a heap on the clothesline and smokes like Saint Nicotine, and that there had been a box of leeks out on her balcony for at least a week.

Next she commented on the news I had shared about Sarah and Ben and Sam, and asked me to give them *bisoux* for her. "Monsieur Mallet and I are holding on to life like crumbling fortresses. But we look forward to the day when you drive down our street for a visit and park in front of our gate, like you used to do before I instructed you to do it the proper way. You're so dear to us and we'll always love you, no matter what the crazy Roches say." She and Monsieur Mallet signed it and taped on five four-leaf clovers from her yard for luck.

At the bottom there was a postscript just for Katie. "The cat Laporte sends his regards to his friend Kettie and would like to add that he misses seeing her on his moonlight strolls."

She added at the end, "We miss all of you," and signed it again, "Affectionately, Astrid."

Astrid. Her first name!

There in the winter's chill, I felt a familiar warmth rushing over me, just like I had felt all those times in our little village in France when the clouds would suddenly pull back behind the hills and all of allée des Cerisiers would light up with sun. I looked at her letter again, cherishing her swirly signature. Astrid. We had finally arrived.

FRENCH BY HEART

READING GROUP COMPANION

ABOUT THIS READING GROUP COMPANION

The introduction, discussion questions, and author bio that follow are
intended to enhance your group's discussion about Becky Ramsey's
French by Heart. We hope that they will provide useful ways of thinking and talking about the book.

INTRODUCTION

In this charming memoir, Becky Ramsey recounts the trials and de-
lights of her young family's four-year stay in "La Belle France." From
the moment she and her husband decide to accept his employer's offer of a transfer to Michelin in France, Becky, Todd, and their three
children are on an adventure that would daunt many in their South
Carolina town.

It's not long before the Ramseys are settled in their new home on
allée des Cerisiers, and gamely venturing forth into new and unfamiliar classrooms, grocery stores, and bank branches. Becky soon learns
that her own neighborhood is no less of an obstacle course, as she and

her wary neighbors feel each other out and establish tricky friendships that are as much a challenge as a comfort. But as time passes and
she learns to accept—and even enjoy—some of the mysteries of
France, pieces of her adopted culture begin to make their way into
Becky's home and heart.

Questions for Discussion:

1) Upon the Ramseys' arrival in France, their temporary neighbors
hear a foreign accent and jump to the conclusion that the Ramseys
are "anglais," much to Becky's chagrin. It's a mistake that's repeated
not infrequently by locals. How does Becky's reaction change over
the years, and what does it say about her comfort level in France?

2) When Becky admits to having her weight criticized by Madame
Mallet, her friends congratulate her: this is a sure sign of friendship in
France. Others advise that friendship among Frenchwomen is not as
easily won as the friendships quickly forged between Americans—a
truth borne out by Becky's experience. What do you make of the
theme of "friendship" in the book? Who do you think Becky's friends
in France are?

3) What prejudices do the Ramseys encounter during their stay in
France? Do you think the negative reactions of some Frenchmen are
due to true xenophobia, simple misunderstandings, or something else?

4) When the tree trimmer arrives at the Ramseys' temporary home,
his incomprehensible French sends Becky into a panic, as she struggles
to answer him and wonders why none of her neighbors will come to
her aid. At her next home on allée des Cerisiers, she receives more so-
licitous knocks on the door from the church missionaries and the
painter. How does her reaction change the longer she is in France?

What does the evolution of her response (and her preparation) say about her changing status in France and in the neighborhood?

5) After some initial hiccups, the Ramsey children seem to acclimate beautifully to life in France. Indeed, by the end of their stay, a delighted Becky is told that they speak French with no accent. What do you expect the children's readjustment to life in the United States will be like? What challenges do you think they might face?

6) How do Madame Mallet's memories of war affect her behavior and ideas in the present? How do the events of September 11 affect her relationship with the Ramseys? Are the two related?

7) Discuss Becky and Todd's experience with the movie club. How does it differ from their expectations? What do you think of their selection of *About Schmidt* as their film? In a book club or movie club, what do you think each member's responsibility is in choosing a discussion piece?

8) The course of the book traces a finite period of time—the four years during which the Ramseys reside in France—yet the narrative does not always follow a strictly chronological path. How does the narrator define the passage of time? How does any full-time mother or father mark the events of a year, as opposed to their office-bound spouses?

9) From the social activities of the local church to the statue of Mary in her home, as well as trips to Lourdes and the family's Joan of Arc pilgrimage, Becky consistently expresses appreciation and interest in the church, if not exactly devotion to it. What role does religion play in the story? What struck you about the difference between her relationship to the local Protestant church and France's Catholic tradition?

10) Madame Mallet repeatedly instructs (and corrects) the Ramseys on the sanctity of private property, and the rules of the impenetrable garden gate. Yet her own behavior toward Becky and the children demonstrates that her feelings about personal privacy and observation are not so restrictive. Discuss some of Madame Mallet's other rules and priorities, and how they could be confusing to an outsider. Are there any that you find simply ridiculous? What do you think your relationship with Madame Mallet would have been like?

11) How does life in France stack up to Becky's expectations? Do you think she was prepared for its challenges? Does the expat life appeal to you? Why or why not?

For free supplementary materials including information on book groups, suggestions for further reading, chances to win books, phone-in author appearances, and much more, e-mail BroadwayReads@Random House.com.

ABOUT THE AUTHOR

After four years of *la belle vie* in Clermont-Ferrand, France, Rebecca S. Ramsey and her family are now settled back home in Greer, South Carolina. Between chauffeuring her children, observing her southern life, and keeping an eye out for French pastries, she writes every spare moment she can.